In 1977 Gilbert Kelland became the sixteenth successive Assistant Commissioner (Crime) at New Scotland Yard, and for the next seven years, until his retirement in 1984, he was responsible for the three and a half thousand detectives who make up the CID of the Metropolitan Police.

GILBERT KELLAND

Crime in London

GRAFTON BOOKS
A Division of the Collins Publishing Group

LONDON GLASGOW
TORONTO SYDNEY AUCKLAND

Grafton Books
A Division of the Collins Publishing Group
8 Grafton Street, London W1X 3LA

Published by Grafton Books 1987

First published in Great Britain by
The Bodley Head Ltd 1986

ISBN 0-586-07300-0

Printed and bound in Great Britain by
Collins, Glasgow

Set in Times

Contents

Acknowledgements

I am grateful to the following for permission to use copyright photographic material as follows:
The BBC Hulton Picture Library for the photograph of Soho in the Fifties; the Press Association for the photograph of Operation Cyril; the Associated Newspapers Group (*Daily Mail*) for the photographs of Jimmy Humphreys, Rusty Humphreys, and the Harrods bombing; the Keystone Press Agency Ltd for the photograph of Ex-Commander Drury; the *Daily Express* for the photograph of the armed bank robbery; and the *Guardian* picture library for the photograph of the Grunwick picket line.

Preface

Crime in London

Crime is a reflection of the society in which it occurs and of the moral and social climate that prevails at any given time. In a democracy these two factors condition the style and methods of policing.

Because of its size, and because it is the seat of government, the residence of the Sovereign and an international and multi-racial city, London has always presented unique and complex problems of policing, and these have increased vastly since the Second World War. Because the Home Secretary is personally the Police Authority for the Metropolitan Police, it is inevitable that it, more than any other police force in Britain, should be the subject of national scrutiny and discussion. This is the essence of accountability, and provided that comment is fair and balanced, the searchlight of publicity can do no harm and often much good to the organization. Being constantly in the public eye is something which members of the force have to learn to live with.

Not all publicity, however, is necessarily helpful. It is probable, for instance, that today organized crime, if it is not continually attacked, could in the long term be far more harmful to society than opportunist burglars or street robbers. The greatest danger comes not from the petty thief or the juvenile lacking parental interest or control but from the fraudsman, the drug trafficker, the armed robber and the vice baron – all of whom, quite consciously, have become professional criminals. They are prepared to corrupt, to threaten and intimidate and, on occasions, to murder in order to achieve their ends. If they are arrested they exploit to the full all aspects of the legal system, and as a last resort they do not hesitate to try to pervert the course of justice by interfering with juries. However the public, as well as many politicians and some senior police officers, perceive the first type of crime far more clearly than the second, which may mean that the lion's share of police manpower and resources tends to be deployed against small-time criminals. Few politicians from any of the political parties have shown until recently any real interest in the long-term measures and strategies necessary to identify, frustrate and control international organized crime. Perhaps this is not altogether surprising if one considers the constitutional position that gives complete operational autonomy to police forces in the United Kingdom where, unlike the USA, there are, with the exception of HM Customs and Excise, no federal law enforcement agencies.

With the growth of organized crime have come great strains on the police. The temptations to which a detective officer in particular is subjected are enormous – I recall one incident in 1979 when a detective chief superintendent dealing with an arrested drug trafficker was offered a bribe of £250,000 in used bank notes. It needs a balanced, well-trained and well-led man to obey all the rules in the face of the revulsion he may feel in the wake of some particularly violent or brutal crime, or to control his anger if he suspects that the person he believes to be responsible may be getting away with it.

Whatever the pressures, however, society rightly expects policemen to work within the rule of law and to maintain complete personal and corporate integrity. There must never be any acceptance or toleration of a philosophy that the end justifies the means as far as their behaviour is concerned. If the law is inadequate or unworkable then it must be for Parliament to change it, or accept the consequences.

The operational and administrative control of New Scotland Yard's Criminal Investigation Department is a demanding responsibility, and as the Assistant Commissioner (Crime) I was answerable to the Commissioner of Police of the Metropolis for this function. In August 1977 after six months as Assistant Commissioner 'A' Department I became the sixteenth successive Assistant Commissioner (Crime),[1] in the aftermath of a crisis at New Scotland Yard in which I had been very much involved.

In April 1973 I had been appointed by the then Deputy Commissioner, Mr James Starritt, to investigate a complaint made by Mrs James (Rusty) Humphreys, a former Soho striptease dancer, whose pornographer husband was at the time a fugitive in Holland. This investigation was to lead to the uncovering of a long-established pattern of corruption and criminal conspiracy between criminals and a substantial number of CID officers.

The inquiry by myself and a small team of personally chosen investigators that never exceeded eight officers was to take three long years. It was carried out against a background of intense interest from the media and Parliament, and members of the team visited Germany, Holland, the United States and the Channel Isles to collect evidence. There were to be many difficulties and frustrations. Potential witnesses were reluctant to offer evidence, some fled the country, one had a heart attack and died, and another committed suicide after having made valuable and detailed statements. It was irritating to have to spend time writing reports for the Home

[1] See Appendix I.

Office, so that briefs could be prepared for the Home Secretary, Roy Jenkins, to answer correspondence and questions from some MPs that suggested a police cover-up was going on.

The evidence eventually obtained resulted in the Attorney-General granting permission for criminal proceedings for corruption offences to be taken against fifteen serving or former officers ranging in rank from commander and detective chief superintendent to detective constable. These trials took place at the Old Bailey in late 1976 and early 1977, and thirteen of the officers charged were convicted and sentenced to substantial prison terms.

It had been a sorry chapter of events, but I had never felt during those three years that it was devoid of hope for the future. If the lessons learned could be remembered, then I believed that the trial of 1976/7 could be regarded as a watershed in the history of the Metropolitan Police. Above all, I had been continuously aware of the support I and my fellow investigators had received from within the force and the determination there to root out and deal with our own problem.

For nearly seven years following my appointment as Assistant Commissioner (Crime) I was responsible for the Yard's some three and a half thousand detectives, including those of the Special Branch. These were exacting but exciting years. Although during three of them there were slight reductions in overall recorded crime, the general crime situation in the Metropolis worsened, as it did in many parts of the country, and particularly disturbing was the ever-increasing use of gratuitous violence by criminals. Thanks to the support of my senior CID colleagues and of the Commissioner and his Policy Committee, we succeeded – despite the saga of the ill-fated, and unfortunately named, 'Operation Countryman'

– in restoring the reputation and morale of the CID which had been disturbed by the corruption trials followed by the scandal of the involvement of members of C.1 Drug Squad in the sale of dangerous drugs which broke just at the time of my appointment. Unprecedented acts of terrorism, kidnapping and armed robbery were successfully dealt with and criminal intelligence systems enhanced, all with little or no increase in manpower. These achievements were due to the professionalism and dedication of many fine officers, and in particular I pay tribute to David Powis, Deputy Assistant Commissioner (Crime-Operations) who was my deputy for most of my period of office.

My own police career has spanned the whole period since the end of the Second World War and during that time there have been enormous changes in society. As a result, the Metropolitan Police today is a very different animal from the force I joined in 1946. I have watched it respond and change – albeit sometimes tardily – to meet the challenges it has had to face in order that it may continue to deal with crime and to keep the Queen's Peace. This book is an attempt to recreate the process as I saw it.

Perhaps the most telling tribute to the spirit of a unique organization was paid by Lord Scarman in his Report on the Brixton Disorders of 1981. He said that he and others who had heard evidence of the Inquiry '. . . will have had many opportunities to marvel at and be thankful for the courage and dedication which was displayed by members of the police and emergency services in Brixton over that terrible weekend. They stood between our society and a total collapse of law and order in the streets of an important part of the capital. For that they deserve, and must receive, the praise and thanks of all sections of our community. Before we pass judgement on the quality of our policing, let us remember their many excellences even while we note and seek to remedy such defects as there may be.'

1
Early Years

I was born on St Patrick's Day, 17 March 1924, in the county of Devonshire. Although I have lived in London for nearly forty years, I have never lost my deep love of the sea and of nature – a worthwhile legacy from my early environment. My home was on that beautiful but then very isolated part of the North Devon coast which faces the Atlantic, a hamlet named Pickwell in the village of Georgeham, overlooking the estuaries of the rivers Taw and Torridge, the setting for *Tarka the Otter* and *Salar the Salmon* by a local resident, the author and naturalist Henry Williamson.

A remote rural village in the 1920s and '30s, Georgeham was very much a closed community. People of necessity helped each other, but although they were poor there was an absence of the feudalism which was typical of many agricultural communities of that period. The spirit of independence probably stemmed from the old-fashioned radical Liberalism which was traditional in this part of North Devon. In those pre-television and early radio days our knowledge of politics and current affairs was mainly gleaned from the BBC, reading the *News Chronicle*, and the words of wisdom from parliamentary candidates at the election hustings that always caused great excitement and interest.

Family circumstances meant that I was mainly brought up by my maternal grandparents. They had hoped originally to become small farmers, but their hopes were dashed when my grandmother's younger stepbrother, indulged by their father, squandered the family's assets and caused the farm they owned to be sold to settle his debts. This meant no dowry or legacy for her and as my grandparents raised a family of eight – three sons and five daughters – they never had sufficient capital to realize their ambition. Despite everything, they remained strong and independent characters, my grandmother in particular being a tremendous influence on everyone. She was very much the focal point of her extended family, corresponding with all its members, including my grandfather's relatives who had emigrated to New Zealand. Her church was very important to her and her strong faith gave her confidence to meet all adversity with understanding and dignity.

The life of the village revolved around the parish church of St George, the Baptist chapel, the village school – which I attended – the vicarage and the two village public houses. Our vicar in the 1930s was the Reverend Harry Sharples, a forthright Lancastrian who exercised considerable influence in his parish. He ran a boys' club at the vicarage and encouraged those of us who were so inclined to use his library. Being an avid reader I benefited from his interest and read everything available, from *Robinson Crusoe* to Macaulay's *History of England*. Just before I joined the Fleet Air Arm at the age of eighteen in May 1942 the vicar raised with me the question of entering the Church. Although as a member of the choir I was a regular church attender, I did not feel I had a sufficiently strong sense of commitment then, and after four years of war service I had no inclination at all.

Before the Education Act of 1944 the school leaving age was fourteen years. Opportunities for children like me in country villages were extremely limited, and I left the new district secondary school shortly before my fifteenth birthday when I was offered a job as a junior clerk by a local firm of agricultural merchants and engineers. Although the salary was small, there was some prestige in having a white-collar job when most of the local male population were manual workers, and I was able to make a contribution to the family finances. Later in the year came the event which was to change so many people's lives, including mine – the outbreak of the Second World War.

Like most of my friends, I could not wait to get into uniform and was afraid that the war would be over before I was old enough to join up. My ambition was to become a Fleet Air Arm pilot and together with two of my former school friends who wanted to become RAF fighter pilots I joined the local squadron of the Air Training Corps. We realized that without the formal educational qualification of School Certificate it would be difficult to achieve our ambitions, and it was our good fortune that the CO of the ATC Squadron was the headmaster of a local private school. In the course of our training activities in the evenings and at weekends he coached us in mathematics, navigation and English, but even more importantly he taught us the discipline of private study. In due course we passed the educational test for air-crew duties.

My two friends became RAF fighter pilots and both survived the war. I was frustrated because slightly defective colour vision made me unacceptable to the navy for flying training. Determined to join the Fleet Air Arm, I accepted the offer of training as an air mechanic (ordnance) and I was called up in May 1942.

After technical training by the RAF on aircraft guns, ammunition, depth charges and bombs, and subsequent service at a Royal Naval Air Station in Scotland, I eventually joined 824 Squadron of the Fleet Air Arm.

Something happened to me during my technical training that was to be a lifelong source of interest and pleasure – I caught the athletics bug. This was through an airman, whose name I now forget, but who belonged to the well-known London club, the Belgrave Harriers, and who organized athletics at the training establishment. I became a member of the track and cross-country team, although the wartime Royal Navy provided few opportunities for athletics and it was not until I joined the Met in 1946 that I was able to become really involved in my favourite sport.

824 Squadron had been a fighter squadron but was re-formed as an anti-submarine convoy protection squadron of Sea Hurricanes and Swordfish biplanes which were affectionately known as 'Stringbags'. We went aboard HMS *Striker*, one of the American-built escort carriers – that is to say, merchant ships with a flight deck – which were literally floating aviation spirit tankers with none of the armour plating of normal naval vessels. Initially our function was to bridge the gap in the Western Atlantic and to protect merchant ship convoys in those parts of the ocean where, as they could not be given shore-based aircraft cover, they were very vulnerable to U-boat attacks. Flying, particularly deck landings in rough seas and at night – the flight deck being only about six hundred feet long – was pretty hazardous, especially for the Sea Hurricanes. We suffered casualties from accidents and there were times when I was not altogether sorry that my colour vision defect was keeping my feet firmly on the flight deck.

There was only one occasion when our Swordfish were armed with torpedoes. We were escorting a convoy in the Western Approaches when a signal was received that the German pocket battleship *Scharnhörst* was leaving Brest harbour. The carrier altered course and calculations were made that their fuel supply would be just sufficient for the Swordfish to reach their target, make an attack and return to the carrier. The air crews were in position and all set to go when the operation was cancelled, the torpedoes replaced with depth charges and normal anti-submarine patrols resumed. Inwardly everyone breathed a sign of relief, for we had realized that it would almost certainly have been a suicide mission – the ninety-knots-an-hour biplanes would have been sitting targets for the land-based fighter aircraft that would have been covering the German battleship.

Air cover for convoys was the turning point in the war in the Atlantic against the German U-boats. With more escort carriers coming into service, the navy went on the offensive and we joined up with corvette squadrons, such as the famous Bird Group, in submarine-hunting operations. Morale was high, but the daily standing to action stations at dawn and dusk – when we were most vulnerable to submarine attack – was a constant reminder of the danger of being aboard a floating petrol tanker. A sister ship, HMS *Avenger*, was lost by enemy action and took only four minutes to sink from the time she was hit.

At the end of the war in Europe a big build-up of naval forces in the Pacific began. Having the necessary seniority and having passed various trade examinations, I was drafted as Acting Petty Officer to join a new fleet carrier, HMS *Theseus*, at Sydney. It was a coincidence to learn some thirty-odd years later from my Commissioner, Sir David McNee, that he had served on the *Theseus* but had not gone with her to the Pacific. Before I reached Sydney VJ day came and thankfully the war was over. I never caught up with *Theseus* and after something of a Cook's tour of the Far East I eventually reached home in the spring of 1946 and was demobilized.

It was on the journey home from Australia that I first heard about careers in the police service. The Metropolitan Police, by far the largest force and responsible for the policing of London, seemed to me to offer the best career prospects, so while I was going through the formalities of being demobbed I sent off my application form to New Scotland Yard.

In due course I was accepted as a recruit and on 1 July 1946, at Peel House, Regency Street, SW1, I was sworn in as a constable. Amongst the forty ex-servicemen who joined on that day and who were to become close colleagues were Colin Woods who thirty years later was to become Deputy Commissioner of the force, receive a knighthood and later be appointed Her Majesty's Chief Inspector of Constabulary, and Dick Pamplin who became a very distinguished chairman of the Police Federation of England and Wales.

For our three months' initial training we stayed at Peel House, which had been founded in 1907 by Sir Edward Henry the Commissioner, but perhaps better known as the Assistant Commissioner (Crime) who introduced the Henry fingerprint classification system to the police service. It was still very much a spartan establishment with its stone floors and dormitories, but these conditions were no hardship to ex-servicemen recruits, although there was one character who arrived with a lot of luggage and his golf clubs but left the same day when he discovered he was not joining as an inspector!

Our initial training was spent mainly in the classrooms learning the theory and practice of law in relation to police duty in London. Our instructors – sergeants and inspectors – were able men who kept us hard at our studies, determined that none of their students would fail their examinations. One or two fell by the wayside but the majority of us successfully completed our training and were posted to our first police stations as probationary constables. I was posted to 'A' Division, Cannon Row police station, in the shadow of the old New Scotland Yard, just off Whitehall, and became PC 548 'A'.

2
Whitehall and the Walworth Road

In the autumn of 1946 Whitehall and the rest of the City of Westminster still bore the scars of enemy bombing, a reminder to those of us who were ex-servicemen of the ordeal the civilian population of London had suffered. Apart from this little had changed from the 1930s. The streets were still lit by gas, with the lamplighters cycling around at dusk and dawn with their long poles to switch the lights on and off. Clean air legislation had yet to be enacted and pea-soup fogs were still a hazard. However, despite post-war austerity that included the continuation of food rationing, there was a feeling of euphoria that the war was over and it was good to be alive and living in the capital city where things were happening. The sights and the sounds, even the most mundane ones – such as Big Ben striking and the tram cars clanking over Westminster Bridge at five o'clock in the morning, disgorging an army of charladies who passed cheery but sometimes ribald comments to the bobbies on the beat as they hurried to their work – added to the excitement. There were, too, moments of unusual peace and quiet, such as just before dawn on a Sunday morning, when standing alone on Westminster Bridge made Wordsworth's sonnet seem very apt.

Cannon Row police station took pride in the fact that all its constables were six feet or more in height, and our recruits training inspector placed much emphasis on good manners and a good appearance. He continually reminded us that we were a showpiece at the centre of the British Empire and that the world reputation of the force was in our hands – somewhat melodramatic perhaps but the advice helped morale because static protection duty in Downing Street and outside the various ministries in Whitehall was not exactly stimulating.

The probationer constables and many of our senior colleagues were war veterans. Although as police officers we were strictly apolitical, I suspect that most of us could be counted among those ex-servicemen who, while admiring Winston Churchill's wartime leadership, had a strong desire for domestic change and were responsible for voting in the Attlee administration. In that immediate post-war period we took a keen interest in current affairs and in the comings and goings in Whitehall, and this helped to prevent boredom from setting in when we were on protection duty. Our Home Secretary, Chuter Ede, was not popular among us because he did nothing about the discontent over the poor salary of police recruits that led to the resignations of many fine men, particularly those who were married and had families, who found they could not afford to remain in the force. A probationary constable then received £5. 5s. per week, plus either a rent allowance of about one pound or rent-free married quarters, if they were available, for married men, and free section-house accommodation for single men. I lived in the Westminster section house just off Victoria Street. A fellow resident was Constable Kenneth Drury and many years later I had the unpleasant task of investigating him after he had retired because of a corrupt association with the pornographer Jimmy Humphreys.

I had somehow imagined that night duty would be exciting, but in reality it was quite often tedious. Between midnight and about 4.30 A.M. when the early morning Covent Garden traffic and the army of charladies began to arrive, the Whitehall area seemed to be mainly inhabited by policemen and cats. During my first month's night duty – 10 P.M. to 6 A.M. – I was learning beats with a senior constable who had just rejoined after service as a pilot in the RAF. One night at about 11.30 we had turned from Pall Mall into Carlton House Terrace when we met an elderly lady housekeeper looking for a ginger cat named Tiddles. It seemed that her Tiddles was not allowed out on the tiles at night; she was concerned about him and asked that if we came across him during the night would we put him through the basement sash window of her house which, because it had iron bars on the inside, she was going to leave slightly open. We promised to do what we could and went on patrolling our beats. In the early hours of the following morning we were again at Carlton House Terrace where we found two ginger cats and about four others of various hues. We caught them all and popped them through the basement window. I could not help wondering whether in the morning the lady blamed Tiddles – assuming one of the ginger cats *was* Tiddles – for bringing home his friends or whether she suspected over-zealous constabulary.

The general political scene was pretty tranquil and, although on some protection posts we carried a revolver, the only threat assessment we were ever given was to be alert to prevent drunks or mentally disturbed persons from throwing a stone through the windows of Number 10 or 11 Downing Street. I remember spending the whole of a three-week tour of night duty in the garden of No. 10. Without a personal radio there was no way of attracting attention other than blowing one's whistle. The next time I was inside No. 10 was some thirty-five years later when, with my Commissioner Sir David McNee, I went to see the Prime Minister, Mrs Thatcher, about personal protection matters.

One of the favourite politicians on the Whitehall beat was Ernest Bevin who as Foreign Secretary occupied the official residence at Carlton House Terrace. Mr Bevin, who was a big man in every sense of the word, owed his popularity to his friendliness, and not infrequently when he returned home late at night he would invite the constable outside on protection duty to join him for a cup of coffee. This practice was known to have caused consternation to supervising inspectors when they found the constable missing and assumed that he had deserted his post.

Our Commissioner at that time was Sir Harold Scott, the first and no doubt the last civil servant to fill the most senior police post in the country. He is chiefly remembered for introducing to the force a competitive examination system for promotion to sergeant and to inspector. After completing four years' service (since reduced to three) and gaining a certificate of competence from the divisional commander, officers could sit an examination, the results of which were published in order of merit. Then, subject to completing five years' service (since reduced to four), promotion followed in that order, within the quota required for the year. I believe the system is an adaptation from an old Indian Civil Service promotion procedure, and it had the merit of eliminating grumbles about nepotism and favouritism that had been constant in the previous system, which relied on candidates who had reached a qualifying standard and completed eight years' service being selected by interview. The Metropolitan Police Federation has since strongly resisted all attempts to revert to the old system, or anything like it. These competitive examinations –

introduced in 1948 – gave the Met an accelerated promotion system long before the introduction in 1964 of the Special Course at the Police Staff College for outstanding young constables. Some thirty years later more than twenty-five per cent of the commissioners and chief constables in the United Kingdom – not to mention numerous deputies and assistant chief officers – were products of the Met system.

One unfortunate feature – which was not put right until 1977 – was that constables and sergeants in the CID were discouraged from taking part in the competitive system because if they were successful they were promoted as uniformed officers with no prospect of ever again going back to CID duties. The great majority of detectives continued to sit the qualifying promotion examination and in due course attended selection boards, where seniority was a major factor. The CID did not therefore get its fair share of young and ambitious officers, since most of these were more attracted by the competitive examination system.

A duty of the constable on traffic point duty in Whitehall at the entrance to the Yard was to assist the progress of the Commissioner and other senior officers when they arrived or departed in their official cars. In 1976, as a Deputy Assistant Commissioner responsible for the complaints and discipline branches, I discovered that Sir Harold Scott had not always been satisfied with our efforts. An old file came on to my desk containing a report dated 1947 by a station inspector, Harold Salisbury, who was responding to a complaint by the Commissioner that constables on the traffic point were not saluting him. In his report the station inspector explained that as most of the constables were recruits just out of the armed forces they did not know what the Commissioner looked like, adding that he was sure no disrespect was intended as he personally was always most punctiliously saluted as he rode in and out of Derby Gate on his bicycle!

Harold Salisbury, a product of Trenchard's pre-war Hendon Police College, had just returned to duty at Cannon Row after service as a Fleet Air Arm pilot and he was well liked by us. It was typical of him that he dealt with this petty complaint and did not mention it to us, correctly judging that it would have done nothing for morale. Later, after service on the directing staff of the newly formed Police Staff College, he left the Met and became the Chief Constable of the old North and East Ridings of Yorkshire Police Force. He retired in 1972 and was then appointed Commissioner of South Australia State Police until 1978 when he had a dispute with Mr Donald Dunstan, then the State Premier, about the activities of the force's special branch.

After two years at Cannon Row I was confirmed in my appointment as a constable and applied for transfer to Rochester Row police station, which is responsible for the Millbank, Victoria and Vauxhall Bridge Road area and where policing was more orthodox. There were ten beats and a number of night crime patrols, but manpower was woefully inadequate and the beats were never full. There were no cars at the station, and I recall parading at 10 P.M. for night duty on one occasion when I was the only constable on duty, supervised by two sergeants and an inspector. I was an authorized cyclist, which meant that when I was using my bicycle on duty I received an allowance of threepence, and on this particular night I was told to get on my bike and to keep cycling around the station territory, ringing in frequently from the blue police telephone posts and boxes, which, until the advent of personal radios in the late 1960s, was the standard means of communication.

The post of station cyclist was a coveted position because while on duty inside the station you were privy to the teleprinter emergency messages from the Information Room at New Scotland Yard. In the absence of any cars it was frequently possible for a keen station cyclist to reach the scene of, for example, a 'suspects on premises' call and make an arrest before the arrival of the single radio car which covered both 'A' and 'C' Divisions. The teleprinter network was extended to all principal police stations in the late 1940s and I was one of a number of constables who attended a five-week operator's course – the target was accuracy with a speed of thirty words a minute. Only a limited number of these courses were held because of the number of trained officers who resigned shortly afterwards to take commercial employment as teleprinter operators. From then on training was given on the job, which generally resulted in two-fingered operators who were not up to commercial standards.

The most troublesome crimes in those early days were shop and office breaking, and thefts from vehicles. Priority was given to shop premises during the night hours and for a constable to leave a shop patrol to which he had been assigned without being relieved by another officer was almost a capital offence. My training in athletics meant that from time to time I made the odd arrest when otherwise the culprit would have escaped. Bearing in mind the lack of any motorized help, it was no bad strategy for a fit PC, particularly if his quarry was running towards the police station, to let him run and partially exhaust himself before making the arrest. Good liaison with the night duty porter at a local men's lodging house often resulted in the clearing up of minor shop breakings. I recall visiting him during the early hours one morning after the discovery of a breaking at a tobacconist's shop and finding a fully-dressed man in bed with several cartons of cigarettes alongside him under the blankets.

Rochester Row station was used as a clearing house where those who were sentenced or remanded in custody at central London magistrates' courts were brought each afternoon to be separated for transfer to the appropriate prison. While on duty one afternoon I was helping a senior sergeant who was regarded as something of a disciplinarian. He was holding the arm of a well-dressed, swarthy-looking man while he took him from one prison van to another, and as they approached the rear steps of the van I heard the man say, 'Take your hands off me, I buy and sell people like you in the West End.' He went up the steps, and the next moment he was sliding down the central corridor of the van on his stomach. As he got up and brushed himself down, the sergeant wagged his finger at him. 'Look here, mister,' he said, 'you may have bought people in the West End but you haven't bought me. You keep a civil tongue in your head, because you'll come through here several times.' He told me the man was Eugene Messina, one of five notorious brothers whose vice empire was destroyed mainly by the efforts in the 1950s of the *Sunday People*'s investigative journalist, Duncan Webb. In a few years I was to have much to do with the West End vice scene and the men behind it, including the property at 49 Curzon Street, W1, which was used for prostitution and still owned by Messina up to the time of his death in Italy in 1971. With his brother Carmelo he had fled the country in September 1950 after the *People*'s exposé of the family's criminal activities, and was never to return. After the Street Offences Act in

1959 outlawed soliciting by prostitutes in the streets or in public places – which was held to include a window – the prostitute living at 49 Curzon Street advertised the oldest profession by means of an illuminated sign in the ground-floor window reading 'French Lessons'.

My fifth and last year as a constable was an eventful one. During the summer I had been selected for clerical work at the Yard and had started relieving duties there, but when in October I was successful in the competitive examination for sergeant, I returned to Rochester Row to prepare for promotion. Some eighteen years were to pass before I was again employed on the force headquarters staff. However, the most important event of 1950, and indeed of my whole career, took place on 12 August at St Stephen's Church, Rochester Row, when I married my wife Edith. The lot of a policeman's wife is a demanding one and I have never ceased to be grateful for all the love, encouragement and support – including the gift of two daughters – that Edith has given to me throughout my police career.

My first five years had passed fairly quickly. I had served my apprenticeship on the streets, dealt with a variety of accidents, suicides, sudden deaths and domestic incidents, learning much about human nature in the process. A policeman rapidly discovers that, regardless of his age or service, the public expect him at all times of emergency or crisis to act with confidence, firmness and discretion. I had learned by experience the physical and moral courage needed to uphold and enforce the law by making arrests and by giving evidence in the courts, including the Central Criminal Court at the Old Bailey.

On the administrative side I had learned about the responsibilities of station duties and, through my brief spell of clerical duty at the Yard, gained some appreciation of the linking between the headquarters of the force and its field stations. Now after completing a pre-promotion course at Hendon I was looking forward to my promotion and additional responsibilities – not least because the increase in salary (£8.4s.10d. to £10.7s.0d. a week) was needed by the newly married Kellands.

One of the pleasant facets of my constabulary life had been the sporting activities that I enjoyed. I had been a regular member of my divisional soccer and cricket teams but my main sporting involvement had been as a member of the Metropolitan Police Athletic Club, representing the force at cross-country running and as a miler and a three-miler on the track. The MPAC had an excellent fixture list with the top London athletic clubs and, quite an event at the time, occasionally went to Belgium for a match with the Royal Racing Club of Brussels and the Belgian Police. The modern all-weather-surface track was of course unheard of, and international athletes were happy to compete for their clubs on the Met's superb 440-yard grass track at Imber Court, Thames Ditton. It was a thrill to take part in those matches as a modest club athlete and, on occasion, to be on the same track as such stars as Sydney Wooderson, Arthur Wint, McDonald Bailey, Chris Chataway and Frank Sando. We had one or two internationals in our Met team including Sergeant David Grigg, a discus thrower who captained the British team on a few occasions. When the 1948 Olympics took place at the brand-new Wembley Stadium I arranged to be on leave and was present every day.

On 1 July 1951 I arrived as a newly promoted sergeant at Carter Street police station just off the Walworth Road, about half-way between the Elephant and Castle and Camberwell Green in south-east London. The Walworth and Elephant and Castle areas were tough neighbourhoods, but they were good places to learn some hard facts about coppering. Violence sometimes flared in the public houses and the odd razor slashing was not unknown, but any use of guns was extremely rare to the point of being almost non-existent. The many back streets of terraced houses, which then were earmarked for demolition and would be replaced by the high-rise estates that were to prove such a social disaster, were friendly places. The corner shop and the public house played a major part in the social life of the residents, old people were respected and street robbery – or mugging, the American euphemism by which this crime is known today – was unheard of.

There seemed to be a proliferation of scrap-metal dealing businesses in the area during this post-war period, for the bomb-damaged property in London contained much valuable lead, copper and other metals waiting to be reclaimed. Sometimes the reclaiming amounted to stealing and 'stops' by policemen under Section 66 of the Metropolitan Police Act in the vicinity of the metal merchants' premises frequently led to arrests.

The scrap-metal dealers were required by law to keep records of their purchases and sales of metal, and their records were liable to inspection by police. This duty was carried out by the CID. Some people in the trade were no doubt receivers of stolen metal – there was a scarcity value at the time – and quite apart from small quantities of scrap the disappearance of complete lorry-loads of valuable metal was not unusual. It did not surprise me that, a decade later, it was in the Walworth area that the Richardson brothers became notorious criminals with extensive interests in the scrap-metal business.

Carter Street police station had a large garden – the only large garden in the Walworth Road – and it was the pride and joy of the chief inspector in charge who, as was usual at most Met police stations at this time, lived in a flat above. I had been at the station some two or three days before I even saw him and then our meeting was somewhat unusual. On a warm afternoon I was on station duty when a man in shirt sleeves and old trousers spoke to me through the open office window overlooking the garden: 'I suppose you're the new sergeant?' He then introduced himself and said he would interview me the following afternoon. Much of this interview was taken up in explaining to me that as street betting in the area was no problem he did not believe in specially employing men in plain clothes to deal with it, but he did not object if sergeants occasionally put on a sports jacket about noon and had a look around the ground.

It has to be remembered that before the Betting and Gaming Act, 1960, which introduced licensed betting shops, all ready-money betting, except on racecourses, was illegal. In most big cities, especially in working-class areas, there was a demand for ready-money betting, and street bookmakers had long satisfied that demand. Betting shops or houses were rare because the fines for keeping such premises were much higher than those imposed for street betting. It was an historic fact that corrupt practices between street bookmakers and some policemen had been – and still were in some places – endemic.

The Met had done its best to face up to the problem and the policy was to attack it by rigorous enforcement of the law. However there were difficulties as the law did not have wide public support. Unlawful betting and gaming were big business with a criminal element frequently involved. Even as a newcomer at that first interview with my sub-divisional chief inspector, I was aware that street betting was rife in the area, with many established pitches. Look-outs were posted at the approaches to a street bookie's pitch to warn him of the approach of policemen, or of any stranger to the vicinity who might be a plain-clothes policeman. Betting normally started about 11 A.M., and ended a few minutes before 2 P.M., which was usually the time of the first race. Specially constructed clockbags were sometimes used to place the betting slips in, ensuring that they were timed and thus preventing the man taking the bets from cheating his employer by adding a slip after the result of a race was known. Business was resumed at about 5.30 to 6.30 P.M., to pay out winning bets and to accept bets on evening greyhound racing. Many of the bets would be as small as a shilling each way, but on a busy pitch about one hundred pounds would be the average daily takings. The bookie invariably had an escape route to be used on the approach of police, usually a nearby house where by arrangement with the occupier he would take refuge until the all-clear was given by a look-out.

There were some senior officers who were naïve enough to believe that if illegal betting activity was ignored it would somehow go away or not cause any trouble. Nothing could be further from the truth and such an attitude was not only stupid but was an encouragement for unscrupulous officers to come to arrangements that in effect unofficially licensed the bookmakers. It is an interesting fact that in the USA, where there is still a resistance to legalizing betting, the 'numbers game' is recognized as a major source of income for the Mafia organized crime syndicates.

The minimum of five years' service before promotion had meant that 1951 was the first year that post-war recruits to the force could become sergeants. We were regarded as some sort of phenomenon by pre-war officers, which of course included all our senior fellow sergeants. There was one other 'instant sergeant', as we were dubbed, at Carter Street, a veteran of the Highland Brigade of the Eighth Army who unfortunately died later that year from some obscure disease he was believed to have contracted during his service in Egypt. He and I conferred and decided that we did not care for the atmosphere at the station about street betting. Although we had not been propositioned, one of our colleagues had commented that 'there was a few bob to be had' from the bookmakers if we were interested. We decided we would show where we stood by arresting a street bookie at the first opportunity.

The next time I was on the early shift I changed out of uniform about noon and went into East Street market where I arrested a 'floater' – a floater was a street bookmaker who did not operate from a fixed pitch with look-outs but, as the name implies, floated or moved about in places like street markets and surreptitiously collected bets. This arrest so upset my shift inspector that he told me I was not to patrol in plain clothes in future without his personal permission. I concluded that an appeal to the gardening chief inspector would not be politic and considered it fortunate indeed when a few weeks later he was transferred on promotion and replaced by a younger man, Chief Inspector John Hill, DFC, from Southwark police station. Mr Hill, who had a fine reputation and was a product of Lord Trenchard's pre-war Hendon Police College which he had entered after a few years' service in the force, later became Deputy Commissioner of the Met and finally retired as Sir John Hill, Her Majesty's Chief Inspector of Constabulary.

His quiet but purposeful style of leadership went a long

way to create confidence and to instil good standards. The young constables and sergeants were encouraged and the bad influence of some of the old regime at the station quickly waned. His philosophy on street betting was 'They won't pay in two places' – meaning that if bookmakers were prosecuted and fined there was no point in paying for police protection. However, this was something of an over-simplification and not as straightforward as it seemed. For such a policy to succeed the senior officer had to be sufficiently experienced and well informed to assess the situation accurately and not be deceived by false factors such as 'stick ups', that is, stooges arranged by the principal bookmakers to be arrested to make the statistics look right. It was also necessary for a few sergeants and constables to share his philosophy and, confident of support, energetically arrest the regular bookmakers, particularly those who were believed to be working for employers with police contacts.

An opportunity to enforce the street betting law presented itself during my first tour of plain-clothes duty. My PC partner and I, both dressed in workmen's overalls, had nearly reached a bookmaker when, warned by a well-dressed man, he ran into his escape house. Looking at the well-dressed man I realized, from descriptions I had been given, that this was not an ordinary look-out but one of the bookmaker barons who controlled a number of local betting pitches. When told he was being arrested for obstructing a police officer in the execution of his duty he said, 'Don't you know who I am?' I replied that I believed that I did but that it didn't matter. His large American car was parked nearby and he suggested that if I was arresting him we went to the police station in it. I refused and walked him to the station via the East Street market, which did not please him. He was doubly displeased when a few minutes after we had reached Carter Street police station my partner arrived with the bookmaker employee whom he had arrested when, in the absence of a look-out, the bookie had unwisely emerged from his place of refuge. If these arrests caused favourable comment in the station canteen, I am sure they caused considerable non-favourable comment amongst the bookmaking fraternity.

Experience is a great teacher. I once had to return to the court a warrant to enter a florist's shop that was being used as a betting house because, despite my taking what I thought were good security precautions, someone had tipped off the bookie who consequently had ceased to use the shop. A long time afterwards I found out that my mistake had been to use a new piece of carbon paper when typing out the warrant application and leaving it in the drawer of the desk. Apparently an inspector, who had retired by the time I discovered this, was able to read the shop address from the carbon paper and presumably passed on the information. This man once remarked to me over a cup of tea in the canteen how stupid it was to chase bookmakers who didn't do any harm and that the 'guvnor' – meaning Mr Hill – was a bloody fool as he could easily be earning fifty pounds a month on the side – at this time a chief inspector's salary was £850 a year. Restricting the use of manpower on enforcing the street betting law, and generally discouraging activity in this direction, was what the inspector had in mind, and he would willingly have organized it. Instead, knowing what the possible consequences for him would be of strict enforcement of the law, he decided to retire while the going was good.

After the betting and gaming legislation of 1960 became law most of the proprietors of street betting businesses applied for licences for betting shops and prospered. One noticeable exception to this rule was Thomas Wisbey, who in 1964 was amongst the men sentenced to thirty years' imprisonment for the Great Train Robbery. His father was the principal of a street betting business at Cook's Road, Walworth, and was most annoyed one winter's evening in 1952 when, by hiding up in a builder's yard near the pitch before dog betting for the night began, my partner and I were able to arrest young Tommy for street betting.

The fact that the West End is only just over the River Thames from Walworth led on one occasion to a big fish, the notorious Billy Hill, self-styled No. 1 gangster in the 1950s, being arrested for keeping a common gaming house in the Walworth Road. It seems that the heat was on Billy in the West End and one afternoon he commandeered a so-called bridge club in the Walworth Road and moved his high-stakes game to it. Unluckily for him a Commissioner's Order in Writing (before the new 1960 legislation the equivalent of a magistrates' warrant) was about to be executed on the club and so he and his clients were arrested for unlawful gaming.

Billy Hill was an international criminal who right up to his death in 1984 at the age of seventy-five was involved in criminal enterprises. In the 1950s and 1960s he tried to organize crime in the American style, using strong-arm protection methods, and he was deported from Australia in 1955 when Scotland Yard through Interpol alerted the police in Sydney before he arrived in the SS *Southern Cross*. He established a niche for himself in our criminal history when in 1957 a prominent barrister named Marrihan was disbarred and expelled by the Bar Council on a charge of 'conduct unbecoming to a gentleman and a barrister' because of his association with him. As the result of evidence given at the disciplinary hearing of conversations between Hill and the barrister on the telephone, which was being tapped on the authority of the Home Secretary, a Committee of Privy Councillors presided over by Lord Birkett was appointed to inquire into and report on the interception of communications. In October 1957 the Birkett Report was published and this lays down the authority and procedures for the interception of communications that still have to be followed.[1]

It is an interesting fact that the enforcement of effective legislation during the 1950s had virtually eliminated gambling for cash prizes from machines, commonly known as 'one-armed bandits', in cafés and shops in the Metropolitan Police area. The almost certain order by the courts for the forfeiture and destruction of the machines, as well as fines for their use, deterred the gaming-machine proprietors from installing them. Previously fifty per cent of the takings from the machines had been guaranteed to them as rental because they held the keys to the mechanism and coin box. On odd occasions an attempt was made to break the embargo, and attention was usually drawn to the café concerned by its suddenly increased popularity. On one such occasion I interviewed the elderly

[1] The most important of these rules, which in 1985, as the result of *Malone* v. *the Commissioner of Police* in the High Court of Justice in 1983 and a hearing in the European Court at Strasburg in 1984, were incorporated in new legislation, were that telephone tapping for the police in England and Wales could only be undertaken by the Post Office with the authority of a warrant signed by the Home Secretary personally. Also, that information discovered must be confined to the authority empowered by the warrant to discover it and not disclosed to private persons or private bodies. In practice information gained by interception is only used for the purpose of assisting investigations and it is not tendered in evidence.

semi-retired owner of the machine which had been seized, and he told me that in pre-Second World War days he could get a 'licence' to install gaming machines in cafés in most of the Met divisions and also in some of the Home Counties police force areas. He deplored the Met's hard-line policy and did not see why the old practice of paying rent to the law – as he put it – could not have continued.

Chief Inspector Hill's good leadership and his policy of interest and encouragement – particularly of his sergeants – was an excellent example of how to motivate personnel. In just over a year the unhealthy relationships between the principals of street betting and gaming businesses and some police officers of supervisory rank, which, I suspect, had existed for many years, were virtually eliminated.

Nevertheless, despite the good morale and a high standard of honesty among the majority of the rank and file at the station, there were undercurrents and sometimes rumours of associations between some officers and local criminals which made me feel uneasy. One incident worried me considerably and although at the time I thought it was probably an isolated occurrence, later on, with the benefit of hindsight, I came to the conclusion that it was symptomatic of a deep-seated malaise that was affecting sections of the CID. The incident concerned the young proprietor of a back-street greengrocer's shop. I had got to know him after I discovered a small fire at the back of the building one evening and called the fire brigade, who put out the blaze before much damage had been caused. He was grateful, and after a fire officer and I had satisfied ourselves there were no suspicious circumstances about the fire and had declined an offer of 'Like some fruit, guv?' I went on my way to complete a fire report. From time to time when I passed the shop on duty I exchanged a few words with the owner, inquiring how business was, whether there had been any good fires lately and so on, and I always found him cheerful. One day, though, I was greeted with a torrent of abuse that ended, 'F— off because all you bleeding coppers are the same: f— no-goods.' After a little while he calmed down and I asked what all the hostility was about.

His story was that a few days earlier an unknown man had come into his shop and offered to sell him some 'bent' (stolen) tea cheap. At this time tea was still rationed and, as was the case with all rationed foodstuffs, a black market existed. He said that he had told the man to push off as he was not interested, and thought nothing more of the matter until the following evening. Then, just as he was closing his shop, the man came back and threw a parcel over the counter, saying, 'The tea you ordered,' and left immediately. The greengrocer said that just as he was going out of the shop door after the stranger, two of the heavy mob (slang for the Flying Squad) grabbed him and accused him of having stolen tea in his shop. At that moment, he told me, he realized that he had been set up, but worse was to come. He was given the alternative of being taken to the nick or coming to an 'arrangement': that he would pay a hundred pounds and they would forget about the tea. He said that he eventually paid the money and the parcel of tea was burnt in his heating stove. When I asked him why he had given in, he said that as an ex-Borstal boy with a bit of form (meaning convictions) he had no choice – he would not be believed and he didn't want to go to prison and lose his business. I could see the logic in this and understood his initial aggression. He was absolutely firm that he would not make an official complaint and that he would deny there had ever been such an incident if I reported the matter and a senior officer came to see him. There was no doubt in my mind that he was speaking the truth and I felt angry, frustrated and ashamed because there was nothing that I could do. A report from me, if it were to be denied by the person concerned, would have served no useful purpose, and in the climate of the times would only have made a fool of me. I had mentally to file away this experience and bide my time. I am fairly sure that some time later I identified one of the detectives concerned, an inspector whose nickname I discovered was 'One Ton Johnny'. A ton is criminal slang for one hundred pounds.

In the autumn of 1952, at the first opportunity, I took the competitive inspectors' police duty examination and was successful. Although I was technically qualified for the rank of inspector, the examination in fact only guaranteed promotion to the rank of station police sergeant. This was a rank peculiar to the Metropolitan Police, a sort of cut-price inspector, because whenever there was a vacancy for a shift inspector a station sergeant was employed as acting – but unpaid – inspector. The rank was eventually abolished in 1970. In 1953 the force was considering doing away with it and consequently made no promotions to the rank during that year but the decision was deferred and promotions again took place, including mine, in January 1954. After passing the examination I was transferred to the South London District HQ, to fill a vacancy there as acting but paid SPS and I remained in this administrative post after my substantive promotion. In 1955 I was one of three post-war SPSs who were among the successful candidates at an Inspectors' Selection Board held at New Scotland Yard and I was allotted a place later in the year on the Junior Command Course at the National Police Staff College, then at Ryton-on-Dunsmore in Warwickshire.

The National Police College, now the Police Staff College, was founded in 1948 after recommendations by the Police Post-War Committee. The objectives set for the college were to raise the standard and efficiency of the police service in a manner which would broaden the outlook, improve the professional knowledge and stimulate the energies of men who had reached or were reaching the middle and higher ranks of the service.

The Junior Command Course A.55/2 at the college in July 1955 had 175 students – nearly all sergeants – representing most of the 126 separate police forces then existing in England and Wales. Among my fellow students was Ronald Gregory, then a sergeant from the Preston Borough force, who retired in 1982 as Chief Constable of the West Yorkshire Metropolitan Constabulary amidst some controversy over his published account of the Yorkshire Ripper murders. Also on the course was Harold Prescott from Lancashire County Constabulary, who while he was an assistant chief constable in that county investigated in 1971 allegations against the Met's C.1 Drug Squad; and two colonial officers, Pengiran Jaya from Brunei and Abdul Rahmin Haji Ismail from Singapore. I enjoyed the company of the last two at Interpol meetings in the late 1970s and early 1980s when they were respectively the Commissioner of Brunei and the Director of CID of the Royal Malaysia Police Force. Abdul Rahmin and I were for a time fellow members of the executive committee of the International Criminal Police Organization, the full title of Interpol.

The commandant of the college, Brigadier Dunn, had been there since its inception. His deputy was Tom Mahir, my local chief when I was a constable at Rochester Row who, besides being awarded the George Medal for gallantry in the Blitz, had a distinguished career, finally retiring as an assistant commissioner and commandant of the staff college. The police members of the directing staff were superintendents and chief inspectors seconded from various police forces in England and Wales. However, it was two members of the small non-police academic staff to whom I, and generations of police students, have most cause to be grateful for furthering our interests in literature and history. They were John Stead and Ian Watt, both of whom moved to Bramshill House, Hartley Witney, when it became the permanent home of the college, where they were responsible for developing the academic side of all higher police training. Perhaps the most significant achievement of John Stead was that through his influence in the late 1960s a number of universities, including Oxford and Cambridge, agreed to accept regularly a number of mature police students to read for degrees in various subjects as Bramshill scholars. Almost without exception the police students have acquitted themselves well and obtained good degrees.

When he retired in 1974 as the Dean of Academic Studies at the staff college, where he was succeeded by Ian Watt, John Stead went to the United States and became Professor of Comparative Police Science at the John Jay College of Criminal Justice at the City University of New York. During his nine years there before retiring in 1983 he promoted regular exchanges between police lecturers from Bramshill and his own university staff, and a visit to him at John Jay became a must for any of his Police Staff College old boys who found themselves in New York. My deputy at the Yard, Deputy Assistant Commissioner David Powis, was a regular visiting lecturer and this was valuable for it enabled us to keep in touch with advanced thinking in the USA about crime and criminal investigation. The professional contacts and associations built up in this way complemented our Interpol relationships and were beneficial both to us at the Yard and to the Federal Agencies of the United States in combating international organized crime.

My six months' residential course at the staff college was enjoyable, the enjoyment being considerably enhanced by promotion to inspector at the end of the first month. The professional studies were not arduous – much of the time was spent in syndicate discussions which were not always particularly stimulating – and there was plenty of opportunity for tennis and other sporting recreation. Above all there was time for reflection, and perhaps for the first time I began to think seriously about the position of the police, particularly the Metropolitan Police, in relation to society. An historical perspective always helps to understand problems, especially ones involving people, and a policeman more than most needs an understanding of human nature.

During the course we were required to write a thesis on a subject of our choice and, influenced by some American literature, particularly the 1951 Senator Kefauver's Committee findings, and my own experiences, I chose as a subject 'Police and Public Corruption'. After discussions with my syndicate director, a superintendent, I was persuaded that as there was insufficient written material on which to base my research I should instead write a paper on crowds and police responsibilities. It seemed that even at the Police Staff College the subject of corruption was not open for discussion. This had been my experience in my own force where, up to that time, the only official reference to the subject I had heard was from the commandant in his final address to recruit constables leaving Peel House, theatrically warning us about the dangers of accepting on a hot day an orange from a street trader and thereby selling our souls. I wondered at the time about his choice of fruit!

What a pity there was such a taboo on open discussion about the problem of corruption at that period, especially among officers being prepared for middle and senior management positions. If an initiative had been taken at the college it might well have had considerable influence and prevented, or limited, much subsequent damage to the police service and to other public sector bodies. The Salmon Commission Report on Standards in Public Life, published after the case of John Poulson *et al*. in 1973/4, showed that the problem was by no means confined to the police service.

3
Vice in the West End

Just before Christmas 1955 I returned to operational duties and was posted to West End Central police station at 27 Savile Row, W1. With just over nine years' service I was very much the junior of the twenty-four inspectors at the station, who were all pre-war men with an average of twenty years plus in the force. West End Central, officially opened in 1941 by King George VI and damaged by enemy bombing shortly afterwards, had replaced the old Marlborough Street and Vine Street stations. It was the chief station of the 'C' or St James's Division – one of the original six divisions when the Met was founded in 1829 – with the responsibility for round-the-clock policing of both Mayfair and Soho. The size and complexity of the command, with some five hundred men working from the same station, made this experiment in centralization a failure. A reorganization that re-established these two territorial commands took place during my service there, albeit with the complication of both administrations functioning from the same building. The difficulty was not finally resolved until 1972 when Vine Street station was reopened.

The dangers, the problems and the temptations that are involved in policing the West End are legendary in the Met's history. In 1886 the Commissioner, Colonel Sir Edmund Henderson, resigned in a storm of criticism after extensive damage to property in Mayfair by an unruly mob that had left a political meeting in Trafalgar Square. In 1887 the Home Secretary of the day, Henry Mathews, resigned in the wake of defeat in the House of Commons after a debate about the unlawful arrest of a Miss Cass, a domestic servant, by PC Endacot of Vine Street for allegedly soliciting prostitution in Regent Street. The PC appeared at the Old Bailey charged with perjury but was acquitted by the jury on the directions of the judge and reinstated as a constable.

In 1929 came the case of the infamous SPS Goddard, who seems to have been on permanent vice squad duty. He was prosecuted and convicted with Mrs Kate Meyrick, known as the London night-club queen, for respectively receiving and giving bribes. Goddard, after serving a sentence of eighteen months' hard labour and successfully claiming £9,000 out of £12,476 found after his arrest in two safe-deposit boxes, went to live in Surrey where he founded the Chessington Zoo.

The conviction of Goddard revealed a grave injustice. Ex-Sergeant Horace Joslin, who by that time was a schoolteacher in Shropshire, had some seven years earlier been dismissed from the Met for supposedly making false allegations against a fellow sergeant. In 1922 Joslin had asked for a personal interview with the Commissioner, Sir William Horwood, to whom he complained that Goddard had asked him to share monies paid as bribes by bookmakers and club owners to save themselves from being arrested and prosecuted. The Commissioner had reported this allegation to the Home Office who conducted an inquiry but, although the findings were not made public, Joslin was obviously not believed because he was subsequently disciplined and dismissed. After the injustice had been raised in Parliament by Jack Hayes, MP, himself an ex-policeman, the Home Secretary offered to reinstate Joslin. Not surprisingly he refused the offer and was paid

£1,500 in compensation and treated as having voluntarily resigned from the force.

The West End acted as a magnet, drawing by day and by night vast numbers of tourists as well as the many thousands who daily commuted to earn their livings in its shops, offices, restaurants, cinemas, clubs and theatres. The number of permanent residents was comparatively small and with such a huge transient populace it was an anonymous larger-than-life place with bustling business activities by day and a frenetic night life. The combination of the people and the environment gave rise to every human predicament that can be imagined, and it was a fascinating but demanding area for policemen to work in. Most tours of duty were full of incident, for truly the place never seemed to sleep.

Regent Street was the dividing line, with Mayfair to the west and Soho to the east. Mayfair, whose fine buildings housed not only the rich and influential, but also the embassies and legations of foreign countries and smart restaurants and night clubs, was a complete contrast to Soho. Despite the overt presence of its prostitutes, Soho, a rabbit warren of narrow streets, passages and alleys, was a warmer and friendlier place than it is today. Many of the small restaurants and cafés, and the one-room workshops where craftsmen such as jewellers, shoe-makers, tailors and musical-instrument makers carried on their traditional trades, have largely disappeared. Strip-tease joints, and sex and pornographic bookshops with garish neon signs advertising their presence had not yet appeared, but the writing was on the wall. As the leases of the premises housing the small businesses expired they were acquired by shady entrepreneurs who let and sublet them at high rentals that could only be met by the burgeoning vice industry. Since the war, in fact, the possession and control of property has been the key to the whole vice situation in the West End and it is pleasing to see that legislation passed in 1983 is at last enabling Westminster City Council to redress the balance by refusing to grant licences allowing premises to be used as sex shops. However, the local authority has a fight on its hands and I am not surprised that the chairman of their environment committee has been quoted as saying that they need more powers to complete their work.

There were characters in Soho with names that seemed to have come straight out of Damon Runyon and some were, or became, notorious – 'Italian Alec', 'Jack Spot', 'The Count', 'Tony the Greek', 'Snowball', 'Big George'. They added colour and sometimes trouble to a cosmopolitan district where violence occasionally broke out, usually between rival factions that were often of different ethnic origins, while the risks of blackmail, extortion and bribery were ever present. The prostitution, seedy late-night drinking clubs and illegal gambling houses attracted a mixed clientele and provided victims – many of them too embarrassed to complain – to be exploited and ripped off.

The publicity attracted by some of the more unsavoury activities in Soho brought political attention, and Royal Commissions and Committees of Inquiry were appointed. As a result sweeping social legislative changes, all of them urgently needed, were to be enacted during the decade after my arrival at West End Central: the Street Offences Act to control prostitution, and the Sexual Offences Act legalizing homosexual relationships between consenting adults followed the Wolfenden Report; a Royal Commission on betting and gaming resulted in a new Betting, Gaming and Lotteries Act licensing betting shops and gambling casinos, and in a new Licensing Act aimed at controlling drinking clubs. The permissive Sixties were fast approaching.

Just before my arrival at the station, some domestic house cleaning had taken place there. Alleged undue familiarity with the proprietors of 'near beer' clubs – disreputable clip joints not requiring a liquor licence because the drinks sold contained less than two per cent alcohol – had led to the transfer of a number of officers. An inspector from the vice squad was under suspension because of his relationships with prostitutes and ponces. He was later found mentally unfit to appear before a disciplinary board and medically unfit to continue to serve as a police officer.

The officer in charge of the whole division was Chief Superintendent Arthur Townsend. He had a reputation as an excellent policeman and a firm disciplinarian who was concerned to ensure integrity among officers working in the West End. It was said that in pre-war days, as an inspector in the East End, he had been responsible for the dismissal of the officer in charge of his station for being in the pay of bookmakers. Bearing in mind the climate of the times, he must have had considerable acumen and no little moral courage. After I had been at West End Central for about a year, he was promoted two ranks in a matter of weeks, a most unusual occurrence, and went to the Yard as deputy to the Assistant Commissioner 'A' Department where he was responsible for operations by uniformed officers and for the Complaints Bureau. During the next ten years or so before his retirement I had many dealings with him and had good cause to admire his professionalism and decisiveness.

My initial briefing from 'A.T.' was comprehensive. He was especially concerned about the welfare and training of the young constables and sergeants serving in the West

End and charged me to provide energetic leadership and to set, and demand, high standards. It was stressed that any association – on or off duty – with undesirable persons in the West End or with premises subject to police supervision, such as clubs and licensed restaurants, would mean an immediate transfer with the consequent effect on career prospects.

He and Sir James Starritt, who was a close colleague of mine for many years until he retired in 1976 whilst deputy to Sir Robert Mark, were two Metropolitan officers who, in my opinion, had an enormous influence for good on the force. They both maintained and demonstrated throughout their careers a deep sense of personal commitment to the values and high standards that are so necessary in the police service. Communication was not so effective then as it is now or their influence would have been greater, but the old adage 'Action speaks louder than words' was certainly true as far as they were concerned. Both were realists and took the view that fine speeches and beautifully constructed memoranda not backed by consistent, determined action and example did not achieve much. They and Sir Robert Mark certainly demonstrated that there is a lot of truth in modern business-study teaching that a company's success is determined more by the personality of its senior executives than by its organization.

As an inspector in charge of a shift it was normal to have upwards of fifty men to deploy and supervise, a high proportion of these being constables on probation who had to be counselled and reported upon every two months until they were confirmed in their appointments after two years' service. This was a satisfying side of my work and in four years I came to know a large number of probationers. Most survived all the pressures and developed into able and confident policemen, and a number of them are now holding senior posts in the Met and in other police forces.

The volume of arrests in the West End was such that it was necessary to employ an inspector from 9 A.M. to 5 P.M. and from 5 P.M. to 1 A.M. on every day of the week except Sunday for the sole purpose of investigating and preferring charges against those who had been arrested. Most were routine cases of soliciting prostitution, drunkenness, shoplifting and so on but there were often more difficult matters to decide, and the seriousness of depriving people of their liberty had always to be borne in mind when we were deciding whether or not they should be kept in custody before their court appearance.

Police duty at this level was very much reactive, for the scale and volume of daily – or even hourly – happenings was such as to keep most of us at full stretch, and our contribution to any long-term planning or strategy was therefore minimal.

Another routine duty was as court inspector at Marlborough Street Metropolitan Magistrates' Court. There we supervised officers attending the court to present their cases, ensured the safe custody of prisoners and generally helped in the smooth running of the court. There was much to learn about the criminal fraternity and about human nature as I watched the daily procession appearing before the stipendiary magistrates. There were some regular attendants – readers may remember the 'Courts Day by Day' column in the *Evening News* which made old Vera, a regular drunk, into quite a celebrity – and the proceedings were occasionally enlivened by unconscious humour.

I remember one case when the late Paul Bennett, VC, a man of military bearing and iron-grey hair, complete with cravat and tie pin – the epitome of a Victorian magistrate – was presiding. A street trader appearing before him pleaded not guilty to causing an obstruction in Oxford Street with his costermonger's barrow. It was common knowledge among policemen that it was necessary to speak very loudly when giving evidence before Mr Bennett because he was slightly deaf and would not wear a hearing aid. The gist of the costermonger's case was that he had been arrested by a 'C' Division PC on the north, or 'D' Division, side of Oxford Street – the street was the boundary between the divisions – and not on the 'C' side, and therefore he should not have been at Marlborough Street Court as all arrests on the north side of Oxford Street were dealt with at Marylebone Court. Mr Bennett was not hearing too well and getting a little testy, so he said to the man, 'Were you in Oxford Street yesterday?' The answer was, 'Yes, Your Worship,' to which the magistrate rejoined, 'Then how could you have been at the seaside – fined forty shillings.'

Another example of Paul Bennett's justice concerned his relationship with Mr James Burge, QC, who specialized in licensing law and often defended club owners in the magistrates' courts. He had something of an antipathy towards Mr Bennett because of his tendency to impose heavy fines in some club cases, and consequently he often made applications for defendants to be taken out of Mr Bennett's list and heard later by another magistrate. The reason given by Mr Burge was always the same, 'Because I submit, with respect, that you are prejudiced in these matters, Your Worship,' and although Mr Bennett did not like these applications he had little alternative but to grant them. One afternoon Mr Burge was representing a club owner summonsed for supplying intoxicating liquor after hours and selling to non-members, and to show cause why the club should not be struck off the register. On this occasion, having agreed with the police solicitor that the 'strike off' summons would not be pressed – a not unusual occurrence – he did not make his usual application but entered pleas of guilty on behalf of his client and told the magistrate that he understood the prosecution was agreeable to the 'strike off' summons being adjourned. With a glint in his eye the magistrate called for the Clubs Officer in the case, a superintendent. In his usual endearing manner he promoted the individual. 'Mr Chief Superintendent,' he said, 'tell me something about this club, how many ladies were in the club when you raided it?' Told that there had only been two or three, Mr Bennett exclaimed, 'I thought so, another of these Soho dens of homosexuality, fined *x* pounds on each summons and the club is struck off the register.'

James Burge rose to make a protest. 'Your Worship, you cannot do this, you did not hear any evidence on oath.'

'Can't I, Mr Burge?' replied the magistrate. 'Very good grounds for appeal, perhaps, but I have done it. Next case, please.'

Mr Burge and his client left the courtroom, but as far as I am aware no appeal was made.

Vice is described in the *Oxford English Dictionary* as 'Evil, especially grossly immoral habit or conduct'. Thank goodness immoral habits or conduct are not necessarily criminal offences and therefore no concern of the police. Another definition is, 'Instrument with two jaws between which a thing may be gripped, usually by operation of a screw so as to leave the hands free for working upon it'. While the first definition is so wide as to be probably only applicable to a clergyman's terms of reference, there have no doubt been occasions when both the man of religion and the policeman would have liked to have had some of their more slippery customers in the instrument with two jaws.

The officer responsible for anti-vice operations in the West End was the Superintendent (Clubs) with a comparatively small number of uniformed officers under his direct control who were temporarily employed in plain clothes while they were on these duties. In the post-war era the problems of the area had grown both in scale and in complexity and there were unpleasant undertones. Superintendent Charles Strath, a dour Scot, was in charge of the Clubs Office and he had been most active in an attempt to deal with the criminal element that was exploiting prostitution by flat farming, that is, letting accommodation at exorbitant rents to prostitutes. The law was, and is, that to constitute a brothel there must be more than one prostitute using a particular set of premises, so the shady agents and landlords concerned were careful to ensure that only the tenant used them.

Among the sergeants then working under Superintendent Strath was Patrick Flynn, who recently retired as a deputy assistant commissioner, and Kenneth Newman, now Sir Kenneth Newman, Commissioner of Police, both of whom were former members of the Palestine Police. As a result of a long and extensive investigation in 1955 by Sergeant Flynn and others on B. Silver and W. Cooper, estate agents with an office in Soho at 34 Romilly Street, evidence was obtained of prostitutes paying exorbitant rents for rooms in Soho used exclusively by them for their trade. Although the legislation had not been used under these particular circumstances before, Mr Strath obtained warrants under Section 1 of the Vagrancy Act, 1898, which made it an offence for a man knowingly to live wholly or in part on the earnings of prostitution.

This was the legislation used before the Sexual Offences Act, 1956, was enacted to prosecute the ponce or pimp who cohabited with and lived off a prostitute.

Warrants for the arrest of Bernard Silver, seven other men and one woman, a prostitute named Albertine Falzon, were executed and they eventually stood trial at the Old Bailey in February 1956. The presentation of the case for the prosecution by Mr Mervyn Griffith-Jones took some thirteen days, but unfortunately the judge, Mr Justice Maud, held that there was no case to answer.

The learned judge ruled that a landlord or estate agent was in the same position as a shopkeeper, doctor or barrister who received money from a prostitute as a customer or client, and that they were living on these monies as their own earnings and not those of a prostitute. He also commented that the court was not a court of morals, and that the problems of prostitution and how to deal with it were infinitely complicated and nothing but a most thorny problem.

The ruling was very disappointing to Mr Strath and his Clubs Office staff who had worked hard to obtain the evidence to bring these people to trial. However, in 1961 in *Shaw* v. *DPP* – the infamous *Ladies Directory* case[1] – the decision was reversed. On appeal in that case the court held that where a man was paid for goods and services supplied by him to prostitutes for the purposes of their prostitution which he would not supply but for the fact that they were prostitutes, he was guilty of living on

[1] *Shaw* v. *DPP* [1961] 125 JP 437; [1961] 2 All ER 446). This case concerns the prosecution and sentence to nine months' imprisonment of a man named Shaw for living on the earnings of prostitutes. Following the Street Offences Act, which removed prostitutes from the streets, he published the 'Ladies Directory' and prostitutes paid him to have advertisements inserted in it.

their earnings. This decision considerably strengthened the hands of the police in their pursuit of the big fish lurking in the murky waters of the vice trade.

Flat farmers noted the evidence in the 1956 *Silver and Others* case and they all, including Bernard Silver himself, took precautions to distance themselves from their prostitute tenants. No longer did these women go openly to an estate agent's office, but dealt through rent collectors and other intermediaries so that the identity of their real landlord was concealed from them. Rent books were misleading documents for they recorded the receipt of a normal rent, while in practice the prostitute tenants paid in cash amounts up to ten times the ones shown, as well as key money of about £100 whenever a flat changed hands.

It is interesting to note here that Silver profited by his escape from conviction and went on during the next two decades to become the evil genius of syndicated vice in the West End and a thoroughly bad and corrupting influence. The Met finally caught up with him in 1974 after a major operation by a Serious Crime Squad team led by Detective Chief Superintendent Bert Wickstead, and an *exposé* naming him and his associates in the Sunday newspaper the *News of the World*. At the Old Bailey in December 1974 I saw him sentenced to six years' imprisonment and fined £30,000 for a similar offence, although on a much larger scale, to the one for which he was acquitted in 1956. Albertine Falzon, the prostitute charged with him at that time, whom he later married, had committed suicide in the 1970s by jumping from the window of her business flat in Peter Street, Soho.

One indication of an organization behind prostitution was the regular appearance of French-born prostitutes on the West End scene. When they were arrested, the police invariably found that they spoke very little English, had obtained a British passport by marriage so that they could not be deported, and gave the address of a Brixton firm of solicitors whom they wished to represent them. Particulars of these women were reported to the Yard and a woman detective inspector from C.1 Branch carried out investigations, usually discovering that the women had been through marriages of convenience with men who had been paid for their services. However, these marriages were legal and as the women were not willing to co-operate, it never seemed possible to establish the behind-the-scenes organizers, although we had our suspicions about them and their links with the flats occupied by the prostitutes.

With hindsight, I am sure now that too low a priority was given to the organized aspect of vice, and at the same time a lack of co-ordination and co-operation between the local operational officers from the uniformed side and the C.1 CID officers worked to the advantage of the vice barons. An attitude that prostitution was something that had existed since time immemorial, that nothing much could be done about it and that it had little to do with real crime even if it was sincerely held, was outdated. Certainly as far as London was concerned, this was a gross misreading of a developing situation that was only fully revealed in the 1970s when the Serious Crime Squad prosecuted members of West End vice syndicates. Most of the individuals who had been involved in the prostitution rackets in the 1950s and their associates during the next two decades diversified by becoming involved in the lucrative striptease and pornography trades.

The Commissioner from 1953 to 1958 was Sir John Nott-Bower. He had been the Deputy Commissioner since 1946, having joined the Met in 1933 from the Indian

Police in the rank of Chief Constable, which would now be graded as deputy assistant commissioner. For a senior officer with such long service he was rarely heard of, or seen, by the rank and file of the force. In his book *The Queen's Peace*, which covers the origins and development of the Metropolitan Police from 1829 to 1979, the historian David Ascoli expresses the opinion that Nott-Bower, above all, was excessively idle, which may account for his anonymity. Certainly with the varied vested interests that were involved, it would have needed the active participation of the Commissioner to have ensured that the organized vice problem was seriously attacked.

I had been at West End Central for about two years and had learned a good deal about Soho and the criminal element that gathered there. A particularly useful time to have a good look around the labyrinth of passages, back rooms and basements used as licensed and unlicensed refreshment houses, card clubs and accommodation addresses was between 6 A.M. and 7 A.M. When I was on early shift, which began at six o'clock, a casual visit to these kinds of premises with a sergeant or constable, both of us in uniform, could be made without arousing suspicion. By using our eyes and having a friendly chat with someone cleaning up or just looking after the place, it was surprising how much useful information could be gleaned. Some of this had been passed to Superintendent Strath and as a result he offered me a tour of duty with his unit.

Superintendent Strath was a fearless and purposeful officer whom we all admired and respected, but he was regarded by many as excessively secretive. He only informed his staff about on-going operations on a need-to-know basis, and I have no doubt that his experiences in his early days in the force had made him regard the wartime slogan 'Careless talk costs lives' as particularly apposite for his present command. On occasions when he was briefing his staff for a club raid in Soho he would instruct officers in advance on what was required of them after entering the club but omit to give its name or address, concluding his briefing with the words, 'Watch, and follow me.' A crocodile of men and women would wander through the Soho streets, and if the officer carrying out that particular observation was not at the place where Mr Strath had arranged a rendezvous, this was taken to mean that the conditions were not opportune for the raid. We would then all return to our base still guessing at our target!

The main duty of the Clubs Office inspector was to organize and direct the work of the constable-and-sergeant teams engaged in detecting cases of men living on the earnings of prostitutes, who were commonly referred to as ponces. At this time there were literally thousands of prostitutes on the West End streets and no doubt nearly all of them had a ponce.

The press publicity given during the 1950s to the vice activities of the five Messina brothers, who although born in Egypt claimed to be British subjects but were eventually declared to be Italian citizens, had alerted the authorities to the continental-style ponce who organized and commercially exploited prostitutes. Two of the brothers, Alfredo and Attilio, were jailed at the Old Bailey in 1951 and 1959 respectively for living on the immoral earnings of prostitutes.

In 1956, after a sensational trial in Belgium, Eugene was sentenced to seven years' imprisonment for procuring women for prostitution, and his brother Carmello, although acquitted on the procuring charge, was sent to prison for nine months for passport and firearms offences.

Much of the evidence in this case was about their vice empire in London and the prosecutor said that ten women, born on the Continent but British by marriage, who were working as prostitutes in London had refused to attend the trial as witnesses.

In Parliament the Home Secretary of the day, Mr Gwilym Lloyd-George, got the backwash of the Belgian trial and came under attack about the blatant prostitution on the streets of London. In a debate he said that the Wolfenden Committee were considering the problem, but no changes in the law were contemplated in the current year. The view expressed by the popular press was that the problem demanded rather more prompt attention than was promised by the deliberations of a leisurely committee.

The Messinas at the time were unique; they were more like big-time racketeers than normal ponces, who generally lacked the brains and the energy to organize large-scale prostitution. It was the opinion of Duncan Webb, a reporter for the *Sunday People* who was principally responsible for exposing them, that they were able to operate so long and so successfully because they were brothers in a family business and a bond existed between them which would have been absent among five independent operators.

When the Vagrancy Act, 1898, was first placed on the statute book its purpose was mainly to prevent men forcing women to become prostitutes by violence. The typical image of the ponce in London was for many years the low type of man who loitered in the street where the prostitute with whom he lived was soliciting, to protect her and also to take from her the money she obtained from her customers. He was not difficult to catch and was seen as a nuisance rather than as any particular menace to society. Times had changed, however, and more sophisticated criminals were turning their attentions to getting rich quick on the earnings of prostitution.

The problem was to be selective and aim for quality rather than quantity by targeting the big fish rather than catching the minnows. To maintain this kind of strategy was not easy, for it is natural to want results and the numbers game has always complicated many types of police work. We had to persuade the observation officers to accept a system of priorities. There were cases where prostitutes shopped their ponces because they were being violent or because they had found out that there was a rival for his affections. There were also those who sought to divert attention from themselves by informing on others – a not unusual phenomenon among the criminal fraternity. It was therefore essential for the inspector to be confident in and to enjoy the confidence of his operational teams and of his boss, the superintendent, through whom the unit's strategy was formulated.

Obtaining the necessary evidence was still difficult. The police procedure to establish that a man was living wholly or in part on the earnings of prostitution required keeping him and the prostitute under observation for five days. This was to establish a prima-facie case by showing their association and that he was not following any normal occupation. It meant literally knowing where the suspect was from the time he woke up in the morning until he went to bed at night. Much tenacity, ingenuity and patience were needed by officers to keep up this sort of surveillance successfully, all desirable attributes in a good detective.

The case of Jean Baptiste Hubert, or Belgian Johnny, as he was known in the West End, illustrates the avarice of the vice merchant and his malignant influence over women. His wife, born in France, and at least two other women worked for him as prostitutes while he lived a life of leisure.

Some time before I began my Clubs Office duties a Soho contact had spoken to me about a man called Belgian Johnny who drove a Jaguar and whom he described as a 'flash ponce'. There was no suspect on our files bearing that name and my informant could only tell me he believed the man lived in St John's Wood.

One morning in 1958 when I came on duty I found a note from the night duty station officer, Sergeant Jim Mace, who had Clubs Office experience, together with a statement from a cab driver. The note told me that a young prostitute, Yeeta Winter, had been brought to the station by the cabby in the early hours of the morning from an address in St John's Wood and that she had a bruised eye, which she said had been caused by her Belgian ponce. When asked to make a statement, she had refused and left the station.

I sent two of my observation officers to locate the cab driver and begin the inquiry. Having established the address and discovered that the tenant was named Hubert, inquiries at the Aliens' Registration Office quickly identified him as Jean Baptiste Hubert, a Belgian subject first registered in the United Kingdom in June 1940 as a member of the Free Belgian Forces. His Belgian record disclosed that he was aged thirty-nine with a number of criminal convictions that included robbery and theft, and in 1953 he had been sentenced in Brussels to one year's imprisonment and fined 1,000 francs for being a ponce. I discovered that as the result of an inquiry from Belgium in 1953 following his arrest there, C.1 Branch at the Yard had replied through Interpol that he was associating with an active French-born but British-by-marriage prostitute named Germaine Borelli, who had a flat she used for her trade in Wardour Street. It was later established that he had, in fact, married Borelli, who was forty-eight years old, at Hampstead Register Office in December 1957.

The observation by constables Calvert and Budworth disclosed that Yeeta Winter and Hubert seemed to have got over their quarrel and were living together at the St John's Wood flat. One afternoon at the beginning of the five-day observation, I went with one of them to interview the prostitute's mother, a respectable widow who lived off the Bayswater Road. While we were there her daughter arrived at the flat and I made the excuse that we were trying to find her because of the assault complaint she had made at West End Central. She said that this had been resolved and that she did not want to do anything more about it, but her mother later made a statement about the association of her twenty-two-year-old daughter with Hubert which had begun about three years earlier. Yeeta's first conviction for soliciting was early in 1958 and there was no doubt that she had been put on the streets by the Belgian, who completely dominated her.

The prostitute's mother also told me that her daughter had said that a few weeks previously two men, claiming to be policemen, had called at the St John's Wood flat early in the morning and demanded £200 from Johnny – which he paid – or they would arrest him. I reported this development to Superintendent Strath. Later, after his arrest, Hubert co-operated over the incident and as the result of extensive CID inquiries, two men with previous convictions were arrested and convicted for this offence and for several others when, masquerading as police officers, they had extorted money from men living with prostitutes.

The observation on Hubert having been completed, statements were prepared and a warrant for his arrest was authorized and obtained. I executed the warrant with constables Calvert and Budworth by arresting Hubert at his St John's Wood flat at about 2 A.M. one morning, a few minutes after Yeeta had returned from the West End with her earnings for the night, which amounted to about £40. She later made a statement in which she said she regularly gave her ponce £30 or £40 a night. An idea of the value of this money may be drawn from the fact that my salary then as an inspector was £75 a month!

Extensive inquiries were made based on letters and documents found at Hubert's flat when he was arrested, and through Interpol it was discovered that he was behind a company formed in Paris which was having twenty-three bachelor flats constructed in the south of France at Villeneuve. Exchange control regulations were in existence at this time so inquiries were made at the Bank of England, but there was no record of any transfer of money in or out of the United Kingdom by Hubert. No doubt he, or couriers acting for him, had smuggled money out of the country to finance the building project.

A court order was obtained to examine his bank account, and this showed that £1,000 had been paid into the account in cash during the first eight months of the year, including some payments by Borelli when he was visiting France. He was a regular gambler at dog-racing tracks, had an account with an off-course credit bookmaker and owned a fairly new Jaguar. It came as no surprise that not much of his vice income was passing through his bank account.

While he was in custody awaiting trial his wife, the

prostitute Borelli who was continuing to practise her trade from her Wardour Street flat, looked after his interests, including making arrangements for his legal representation.

In addition to the charge of living on the earnings of prostitution, he was dealt with for assaulting PC Calvert at the time of his arrest when he lost his temper and kicked the constable in the leg. In October 1958 at the County of London Sessions he was found guilty on both charges and sentenced to fifteen months' and three months' imprisonment, the sentences to be consecutive. His counsel, in mitigation, stressed that his client's greatest punishment would be that as a convicted alien he was certain to be deported. The judge made no specific recommendation on this point but I, too, thought that Hubert would be deported as an undesirable alien. For some reason this did not happen.

I was again aware of Belgian Johnny's continued presence in this country in March 1960, some eighteen months after his conviction. At this time I was a chief inspector at Notting Hill and in the early hours of one morning had just led a raid on the Betavon Residential Club in Westbourne Grove, one of the many disreputable drinking clubs that troubled the district. Only a barmaid was in charge of the sleazy place, the ground floor of an ordinary house, and when asked who owned the club she said it was a Mr Herbert but that he was out and did not live there. After seeing the customers off the premises and reporting the barmaid, we left the club. I was standing outside on the pavement with a colleague when I saw a man walking towards me who looked vaguely familiar. As he reached us the penny dropped; Mr Herbert, the club owner, was none other than Jean Baptiste Hubert, alias Belgian Johnny.

'Hello, Johnny, how are you?' I said to him.

He stopped. 'OK,' he replied cautiously.

'I believe you are doing very well with the club here.'

'Yes, it's OK.'

I could see that he was puzzled so I said, 'You don't remember me, do you?' and as there was no answer, 'London Sessions, 1958.'

There was instant recognition and he said angrily, 'I suppose you do like the bloody last time, send me to prison.'

We went into his club with him where he was formally cautioned and reported for various licensing offences, and afterwards we returned to Notting Hill police station. As was our practice at this time in an attempt to put these troublesome clubs out of business, we visited the club again about an hour later. Finding that there were people inside we raided it once more, and this time Belgian Johnny was behind the bar. About three days later we again raided the club when drinking was taking place after hours.

The sequel to this was that the paper work was expedited and an early date of hearing arranged at Marylebone Magistrates' Court. Hubert appeared, pleaded guilty to all summonses and was fined about £200, which he paid immediately from a roll of bank notes. I then submitted a comprehensive report to the Home Office Aliens' Department, expressing the opinion that his presence in the United Kingdom was not conducive to the public good. The Home Secretary made a deportation order and the country was at last rid of the international *souteneur*, Jean Baptiste Hubert. As for the prostitute Yeeta Winter, to the best of my knowledge she did not come again to our notice and it is to be hoped that, free from the evil influence of the Belgian ponce, she responded to her mother's love and concern by leaving the West End vice scene.

The extensive surveillance that was necessary to collect evidence to prosecute men living on the earnings of prostitution gave those engaged on it an insight into a sordid world. Prostitutes who were fortunate enough to have a business flat jealously guarded the asset and had no wish to be convicted of brothel-keeping by letting other women use their premises. On odd occasions, however, an observation would show that in order to cater for the sexual deviances of some of her customers a prostitute would regularly arrange for a second woman to join her at her flat, thus in law turning the premises into a brothel.

Some idea of the amount of money earned by a Soho prostitute can be seen from a particular case where the prostitute of a ponce we arrested solicited her customers in Broadwick Street and took them to her flat in nearby Duck Lane. When the man was arrested I found a little red notebook in which her maid had kept a daily record of the prostitute's earnings on an hour-by-hour and client-by-client basis. The book showed that in twenty days in March 1957 some £928 had been earned – a tax-free income of over £15,000 a year. Allowing for inflation this would be in the region of £140,000 today. A typical working day for this prostitute began at 6.30 P.M. and finished about 12.30 A.M., during which time she entertained about thirty customers.

It does not need much imagination to realize the importance that Soho vice merchants attached to finding out the identities of the officers employed on observation duties, the cars they were using and who their targets were. Cunning had to be matched with cunning; for instance, when we discovered that the registration numbers of our official cars were being logged and passed around, arrangements were made to use private-hire ones which were changed fairly frequently and not parked near the police station. To retain the element of surprise and because of the unpleasant nature of the work, constables and sergeants were limited to a three months' tour of duty in any one year and they were carefully briefed, especially on the need to guard against the leakage of information. In general the officers selected for this duty enjoyed the challenge and showed great stamina and strength of character.

A perennial problem in the West End, especially in connection with clubs, restaurants and licensed premises in general, has been protection rackets. The methods of the criminals involved in the 1950s and 1960s were not particularly subtle. Strong-arm men caused disturbances to disrupt trade and then an accomplice offered to 'mind' the business to stop such incidents happening again. Of course, regular payments were demanded for their services. Fear of personal violence and the fact that the proprietors of these types of business were often skating on thin ice as far as the licensing and other laws were concerned made them reluctant to complain to the police. To combat this type of crime it is necessary to be well informed and to inspire confidence in the victim in order to gain his or her co-operation. The Clubs Office staff and all the senior officers continually monitored reports of assaults and, especially when they were on inside observation duties, were alert to identify such cases.

Before the 1961 Licensing Act anyone could start a members' club by paying a five-shilling fee at the local magistrates' court to have it officially recorded in the register. It was not uncommon for fictitious names and addresses to be given, and some criminals and their nominees were always trying to get rich quick by running shady drinking clubs in the basements and back rooms of Soho. Any disputes that these individuals had with each other, or with their customers, were likely to be settled by force, and the only law they recognized was the law of the jungle. These so-called clubs were a continual source of trouble and to keep control of the situation much time, energy and police resources had to be used. There is no doubt in my mind that liquor, prostitution and illegal gaming were, and still are, inextricably linked with crime and criminals. This, quite apart from any social reasons, fully justified the high priority given in the West End to enforcing the law – inadequate though it was. It is a pity that when porn shops mushroomed in Soho in the 1970s the enforcement of the law to control them – the Obscene Publications Act – was not made the responsibility of the Clubs Office. However, that is another story of which more will be said later.

After my six months' tour of duty with the Clubs Office I went back to my normal duties at West End Central much better informed about the criminal fraternity of the West End, how they operated and the dangers they posed. There had been no blatant direct offer of bribes because criminals do not work that way – they make their own inquiries about the reputation of individual police officers and this very much conditions their behaviour. I did on occasion receive the usual oblique approaches from arrested ponces or their associates such as 'We can meet for a talk, can't we?' and 'You do drink, don't you?' 'Drink' in this context is the London criminal slang for a bribe, and of course any indication on my part of a willingness to be corrupt would have been welcomed.

The report of the Wolfenden Committee had highlighted the growing problems arising from prostitution, especially in the West End, and the need for new legislation. The overt presence of thousands of prostitutes on the West End streets was a disgrace to the capital city, and foreign visitors often passed comments about this to policemen. The law under the Metropolitan Police Act, 1839 – a maximum fine of forty shillings (£2) for soliciting to the annoyance of passengers or residents – was completely inadequate. The police were expected to control the situation by making arrests, but although complaints were received from residents few of them were willing to come forward and attend court to prove a case. Although very few of the prostitutes arrested ever pleaded not guilty, constables were becoming concerned about giving evidence in cases where in their opinion the men solicited appeared annoyed, when the public view was that men were fairly indifferent to these approaches.

Prostitutes appeared on the streets as if organized in shifts. The first of the day, usually about noon, would be the very well-dressed and well-groomed frequenters of Bond Street and Chesterfield Gardens, many of whom commuted from as far away as Brighton. Some of the Soho regulars who had flats nearby were also on the streets by lunch time but from 5 P.M. onwards, as offices and shops began to close, the prostitute army steadily increased, occupying Mayfair, Piccadilly and virtually every street in Soho. Last of all was the midnight shift in Glasshouse Street outside the Regent Palace Hotel, who were mainly older professionals with heavy make-up who plied their trade until nearly dawn – all in all not a pretty sight. I remember one night walking along Shaftesbury Avenue after midnight and counting, between Piccadilly

Circus and Charing Cross Road, over one hundred prostitutes.

In the Metropolitan Police District in 1958 there were 16,990 arrests for prostitution involving some 2,000 individual women, the great majority of these being dealt with at West End Central. At this time it was estimated that there were about 5,000 prostitutes on the streets of central London.

The Conservative Government's answer was to introduce the Street Offences Act, which removed the need to prove annoyance before a prostitute could be arrested and increased the penalties to £10 for the first offence, £25 for the second and three months' imprisonment for a third or subsequent offence. It also increased the penalty for a man living on the earnings of prostitution from two years' imprisonment to seven years.

There was a lot of opposition to this new Act and one of the main objections was that the removal of the requirement to prove annoyance would result in policemen arresting innocent women. The ministers concerned with the legislation were anxious to counteract this rather emotive point, which probably accounted for my being told one evening before the Act received its final reading to collect the Attorney-General, Sir Reginald Manningham-Buller, QC, and the Right Honourable David Renton, QC, the joint Parliamentary Under Secretary of State at the Home Office, from the House of Commons and give them a tour of the West End prostitution scene.

Sir Reginald told me that when he was a young soldier in the First World War Villiers Street beside Charing Cross Station was the notorious prostitute area. The situation had changed because there was now no prostitution south of Piccadilly and Coventry Street, and I took them through Villiers Street to demonstrate this. Shortly afterwards, when we were driving along Shaftesbury Avenue towards Piccadilly Circus so that they could see the prostitutes standing on the pavement and in doorways, I pointed out one prostitute who, with a man, was getting into a taxi on the Windmill Street cab rank. There were a few cabbies on this rank who allowed prostitutes to use their cabs for the purposes of their trade and this was one of them. We followed behind the taxi and before it had gone many yards the man was facing the rear window and his movement clearly indicated what was going on. This facet of prostitution was new to my distinguished passengers and they asked what we did about the cab drivers. I explained that we withdrew the licences of any drivers involved but that to prove their guilty knowledge it was necessary to observe them over a few days to establish a regular pattern of conduct.

Finally, just before midnight, I took them to Curzon Street and parked the car. Among several women busy soliciting passing men there, particularly noticeable was Marie Smith, a French-born prostitute, who was working from her flat at 49 Curzon Street, a house owned by Eugene Messina who at that time was imprisoned in Belgium. Smith, who was wearing a skin-tight pink suit, persistently accosted nearly every man who passed along the street and when she was successful she took her client to No. 49 and was back again on the street in about ten minutes.

When I finally returned the learned gentlemen to the House of Commons, the Attorney-General thanked me for my help and remarked, 'Even I would recognize a prostitute now!' Their experience of the situation on the streets that night was reflected in their subsequent speeches in the House of Commons supporting the new Act and firmly rejecting the mistaken identity theory.

After Eugene Messina's death in Italy in 1970, Marie Smith, who for many years had practised as a prostitute at 49 Curzon Street, took an action in the High Court claiming half of his £1 million fortune. She lost her case because the judge held that her marriage to him some six months before his death was invalid and that her marriage of convenience in 1954 to William Smith, a British subject and former Shanghai policeman, was still legal. He cancelled a decree nisi granted to her in June 1970 on the basis that her case was false and misleading: she said she had not realized her marriage to Smith at the Paddington register office was a marriage ceremony. She was ordered to pay costs – unofficially estimated at £7,000 – to Salvator Messina, Eugene's eldest brother.

The government obviously attached importance to the women's lobby on the Street Offences Act because a few nights after my evening with the Attorney-General I was detailed to give Miss Patricia Hornsby-Smith, then a Parliamentary Under Secretary of State at the Home Office, and Miss Joan Vickers, MP for Devonport, a similar guided tour. At the end of the evening, after returning Miss Vickers to the House of Commons, I took Miss Hornsby-Smith to her Westminster home and she told me that she thought her parliamentary colleague was too committed to her particular women's pressure group to vote for the Act, despite what she had seen on our tour.

It is now history that the Street Offences Act came into force in August 1959 and overnight the vast majority of an estimated population of 5,000 prostitutes left the streets of central London. Why did this legislation have such a dramatic effect? I am quite sure it was not the fear of increased fines but rather the threat of imprisonment that caused these women to leave the streets and for some to leave the oldest profession altogether. As one prostitute remarked to me, 'I don't mind paying fines and giving money to my ponce but I am not going to prison for him.'

Over the years there has been some return of prostitutes to the streets, but in comparison with the thousands appearing daily in the pre-1959 period the numbers are infinitesimal. In the years immediately following the Street Offences Act there was much ill-informed comment to the effect that there had been no reduction in the number of prostitutes because they had been driven underground – wherever that may be – and into clubs. This was not the case because in order to exist prostitution has to find customers among the public and the publicity generated would inevitably bring the activity to the notice of the police.

Legal prostitution, that is one woman in one flat, still of course went on and continues. Illuminated doorbells in Soho advertise the prostitute occupant, and the scarcity of available flats has added to their value, which means that the people controlling such property are still making a lot of money out of vice. Sophisticated so-called escort agencies and high-price 'call girl' systems have developed to satisfy demand, but again the number of individual women involved is comparatively small. The hostesses of certain night-clubs might when the clubs close take their partners for the evening home or go with them to a hotel, but this type of prostitution existed before the Act and has not noticeably increased.

There is no doubt that the Street Offences Act, even if by almost negative means, was far more effective than was ever anticipated in reducing prostitution. This must be of benefit to society and particularly to the residents of parts of Mayfair and Soho whose environment has been very much improved by the absence of a street nuisance.

In May 1964 *The Justice of the Peace and Local Government Review* carried out an extensive survey of the Street Offences Act after five years. They concluded that there had been an enormous decline in the number of women engaged in prostitution and made this interesting comment about demand and supply:

> There are grounds for asserting, indeed, that the Street Offences Act has given the lie to the assumption that the supply in this field is invariably created by the demand. While certainly true up to a certain level, beyond this level it is more likely that the supply, through the advertising it generates, in fact creates the demand, an assertion, incidentally, that few engaged in the advertising field would be unable to accept.

Early in 1959 there was concern about the growth in the number of illegal *chemin de fer* gaming parties which were said to be taking place in Belgravia and Chelsea. There were rumours that strong-arm criminals had on at least one occasion robbed an organizer and his punters, who because of the illegality of the party were unwilling to complain to the police.

The commander of 'B' Division, who was responsible for policing Chelsea and Belgravia, was John Wray and at this time he occupied a police house at Brixton, while I lived in a police flat nearby. One day early in March 1959 he called to see me and explained that he had the approval of the officer in charge of central and west London to employ me and a sergeant of my choice to investigate unlawful gambling parties he believed were taking place on his territory. For security reasons he did not wish me to go to his office at Chelsea for the time being. I chose Sergeant 'Spike' Hughes, an experienced vice investigator, to work with me, collected a hire car from the police garage at Lambeth and, as they say, we commenced our inquiries.

We fairly quickly established the organization behind two separate *chemin de fer* syndicates, one patronized by a wealthy clientele from Chelsea, Belgravia and the City and the other by Warren Street car traders, bookmakers, publicans and their friends, including the notorious Billy Hill. This latter group often used the Star Tavern in Belgrave Mews as a meeting place and the gaming party could be located by following them when they left.

By surreptitiously removing the contents of rubbish bins put outside after a gaming party was over and piecing together torn-up cheques, bank note wrappers and similar debris, we secured some useful evidence. However, this and other evidence that was gathered as the result of our surveillance seemed of little use because the organizers kept changing the venues of the parties, making it impossible to prove – as we were required by the Gaming Act of 1845 – habitual use of the premises. The law was being brought into disrepute and the need for new legislation to license certain types of gaming was self-evident. I was about to recommend that because of the precautions being taken by the gaming party organizers our investigations should be temporarily discontinued when we located a house at Netherton Grove in Chelsea which was being used for regular *chemin de fer* parties.

We kept observation and found that the ground-floor garden room was used for gaming on Wednesday, Thursday and Friday nights and that between twenty and thirty people were regularly attending these parties. It was decided that, under the legislation then applicable, the Commissioner was justified in signing an Order in Writing authorizing the local superintendent and other officers named in the Order to enter the premises as an alleged common gaming house.

On Friday 20 March a raiding party was assembled and briefed by Superintendent Tom Thomas of Chelsea. In this type of raid, where no inside observation had taken place, it was important to enter the house quickly and quietly in order to get detailed evidence. From our observation the previous week we had identified a number of gamblers, including a man whose christian name was Norman, who usually left the parties shortly after midnight. Just before 1 A.M., accompanied by Woman Sergeant McCann, I rang the front door bell and the door, secured by a safety chain, was opened about three inches by a man. 'We are friends of Norman,' Miss McCann said, whereupon the safety chain was removed and the door opened, allowing us to enter the house, followed immediately by the raiding party. We went quickly to the rear garden room – passing a couple who, quite oblivious to our entry, were kissing on a *chaise-longue* on the landing – and took up positions around the chemmy table while the game was still in progress. Superintendent Thomas then introduced himself, read the Order in Writing under the Gaming Act and cautioned everyone in the room. They all looked pretty surprised at the arrival of the police and even more discomfited when they were told they were being arrested and taken to Chelsea police station.

Twenty-two people, including four women, were arrested and all charged with being found in a common gaming house. Five of the men, including the Old Etonian tenant of the house and a professional croupier, were additionally charged with keeping a common gaming house. Some eight hours later they appeared at West London Magistrates' Court. The presiding magistrate, Mr

Kenneth J. Barraclough, remanded the five men on bail, who said they wished to plead not guilty. All the frequenters agreed to be bound over for twelve months in the sum of £25 not to frequent gaming houses. One of the frequenters, the nephew of a countess, was quoted in a daily newspaper as saying, 'This is the end for me, boy. I never want to see a gaming party again.'

The men charged with keeping a common gaming house elected to be tried by a judge and jury and on 12 May at the County of London Sessions they were found not guilty. However, the publicity from this case and about illegal gaming parties in general hastened the introduction of the Betting and Gaming Act, 1960, which for the first time introduced licensed gambling casinos to this country.

In the course of our investigation we located gaming parties in Belgravia at addresses in Eaton Place and Grosvenor Crescent, and in Chelsea at Sloane Street, Sloane Gardens, Pont Street and Elm Park Gardens. It was sheer chance that after obtaining a Commissioner's Order in Writing to enter a flat in Grosvenor Crescent I did not see Billy Hill in the charge room for the second time in my career. A party attended by Hill and others was held at the address on two successive Saturday nights, and justified the Order, which was valid for one month, but then, as was often the pattern, there was no further use of the flat. On a Sunday of the last weekend that the Order could be legally executed, although this was usually our leave day and not normally a day when gaming parties were held, I had a premonition that the Hill party might decide to break their two weeks of inactivity. I telephoned Sergeant Hughes and we met near the Star Tavern at about 9 P.M. A quick look at the cars in Belgrave Mews revealed that Billy Hill's Ford Consul and motor cars belonging to two or three of his associates were parked there. It looked as if we might be in business.

We took up observation on the flat and shortly after closing time Hill and two of his friends, one of whom we believed was a croupier, arrived. A telephone call was made to alert the chief superintendent who held the Order to enter the flat and he asked to be contacted again when ten or more people were there – it was customary to require at least ten people to be present before entering an alleged common gaming house to counteract any defence that it was a private party. We waited patiently and just before midnight, when three men entered the flat, there were at least twelve people inside. Almost immediately one of the three men came out again and sat in a car parked outside, clearly acting as a look-out.

I telephoned the chief superintendent at his home with the latest information and he said he would go to the police station, organize a small raiding party and join us in about an hour. Just on the hour two more men left the premises, which left nine inside, and a few minutes before our senior officer arrived another two men came out. After a short on-the-spot conference I was not surprised when the chief superintendent decided against executing the Order – it was Billy Hill's lucky night.

Shortly after completing the plain-clothes assignment and returning to duty at West End Central, I appeared before a selection board at New Scotland Yard and was among those selected for promotion to chief inspector. After this I was employed for several weeks as acting chief inspector and during this time I was asked to select some experienced constables living in west London for transfer to Notting Hill to reinforce the manpower there after the 1958 race riots. Although the violence had been on nothing like the scale experienced in Brixton in 1981 and at Brixton and Tottenham in 1985, the riots were the first racial disturbances in London and there was concern about the situation. It is an interesting fact that after the 1981 Brixton riots – although, unlike Notting Hill in 1958, the station was not under strength – a similar tactic of drafting in experienced constables was employed.

At the time I arranged their transfers I was unaware of my own pending move and the fact that, very shortly, it was to be my good fortune to have the services of these experienced constables again, but on 1 June 1959 I was promoted to become the first post-war Met chief inspector and appointed an assistant to the superintendent in charge of Notting Hill.

4
Notting Hill Gate – Riots and Rachmanism

The Notting Hill police station area, divided between the old London boroughs of Kensington and Paddington, was a very mixed one with plenty of policing problems. The elegant and expensive houses of the streets and squares just off Notting Hill Gate and Holland Park Avenue and their well-to-do occupants were in complete contrast to the large, run-down and multi-occupied Victorian properties of North Kensington and Paddington that were tenanted by people of many different ethnic origins. Notting Dale, bordering on Shepherd's Bush, with its streets of mainly terraced houses and some new council flats, was a white working-class enclave with a reputation for toughness and an inclination to settle disputes by violence, and presented a further contrast.

The nearness of the West End and Paddington, and the fact that at that time street prostitution extended west from Marble Arch to Shepherd's Bush, meant that the seedy rooming houses and other property in the area had become increasingly coveted by various operators in the vice trade. The spread of bogus drinking clubs was endemic and these shebeens were attracting criminals and other undesirables from all over London. The district had gained an unwelcome notoriety and had begun to be referred to as Jungle, W11.

The race riots of 1958 had focused attention on Notting Hill and had highlighted the housing problems of the newly arrived West Indian immigrants and their vulnerability to racketeering landlords, such as Perac Rachman, of whom more will be said later. To add to the complications and to the volatility of the neighbourhood Sir Oswald Mosley had established the headquarters of his Union Party at Kensington Park Road and it was from this office that he and his lieutenant Geoffrey Hamm conducted their 1959 general election campaign.

Before taking up my post at Notting Hill I was sent for and briefed about its problems by Jim Evans, the Commander (the rank would now be Deputy Commissioner) of No. 1 Area. He particularly emphasized the need to control violence and racial attacks, and to prosecute the bogus drinking clubs. He told me that within a week or so a second chief inspector would be posted to Notting Hill so that alternately for six-month periods one of us could concentrate on anti-vice work while the other dealt with all the normal duties of the assistant to the superintendent in charge. This was the first police station in the force, other than West End Central, to be organized in this way.

On my first day at the station Mr Douglas Webb, the Deputy Commissioner, paid us a visit. After a talk with the superintendent he told me this officer needed a break – he had not taken any leave for some time – that he would be going away immediately and that I would be in charge during his absence. He added that the second chief inspector had been selected and would soon be joining me. In due course he arrived. It was John Gerrard, MC, a post-war entrant, known to me only by name, who had also just been promoted. We shared the same small office, striking up such a rapport that we worked in complete harmony and developed a lasting personal friendship. This relationship was particularly valuable in the latter years of our service when, with John as Assistant

Commissioner 'D' Department, we were both members of Sir David McNee's Policy Committee.

Possibly because of the experience that had been gained during the riots and disturbances by those who were at the station, as well as the quality of the experienced constables drafted in, the general standard of the personnel was well above average. I briefed myself by talking to the officers who had served at the station for a long time – particularly the four uniformed inspectors and their detective inspector colleague, who were all experienced and able policemen – and by patrolling the streets at different hours of the day and night. Having been given the anti-vice responsibility initially, I decided as a strategy to form a mini Clubs Office on the West End Central pattern, and I was helped by the fact that one or two constables I already knew with West End Clubs Office experience were among the recent reinforcements.

One of them, Constable Frank Pulley, whom I had known since he was a probationer, became one of the most outstanding operational officers the force has ever known. An intelligent, energetic and thoroughly dedicated man, he became something of a legend at the station. During his service there he was awarded several Commissioner's commendations and the BEM for gallantry in arresting an armed man who assaulted and threatened to shoot him. He also had the unpleasant experience of being the subject of a sustained slander campaign alleging that he was racially prejudiced which was taken up by some newspapers. Eventually, supported by the Police Federation, he took a civil action for libel against a national Sunday newspaper. He won and was awarded substantial damages, which vindicated him and put a stop to the slander. In his book, *In the Office of Constable*, Sir Robert Mark, commenting on PC Pulley's successful action, says, 'I was anxious that he should pursue similar action against everyone involved in this unscrupulous campaign but he felt that honour was satisfied.' Although an active and fearless policeman, compassion and magnanimity were part of his make-up – as was a reluctance to sit promotion examinations! As Assistant Commissioner (Crime) I was delighted to have his services as a detective in a newly formed special intelligence section at the Yard for which his wide knowledge of Notting Hill and the West End and his integrity made him eminently suitable. When he retired his expertise on international crime and criminals got him a job on the team of the journalist Martin Short which produced the much-praised series of programmes on the Mafia in the USA, *Crime Incorporated*, which was shown during 1984 on the ITN network.

Another outstanding young constable in the Hill's vice squad was Alan Grant, a Scot who joined the force as a junior cadet. Unlike Frank Pulley he had no antipathy towards examinations, winning a place on the Special Course at the staff college and later as an inspector being awarded a Bramshill scholarship. He went to London University, got a first class honours law degree, and some time after returning to duty he was head-hunted by the University of Ontario, Canada, where he is now Professor of Law. Young men of his calibre and their colleagues welcomed an intensive operational programme; it was a pleasure to see their response and rewarding to work with them.

Although there were some West Indian clubs which flouted the law by after-hours drinking and gaming, it was from the bogus clubs run by the indigenous criminals and their stooges that most of the trouble and violence came. Their method of operation was to rent a couple of rooms – often in a basement – register the club by paying the five-shilling fee, get liquor on credit and then open for business. Unlike the West End, where at least there was a pretence of keeping to correct licensing hours and membership formalities, these shebeens rarely opened until after 11 P.M. and blatantly ignored the membership requirements. Being registered as members' clubs – although this was often a complete sham – there was no right of entry by police without a warrant. The proprietors calculated that if they stayed open for a minimum of one month it was a profitable business. Of course, prices were high, the income was tax free and drunkenness and violence were habitual.

The licensing branch at the Yard and our solicitors were persuaded that the normal procedure was ineffective. This involved three nights' observation, the preparation of case papers, getting authority to apply for a warrant, followed by its execution, and reporting the club secretary/owner for a summons. It was agreed to shorten the observation period and where there was evidence that the members' club was a sham – which could usually be shown – a warrant could be applied for under the section of the Licensing Act which authorized the seizure of the intoxicating liquor.

This procedure was effective, but the get-rich-quick-by-opening-a-bogus-club attitude had become so well established that it was over a year before these entrepreneurs began to realize that the climate had changed. Initially we had to store large amounts of confiscated liquor, but then the brewers, finding that they had a lot of bad debts, stopped supplying on credit and the stocks held by the clubs diminished. The licensing warrants were valid for a month and it was frequently necessary to raid some of the premises several times before the proprietors got the message. Late-night raiding teams of up to forty men, with about half of them in uniform in order to deter or deal with any disorder, had quite often to be organized two or three times in a week. This sort of commitment from a total manpower strength of 144 officers really stretched resources, but enthusiasm and morale were so high that there was never any shortage of volunteers. The necessary administrative burden of preparing legal aid papers on these and other vice operations was considerable, and the tempo of work was only sustained by John Gerrard, myself and sometimes our superintendent sharing out the cases between us.

There were odd occasions when we had some anxiety about the possibility of violence when clubs were raided, though in the main good humour prevailed. One such was a notorious club at Notting Dale run by a local criminal named Bell, where it was not thought safe to attempt an inside observation by our 'under cover' officers. During outside observation a man was seen to be thrown out of the house early one morning badly beaten up, and our watchers reported that they thought the doorman might have a gun. When a warrant had been obtained entry was secured by playing the old schoolboy game of 'knock down ginger', that is to knock on the door and run away. This worked because after two or three knockings the doorman, the proprietor's teenage son, Sydney Bell, came outside and walked to the corner of the street to see who the prankster was. He was held and searched while the raiding party quickly entered the house and the drinking club, an adapted living room. At this point young Sydney Bell came back into the club in a temper and with venom in his voice shouted at us, 'If I had a gun, I'd shoot the f—g lot of you.' I believe he meant it.

Some time later, in May 1960, as a result of a long-standing feud between the Bells and another local family named Smith, James David Smith was shot dead in the street. Ernest Bell, the former proprietor of the club, his three sons, Ernest, Sydney and Peter, and a neighbour, George Baker, were arrested and charged with murder. Ernest Bell junior and George Baker were eventually convicted of manslaughter and sentenced to seven years' and five years' imprisonment respectively. The others were acquitted.

Another club connected with a notorious murder case which features in the Yard's Black Museum was the Celebrity Club at 10 Ruston Close, owned by a man named Charlie Brown. He was the doorman of a club at Kingly Street, Soho, who when it closed each night used to send some of the patrons on to his house. Ruston Close was formerly Rillington Place, but had been renamed after the trial of the ex-War Reserve policeman, John Reginald Haliday Christie, who had lived at No. 10 and had murdered six women and hidden some of the bodies in a cupboard which he concealed by papering it over. Although the murders had been committed between 1943 and 1952, when Christie was arrested, the bodies had been preserved by mummification because of the wallpaper sealing the cupboard. When we raided the Celebrity Club at 2 A.M. one morning in June 1960 we found the patrons quite oblivious of its macabre history, using as a bar the room where Christie had concealed the bodies.

Christie was convicted before the abolition of the death penalty and was hanged for his crimes. At that time it was the practice of the pathologist carrying out the post-mortem examination to retain, if he so wished, the murderer's organs for medical purposes, and I understand that generations of medical students at a famous London teaching hospital have learnt their testicular histology from part of Christie's anatomy.

The exploitation of tenants, particularly recent immigrants from the West Indies, by a landlord in the Notting Hill area during the late 1950s and early 1960s gave birth to a new word – 'Rachmanism', which was commonly used to describe the blatant abuse and intimidation of tenants by rapacious landlords.

Perac Rachman was born in 1920 and came to England during the Second World War as a penniless refugee from his native Poland. When he died in London in November 1962 he was reputed to be a millionaire. After some casual work in the East End he obtained a job as a clerk in a Shepherd's Bush estate agent's office but soon branched out on his own, taking advantage of the severe post-war housing shortage. The twilight world of the Notting Hill vice scene and the settlement of immigrant West Indians in the district was the market that he exploited. After the passing of the 1957 Rent Act it became possible to charge new tenants much higher rents than those paid by existing sitting tenants whose low rents were legally protected. The newly arrived immigrants were very vulnerable because there was little rented accommodation available; they were not eligible or had low priority for council housing, and they were ignorant of the laws of this country.

From about 1957 Rachman began to buy up large Victorian terraced properties, many of them on short leases, in the streets and squares of North Kensington and Paddington. He was helped in his enterprise by the Eagle Star Building Society which had been founded only a year earlier. The records of this society showed that in 1957 it lent Rachman over sixty per cent of its total loans, amounting to some £59,895, and that by the end of 1959 the amount loaned to Rachman companies was over £220,000. These figures came to light much later because at the time the loans were arranged so that no one person or company owed over £25,000, and only details of loans above this figure had to be disclosed in the society's annual returns.

To maximize the value of his properties as lettings Rachman schemed to get sitting tenants out. His first approach was to offer them fairly modest lump sums of money to go. If that was refused, the next move was to let adjoining rooms to selected acquaintances of his team of lieutenants and give them *carte blanche* to have all-night parties with loud music and generally to make living conditions intolerable for the established tenants. If this in turn did not work then his strong-arm agents would cut off the water supply and electricity, break shared lavatories and damage locks to external doors to make the flats insecure. Some courageous tenants took cases to the local rent tribunals and considered other legal action, but in the main they were people of only modest means and the complexities of civil law, as well as the difficulty of establishing who was legally responsible, meant that they sooner or later gave up the fight and vacated their flats. A few modest repairs would then be carried out and the accommodation re-let at a higher rental, often subdivided to create more lettings.

By 1959 allegations about strong-arm methods with tenants and the use by prostitutes of properties owned by Rachman companies began to cause concern to local and central government authorities. At this time Rachman was living in opulent style in a large detached house named 'Bishopstone' at Winnington Road in Hampstead, with a woman business associate, Audrey O'Donnell, whom he married in March 1960. His domestic establishment included two residential maids and a gardener, and he moved around London in either his company Rolls Royce or a Jaguar owned by Audrey O'Donnell Ltd, usually driven by one of his Polish employees.

There were high-level conferences at the Yard and at No. 1 Area Headquarters at Kensington and I was deputed in August 1959 to mount an intensive investigation into Rachman and his vice activities. I had suggested, because our local manpower resources were limited and already committed, that such an investigation should be undertaken by the Yard, but this had been turned down. To reinforce my local team of a sergeant and four constables I was allowed to borrow from a neighbouring division Inspector Reginald Doak, an officer with much experience of vice investigation. Mr Doak had a distinguished career, retiring in 1969 when he was the commander in charge of the West End District and becoming the first chief inspector of the then newly formed Gaming Board of Great Britain.

The aim of the investigation was to get evidence – if it was available – to prosecute Rachman and/or any of his associates under the Sexual Offences Act, 1956, for living on the earnings of prostitution and knowingly permitting premises to be used as brothels. It was organized in three main phases: first, a survey and observation on a sample of fifty properties with about three hundred separate lettings owned by Rachman companies; then an observation on his estate agents' office at Westbourne Grove; and finally surveillance on Perac Rachman himself. Although it resulted in two prosecutions for brothel-keeping against prostitutes and the gathering of much intelligence, the inquiry did not produce sufficient evidence to justify any proceedings against our main target.

This was not surprising for Rachman was a cunning operator, well briefed by his legal and financial advisers. He had also been put on his guard by an Inquiry started earlier in the year by Detective Inspector George Taylor, the senior CID officer at Notting Hill, arising out of allegations made by tenants at rent tribunal hearings. This inquiry, while curbing the activities of Rachman's strong-arm men, failed to provide the evidence to prosecute him personally.

Our investigation identified thirty-three separate companies with Rachman as a director and principal shareholder, and in many cases the company secretary was Brian O'Donnell, a brother of the woman with whom he was living. In some cases the returns required to be submitted to the Registrar of Companies were two or three years overdue, but that was, and still is, a common failing of many small businesses. It was estimated that a tax assessment on his companies would probably have forced him into bankruptcy, but as the assets were only a nominal share capital this would not have been very fruitful for the Inland Revenue.

Rachman made a fortune out of charging exorbitant rents for poor and squalid accommodation, but he was careful to avoid personal contact with individual tenants. He operated by remote control through agents and strong-arm rent collectors whose loyalty he bought. Eventually, however, early in 1960 the time came when for some reason he decided to dispose of his Notting Hill properties. Much to the consternation of the owners of the freeholds of some of the short-lease properties, he sold them to men of straw. This meant that when the leases expired the owners were not able to enforce repair and maintenance agreements and had themselves to meet the cost of the extensive repairs needed to restore the houses to a reasonable standard.

One of the brothel convictions we had secured was in respect of a house at Chepstow Road where, according to the Paddington Borough Council records, the rateable occupier was Mr Perac Rachman. There was no evidence of any guilty knowledge by him as to the use of the house, something we would have to prove in order to bring him within the reach of the law. However, in the remote hope of providing this vital evidence should the house again be used as a brothel, I decided to serve a written notice of the brothel conviction on him personally.

On 11 September 1959 at about 11.30 A.M., I went with Sergeant McDonald and Constable Spooner – the officers who had carried out the brothel observation – to Rachman's home at Winnington Road. His Rolls Royce and Audrey O'Donnell's Jaguar were parked in the drive and a gardener was working on the flower beds. The door bell was answered by a maid wearing a black dress with a starched white apron and cap who, after I had shown her my warrant card, invited us in. She asked if we would like a whisky, a brandy or some tea or coffee, and we refused. From the doorway of the room where we were waiting I watched her go up the wide staircase and, after knocking, enter a door about half-way along the balcony which extended round three sides of the large entrance hall. Almost immediately Perac Rachman came out of the room, down the stairs and joined us, wearing silk pyjamas, a towelling dressing-gown and slippers. He was a rather short, bespectacled, balding and podgy-faced man with a dissolute air that suggested he was suffering from a hangover. He had the reputation of being a womanizer, and I could not help wondering what women could possibly see in this unattractive individual. He seemed rather nervous and apprehensive which, in the circumstances, was I suppose hardly surprising.

I explained the reason for our visit and handed him a letter notifying him of the brothel conviction about his Chepstow Road house on 7 August, which had been also preceded by a conviction for habitual prostitution at the same house on 23 January.

Rachman read the letter. 'It's not my property, it's leased to a coloured man named Hunte,' he said.

I pointed out that according to the records of Paddington Borough Council he was the rateable occupier of the house. He picked up a telephone and dialled a number. When the call was answered he said, 'Mr Edwards? Fifty-eight Chepstow Road, that's Hunte's property, isn't it? Well, tell him to get the place cleared by twelve o'clock today or I'll get my solicitor to cancel the lease. I've had a letter about a brothel at the house. I will send Serge to change the locks, I'm fed up with all this.' His voice while he was speaking to his agent was much more strident and authoritative than his former quiet tone. Putting the telephone down he said to me, 'There, you heard what I said, the place should be right soon.'

As we had completed our business I decided to leave and Rachman walked to the door with us, and though he did not speak I could sense that now that we were leaving this thirty-nine-year-old Polish refugee had regained his confidence, well aware of our difficulty in proving that he knew about the immoral use of his property.

Rachman had by this time, although his business methods were odious, a legitimate income from his property interests and was taking good care not to put himself within reach of the criminal law. Having disposed of his Notting Hill interests he kept a fairly low profile right up to his death three years later. Some of his young protégés did not take the same care and over the years I was personally involved with three of them, who paid the penalty for their criminal activities.

The first two, Raymond Naccachian, alias Nash, a Lebanese who was Rachman's principal lieutenant in the 1960s, and George Piggott, a strong-arm rent collector, will be mentioned again later in this book. Nash developed interests in Soho clubs and was reputed to be a millionaire when in 1965 he was barred from the United Kingdom after being sent to prison in Japan for handling and smuggling gold. Piggott, who became an armed robber, is at present serving a life sentence for his part in a contract murder by shooting a man named Zomparelli, known as 'Italian Toni', in the Golden Goose Amusement Arcade in Soho in September 1974.

The third man, Michael Campbell De Freitas, a Trinidadian who became well known as Michael X, a self-appointed Black Power leader, was hanged for murder in his native land early in 1974. In 1960 he became well known to me as an agent for Rachman in the Powis Square and Colville Terrace area off Notting Hill. He was frequently seen in the local cafés and drinking clubs, appeared quite affluent and I was told by a local West Indian that for the right price he would provide flats for prostitutes.

In late September Sergeant Robin Duff-Cole and his plain-clothes partner, Constable Peter Main, kept observation on 24 Colville Terrace where De Freitas lived with his wife and small child in a fourth-floor flat. They established that the basement flat was not occupied permanently but was used in the evenings by two prostitutes, thus in law becoming a brothel. De Freitas was seen around when the women were taking men to the flat and he must have been aware of what was going on. Inquiries disclosed that other tenants in the house had rent books supplied by De Freitas showing him as their landlord. The details of the observation were reported, as was the practice, to the Kensington Borough Council whose solicitor approved that a warrant be applied for to arrest De Freitas for being the lessor or landlord of a house where the basement flat was used as a brothel.

On the evening of 19 October, with a warrant under the Sexual Offences Act, 1956, to arrest De Freitas, I joined Sergeant Duff-Cole and Constable Main at Colville Terrace. They told me that De Freitas was at home and that a prostitute was using the basement flat. A few minutes later after we had seen the prostitute successfully solicit a man and take him to the house we entered it, went to the top-floor flat and knocked on the door. The door was opened by Desirée De Freitas carrying a small child in her arms. She called her husband and at my request he came with us to the basement. We pushed the door of the flat open and there, in the presence of his wife, he was confronted with the prostitute and her client, and I formally arrested him.

Desirée, who was quite a pretty young woman, began to cry but De Freitas showed no emotion. He asked to see the warrant and after reading it he turned to his wife saying, 'I have to go, darling, but get on to Sheridan [his lawyer] and he will come to court and get me bail.' Weeping and shouting abuse, she followed us out of the basement. De Freitas told her to go to bed, and the prostitute, who a few minutes earlier had denied knowing who he was, said, 'All right, Michael, I'll stay with her.'

Later at Notting Hill police station De Freitas was charged as the landlord of the basement flat wilfully being a party to its use as a brothel. On the following day he appeared at Marylebone Magistrates' Court and was remanded in custody, but later he was granted bail subject to finding two sureties in the sum of £250 each, surrendering his passport and reporting to the police daily. On 6 December the case was heard and the magistrate upheld a submission by De Freitas's counsel that in law he was not the landlord of the property because he had never owned it, and therefore found him not guilty.

Briefly, the defence was that in February 1960 De Freitas had entered into a contract with the Eagle Star Building Society to purchase 24 Colville Terrace and was given authority, before completion of the conveyance, to collect rents and to manage the property. The house was not conveyed to him and in August he agreed to sell his interests to a man named Daly. As this man was unable to raise a mortgage the sale was not completed and De Freitas went on collecting the rents from the tenants. However, as the property was still owned by the Eagle Star Building Society, it was contended that they, and not De Freitas, were the legal landlords.

There is no definition of a landlord in the Sexual Offences Act and Kensington Borough Council agreed to obtain the opinion of counsel on this point. As the opinion supported my own view that a person who issues rent books, collects rents and is regarded by the tenants as their landlord has that legal contractual relationship, an appeal, by way of case stated, was made against the magistrate's finding. The appeal was heard in the Queen's Bench Division at the Royal Courts of Justice on 20 April 1961 before the Lord Chief Justice, Lord Parker, and two other judges. They allowed the appeal and directed that the magistrate should hear and determine the case. However, De Freitas could not be found until October, when he was arrested and again brought before the court.

He was found guilty of the brothel offence, given a conditional discharge for twelve months and ordered to pay ten guineas costs.

By this time De Freitas had become a Muslim calling himself Abdul Malik and was interested in the Black Power movement in the USA which was led by a man known as Malcolm X. He later adopted the name Michael X and founded a 'Racial Adjustment Action Society', becoming a self-appointed Messiah to a community running a Black Power commune at Holloway Road in Islington. He became something of a cult figure with a number of wealthy patrons, both male and female, who failed to identify him for the criminal he was. Even a sentence of twelve months' imprisonment under the Race Relations Act in 1967 for publicly urging the shooting of any white man seen with a black girl did not seem to lessen his popularity with his supporters.

His final downfall began in 1969 when with four of his Black Power colleagues he was committed for trial at the Old Bailey on charges of robbery and demanding money with menaces. The proprietor of an employment agency at Newburgh Street, Soho, had money forcibly taken from him and at the Black House in Holloway was humiliated by De Freitas and his associates by having a dog collar put on his neck and being made to crawl on all fours. De Freitas jumped bail and ran away to his native Trinidad where some of his followers joined him, including a young girl called Gale Benson whose father was at one time MP for Chatham.

The Director of Public Prosecutions did not seek to extradite him and he linked up with local criminals, developed a Black Power party and became a thorn in the side of the Trinidadian authorities. In February 1972 a member of his criminal gang called Joseph Skerritt refused to carry out a raid on a country police station ordered by De Freitas, and a few days later he was murdered. Members of De Freitas's gang, including Skerritt, were told by him to dig a trench in his garden which he said was to improve the drainage. When the task was completed he decapitated Skerritt with a cutlass and buried him in the trench. Shortly afterwards another member of the gang was drowned in a bathing 'accident' in a quiet inlet, Gale Benson was missing and, according to subsequent reports, his criminal associates became nervous and edgy.

De Freitas and his wife went on a lecture tour to Guyana but no sooner had he left their bungalow than a disgruntled member of his gang set fire to it. After the fire had been dealt with, a police inspector examining the garden was suspicious about some lettuces which were abnormally tall and yellow. He had the ground dug up and the decapitated body of Joseph Skerritt was found. Two days later after further digging the body of a woman, later identified as Gale Benson, was found buried some five feet deep in another grave.

The Trinidad authorities called on the services of the eminent British pathologist, Professor Francis Camps, who visited the scene of the murder and carried out the post-mortem examination on the dead girl. He gave evidence that she had resisted her attackers, that the fatal stab wound was from a knife with a blade capable of penetrating over six inches and he deduced from the fact that there were soil particles in her air passages and stomach that she had been buried while she was still alive. Two of De Freitas's gang, Stanley Abbot and Edward Cheddi, were convicted of her murder and sentenced to death.

De Freitas was arrested in Guyana, brought back to

Trinidad, tried and found guilty of the murder of Skerritt. After exhausting all the appeal procedures, including an application to the Privy Council in London who refused to hear his appeal against the death sentence, he was hanged in Trinidad in 1974. He had also been indicted for the murder of Gale Benson but never stood trial for this crime. The brothel keeper from Colville Terrace, Notting Hill, had indeed proved to be a most evil person.

During 1959 and 1960 the increased police presence on the streets, firm action against all forms of violence, and sustained pressure against bogus drinking clubs and vice pedlars, had reduced racial tension and general anxiety in the Notting Hill area. We were much encouraged when, despite a vigorous campaign of street meetings by the Union Party led by Sir Oswald Mosley from their local headquarters, the run-up to the 1959 general election passed without any serious disorder.

The Commissioner by this time was Sir Joseph Simpson, and he was a complete contrast to his predecessor, Sir John Nott-Bower, whose departure had hardly been noticed by the force. Joe, as he was affectionately known, was a workaholic who got around the force and kept in touch with the grass roots. He was the first commissioner to begin his career as a constable and as that was at Bow Street police station he was a real son of the Met. His wide interest and support for sport, particularly athletics and rugger, gave him many informal contacts, and his friendly relationships with a number of junior officers with whom, as a young man, he had competed or played was, for me, a splendid example of effective leadership.

One Saturday night during 1960 I had gone to the police station at about 10.45 to brief a club raiding party at midnight. I was filling in the time by clearing some routine correspondence when Sir Joe walked into my office. He had called at the station to see how things were going and the night duty station sergeant had told him that I was in my office. We discussed the local situation, and after about fifteen minutes he got up to leave and I walked with him to the station yard, expecting to find his official car and driver waiting there for him. There was no official car – apparently, as was often his practice at weekends, he had given his constable driver the day off. He got into his private estate car, which had a couple of labradors in the back, wished me luck with the club operation and drove off.

His premature death from a heart attack in 1968 was a sad loss and I found it a very moving experience to be among the officers who, in ceremonial uniform, followed his cortège from the Yard to Westminster Abbey for his funeral service.

During the autumn of 1960, although comparatively junior in our rank, both John Gerrard and I appeared before a superintendents' selection board at the Yard chaired by the Commissioner and were successful, though owing to our lack of seniority it was not until September 1961 that we were promoted. It was with mixed feelings that we went our separate ways because we had both enjoyed the challenge of Notting Hill and of working together with some really first-class policemen.

5
Return to the West End

My initial posting was as the superintendent in charge of Lavender Hill police station, which covered the Clapham Junction and Battersea districts of south London. However, my stay there was short because two months later, on 1 November 1961, with only two days' notice I was transferred back to the West End. My command was West End Central (2), the division responsible for policing Soho and parts of Mayfair, including the United States Embassy in Grosvenor Square. Although I had begun to get used to the quieter tempo of life at Lavender Hill, with the added bonus of being able to spend more time with my young family, I must admit I felt elated at returning to take charge of an area where only just over two years earlier I had been one of a number of inspectors.

The most obvious change was that as the result of the Street Offences Act, the army of prostitutes had virtually disappeared from the streets. Vice, however, had not vanished. The shadowy figures busy securing a corner on the Soho property market had already begun to exploit the new situation. Striptease clubs were their latest innovation, while 'clip joints' where near-beer and fruit cocktails were sold at inflated prices on the implied promise of sex that in fact never materialized were a bigger nuisance than ever.

The Betting and Gaming Act of 1960 had resulted in the birth of the legal gaming industry. The licensed betting shops opened and functioned without causing any difficulties, but the gaming legislation had many teething troubles. Although it was an improvement on the old Victorian law the new legislation was wide open to interpretation, and enforcement was, of necessity, based largely on the technicalities of the law.

The long and tedious process of testing the law in the courts, with the gaming clubs seemingly always one jump ahead, was expensive in terms of time and money. *Kelland* v. *Raymond* in the Queen's Bench Division of the High Court was one such case, when an appeal by me was allowed against a decision at Marlborough Street Magistrates' Court that making a charge of ten shillings for a twenty-minute session of roulette at the Raymond Revue Bar Club at Walkers Court in Soho was not contrary to the Act. The constant invention of new systems to circumvent the intentions of the gaming law made new legislation inevitable. In September 1966 the Home Secretary, Roy Jenkins, said, 'The Betting and Gaming Act, 1960, has led to abuses, particularly in the field of gaming clubs, which were not foreseen by its promoters. This country has become a gamblers' paradise. There is a close and growing connection between gaming clubs and organized crime, often violent crime, in London and other big cities. The fat profits made by the proprietors make them a sitting target for protection rackets.'

In 1967 Raymond Blackburn, a former MP, made an unsuccessful application in the Queen's Bench Divisional Court for an order of *mandamus*[1] requiring the Commissioner, Sir John Waldron, to reverse a policy decision of April 1966 that the time of police officers would not be spent on enforcing provisions of the Betting and Gaming

[1] *Mandamus*: a prerogative order from a superior court commanding an inferior tribunal, public official, etc., to take specified action.

Act. An appeal against this decision was heard in the High Court by the Master of the Rolls, Lord Denning, Lord Justice Salmon and Lord Justice Edmund-Davies. Lord Denning, giving judgment, said that as the Commissioner had given an undertaking to the court that his policy decision would be officially revoked there must be a dismissal of the appeal, but Mr Blackburn and his supporters might well feel that in truth theirs was the victory. His Lordship also made an important observation about the Commissioner's constitutional status, which had never before been defined in statute or by the courts. He said:

> I have no hesitation in holding that, like every constable in the land, he should be, and is, independent of the executive. I hold it to be the duty of the Commissioner, as it is of every chief constable, to enforce the law of the land. He must take steps so to post his men that crimes may be detected and that honest citizens may go about their affairs in peace.
>
> He must decide whether or not suspected persons are to be prosecuted and, if need be, bring the prosecution or see that it is brought. But in all these things he is not a servant of anyone save of the law itself. No Minister of the Crown can tell him he must or must not prosecute this man or that. Nor can any police authority tell him so.
>
> The responsibility for law enforcement lies on him. He is answerable to the law and the law alone. He has a discretion in many fields with which the law could not interfere. But there are some policy decisions in which the court could interfere.
>
> It might well be a question of machinery to know how he can be compelled to do his duty. Once a duty exists there is a means to enforce it, perhaps by suit of the Attorney-General or the prerogative writ of *mandamus*. *Mandamus* is a very wide remedy which had always been available against public officers to see that they did their public duty. No doubt the person applying has to show that he has sufficient interest to be protected and that there is no other equally convenient remedy.

Mandamus, in case of need, is available even against the Commissioner.

Some five years later, in 1972, Raymond Blackburn again applied for an order of *mandamus* directing the Commissioner, Sir Robert Mark, to enforce the laws relating to pornography. He was once again unsuccessful in his action and in his subsequent appeal against the High Court decision.

Part III of the Licensing Act, 1961, was more effective than the gaming legislation and was very helpful in eliminating bogus members' clubs but, as will be mentioned later, it also made premises available which became striptease clubs. However, the new legislation modernizing the laws relating to licensing and betting and gaming – despite the problems of the gaming aspect – were welcomed by the police because they required less enforcement and were more in accord with public opinion. The inadequate gaming laws were eventually rectified by the Gaming Act, 1968, which became effective the following year. It set up a statutory authority, the Gaming Board of Great Britain, with a system of control that required casino operators to obtain a certificate of consent from the Board before they could apply to the licensing justices for gaming licences. Regulations prescribed new rules for the gaming and a system of supervision by the Gaming Board's own inspectors was introduced which reduced the need for enforcement by the police to a minimum. This Act, which drastically reduced the number of gaming clubs, has proved generally satisfactory.

The pornographic bookshop businesses in Soho, which were to proliferate in the 1970s, were beginning to expand as a sort of natural consequence of the permissive society.

However, a few more years were to elapse before our more sophisticated criminal intelligence analysis systems established the link between this trade, strip clubs and prostitution with organized and international crime.

The West End of London, as always, was affected by world political events and the era of anti-nuclear protest had begun. Major demonstrations, marches and vigils, with the American Embassy the focal point, were frequently organized by the Committee of 100. Protection of the embassy was a particular responsibility and a constant drain on manpower. After a sit-down demonstration at Grosvenor Square on Easter Monday 1961 that led to a large number of arrests, including one of the organizers, an American called Ralph Shoenman, I was relieved when a visit to the embassy on 5 June by President John F. Kennedy took place without incident.

It was essential for efficiency at a busy station like West End Central, the base for two separate territorial commands as well as the Clubs Office anti-vice unit, that senior officers in charge and their chief inspector deputies co-operated with each other. My colleagues were thoroughly professional, and two of them, James Starritt and Colin Woods, were to become deputy commissioners of the Met and receive knighthoods in recognition of their public service. Sir Colin Woods was the last deputy commissioner to be so honoured and the award of knighthoods to deputy and assistant commissioners, once fairly commonplace, is now no longer made. Although there are varying views on the honours system, there is little doubt that individuals, and the organizations they represent, appreciate such public recognition. In recent years there has been much comment in the force about the reduction in both the number and grade of honours awarded to its members, and the scale of awards to the police service is often contrasted with that of the armed forces. Perhaps the validity of this comparison is open to question, but there does seem to be a great numerical disparity.

On 1 August 1962 the superintendent (Clubs) post, which normally changed hands each January, became vacant and I was appointed to fill the vacancy. Thus began an extended tour – it lasted until January 1964 – in the hot seat of the head of the vice squad.

When I took up the job I was very mindful of the professionalism of my old chief, Charles Strath, but I did decide to be more communicative with my staff than he had been and to say just a little more than 'Follow me!' My own personal experience, and the conclusions of historians and sociologists, had taught me that the basic principle of supply and demand applied to vice offences and that, on the basis that most customers would either be satisfied or too embarrassed to come forward, there would be few complainants. Apart from the duty of police to enforce legislation enacted by Parliament, the importance of combating vice offences – which, on any scale is a problem mainly peculiar to large centres of population – is the connection they have either directly or indirectly with major crime and criminals. The prospect of obtaining a large untaxed income by exploiting human weaknesses always attracts criminals, who are people usually devoid of any moral scruple and dangerous to deal with.

The selection of personnel for anti-vice duties is particularly important and although there was never any shortage of volunteers, officers were carefully screened and thoroughly briefed before employment. Leadership from inspectors and sergeants was recognized as being of vital importance and because of this a policy had been formulated and approved at the Yard by Sir Joseph Simpson specially to select a number of outstanding inspectors for duty in the West End. Amongst the inspectors I was fortunate enough to have until they were promoted were Kenneth Newman (now Sir Kenneth Newman, Commissioner), Alan Goodson (lately Chief Constable of Leicestershire), Patrick Flynn and David Powis, who both retired as deputy assistant commissioners in the Met.

The policy of hand-picking supervisory staff, apart from developing the careers of individuals, was aimed at ensuring high standards of integrity and it paid dividends. In the years 1973 to 1976, when I was investigating the pornography scene, I discovered only one instance of an inspector who had served in the Clubs Office being improperly involved with the pornographer Jimmy Humphreys or his associates. This man had been identified by his senior officers as a weak link and transferred away from the West End before he ever came to my notice.

The daily and nightly round – because most of the activity of our customers was nocturnal – went on against clubs, brothels and ponces in a seemingly never-ending operation to keep a measure of control in the West End. The strategy of being as selective as possible in identifying and targeting the vice barons and their front men meant that we had to be well informed and have motivated key staff. In addition to demanding, and getting, absolute frankness from my selected officers – which was supplemented by information from street duty officers, some with vice squad experience – my own West End contacts, including some from my inspector days, were useful sources when I was checking and assessing the scene.

During 1962 John Gaul, a reputed millionaire director

of several property companies, and his company secretary, a man named Young, both of whom had been investigated by my predecessor, were convicted at the Old Bailey of living on the earnings of prostitution by letting flats at exorbitant rents to prostitutes and were fined £25,000 and £2,500 respectively. These convictions were particularly encouraging because they reversed the disappointments of the 1955 *Strath* v. *Silver and Others* case at the Old Bailey.

John Gaul was once again in the headlines when in 1976 his fourth wife, Barbara, was murdered in the car park of the Black Lion hotel at Brighton. Two London brothers, who claimed that they had been paid £5,000 for the killing though they refused to say who had hired them, were later arrested and convicted of Mrs Gaul's murder. Gaul himself fled to Malta where he lived on his luxury yacht and successfully resisted attempts by the Sussex police to extradite him in connection with the murder. In 1984, after a ruling by the Director of Public Prosecutions, presumably after a lapse of years for evidential reasons, the warrant for his arrest issued by the Brighton Magistrates' Court was withdrawn. In September, after eight years' absence, at the age of seventy-three and having married for the fifth time, he returned to England for the wedding of his son Simon. He was interviewed by John Chapman of the *Daily Mail* as to why he fled the country after the shooting of his fourth wife and he said, 'I did not come back to face charges because when the time comes to die, I do not wish to be kicked to death in a police cell. It has happened to others.' He added that he had not made up his mind whether to live in Britain permanently. Although this is what Gaul is quoted as saying, I very much doubt if it was the fear of what might happen to him in a police cell that made him contest the extradition proceedings.

It is said that nature abhors a vacuum and that was the case in 1962 with John Gaul's prostitute flats in Soho. After his conviction and that of the property company's secretary, their rent collectors, some of whom had given evidence for the prosecution, ceased to collect the rents for the prostitute occupiers. The news reached another citizen of Soho, Alec Kostanda, alias Kay and nicknamed The Count, a man with a considerable criminal record. He showed his entrepreneurial instincts by changing the locks on the doors of some of the flats, informing the occupants that he was their new landlord, claiming the traditional key money and issuing them with standard printed tenancy agreements which were absolutely worthless.

Enough of these facts reached our ears to justify putting an observation team on to The Count, but he proved very surveillance-conscious and, without running the risk of alerting him, it was impossible to discover exactly where he was living. However, while in Soho, where he could be found for most of the hours of every day, he was habitually in the company of a prostitute, which meant that a warrant under the Sexual Offences Act could be obtained for his arrest. When he was arrested, bogus tenancy agreements were found in his briefcase and the prostitutes confirmed what we had heard. The Count pleaded guilty at Marlborough Street Magistrates' Court to living on the earnings of prostitution and was sentenced to six months' imprisonment – a typical case of a jackal feeding on the refuse of Soho.

The new Licensing Act had resulted in a tremendous amount of work, for the police had to make inquiries into the characters of the applicants and into the bona fides of the clubs applying for registration. The existing clubs had the option of applying for re-registration under rules designed to ensure they were genuine members' clubs or of applying for a Justices' Licence to sell intoxicating liquor as a proprietary club. In the latter category the licence holder had to be of good character, the club hours were restricted to the normal public house hours and police had right of entry without a warrant.

At the time the Act became law there were nearly 400 registered clubs in the West End and it was estimated that about seventy-five per cent of those were one-roomed, proprietary drinking clubs whose operation was probably unlawful even under the earlier 1953 Licensing Act. Some seventy-odd failed to register and included among them were many of the worst type of club whose proprietors realized that they would not measure up to the new requirements. Eventually the number of clubs diminished by about a hundred, and of those remaining only about fifty per cent received registration certificates as genuine members' clubs while the others operated under a Justices' Licence.

Since one of the effects of the 1961 Act was to put a number of drinking clubs out of business their premises thus became available and were taken over as striptease clubs. Although, almost without exception, these were clubs in name only because the public was admitted after paying an entrance fee, a few of them in the early days went through a charade – which incidentally brought them extra income – of charging a separate membership fee and filling in application forms for membership.

Many of the clubs were in basements with no emergency exits and it was indeed fortunate that no fires occurred or there must have been loss of life. The seating capacity varied between sixty and one hundred, the entrance fee from seven shillings and sixpence to fifteen shillings and the entertainment, consisting of a female dancing to music while she removed her clothes, was continuous from early afternoon until after midnight. These striptease artistes – who were not prostitutes – went from club to club and were paid a fee for each individual performance.

The licensing authority for public music and dancing entertainment was the old London County Council and as a matter of policy they would not grant licences for such entertainment. The problem of controlling these clubs was a pretty intractable one. The clubs were usually run by 'front men' paid by the real owners to accept responsiblity whenever the question of proceedings for unlicensed music and dancing performances arose. None of the normal records associated with a proper business, such as the names of employees and insurance and tax particulars, were kept and clearly the revenue authorities were being defrauded. We were concerned because most of the people behind these dozen or so very lucrative clubs – some of them in partnerships drawn up in the privacy of their solicitors' offices – were of bad character. The regular, large, untaxed cash flow presented the obvious and real dangers of being used for criminal enterprises and of furthering the sinister influence of the criminal owners.

The procedure of regularly reporting various 'front men' for permitting unlicensed music and dancing and subsequently, after the service of summonses, giving evidence at the magistrates' court, was most unsatisfactory. It was costly in terms of our resources and open to the interpretation that the police were only interested in raising revenue from fines rather than taking really effective action. The maximum fine was £100 and, although this was usually imposed, the difficulty of serving summonses and getting the defendants before the court meant that, at best, the clubs were only prosecuted about ten times a year which was not a real deterrent.

The clubs were a novelty and with the daily influx of visitors to Soho the profits for the owners were enormous. I got some idea of their income when in August 1962 I executed a warrant under the Licensing Act at the Carnival Strip Club at Green's Court in Soho. The proprietors, two semi-illiterate Maltese both with convictions for brothel-keeping, had ignored the requirements of the new Licensing Act and were selling intoxicating liquor in their club without a licence. When we entered the club they were examining a notebook which I seized as evidence. It was later admitted by one of their employees, who had been sent to the station to make a copy of the entries in the book, that it was the authentic record of the entrance money taken for the first sixteen days of August which, at 12s.6d. a head, showed takings of £2,396. Allowing for inflation this would be about £22,000 today. Between September and January these two men paid fines amounting to £2,300, but the striptease shows continued until February, when the superior landlord secured repossession of the lease by winning a vigorously contested civil action.

Two of the major entrepreneurs in Soho, the already well-known Bernie Silver and one of his partners, a Maltese called Mifsud who was known as Big Frank, controlled striptease clubs and other premises. However, Silver, who was rapidly becoming a godfather-type figure, was careful to operate through nominee managers and other front men which made it difficult, if not impossible, to prosecute him personally. Knowing his propensity for cultivating police officers in the hope that he might corrupt them, my Clubs Office staff were well briefed about him and instructed to report any personal contacts or information coming to their notice from him or his known associates. At the same time, to indicate both to the jungle of Soho and to police officers where we stood, a number of prosecutions were taken against clubs believed to be owned or controlled by Silver and Mifsud.

One interesting prosecution in the autumn of 1963 against the Striperama Club, which opened from 1 P.M. to 1 A.M. daily in Greek Street, resulted in Frank Mifsud and another Maltese, Big George Caruana, being convicted and fined under Section 46 of the Metropolitan Police Act for this offence. This line of attack was discontinued because the Lord Chamberlain's Office, at that time operating as the licenser of theatre buildings in central London by virtue of the Theatres Act, 1843, made it known that they did not consider that striptease dancing amounted to a stage play or dramatic entertainment.

Silver was not at the Striperama when we raided the club but I did speak to him later in the foyer of Bow Street Magistrates' Court when he was with Mifsud after the latter's conviction for assault on PC Saunders which will be mentioned later. When I told him he would be reported for keeping an unlicensed theatre and for unlicensed music and dancing, Silver said, 'I understand your position, Mr Kelland. I must say I have only a rental interest in the premises. I don't mind the music and dancing but I'm having a battle with the tax people.' At his trial at the Old Bailey in 1974 he admitted that he had paid no income tax for over ten years. I am sure that he did understand what my position was, then and subsequently – for I later interviewed him in Wormwood Scrubs Prison during my corruption inquiry. We were on completely opposite sides of the fence and he took good care, with the help of his advisers, not to provide any evidence which would enable me to prosecute him.

The administrative policy of rotating the junior ranks of the Clubs Office at three- and six-monthly intervals and the superintendent annually was understandable because of the nature of the duties, but it did hinder the long-term commitment and continuity of effort that was needed to investigate a major conspiracy successfully. Our efforts were very much the result of local initiative rather than central strategy, and because we were aware that some senior CID officers at the Yard insisted that Silver and Mifsud were good informants and ridiculed the proposition of a connection between them, vice and other crime, there was a lack of trust and no incentive to enlist central office assistance. To be blunt, there was a complete lack of confidence on my part and a feeling that any information about these two men that passed through the official channels would soon be known to them. I proved this theory on one occasion by sending to the Yard for the official criminal-record files of Silver, Mifsud and some of their Maltese associates, giving as my reason 'required in connection with a Clubs Office inquiry'. Shortly after this their solicitor Norman Beach, who some years later was struck off for unprofessional conduct, wrote a letter to the Yard to the effect that his clients, who had committed no offence, understood that I was investigating them and he wished to be assured that they would not be persecuted. I suppose he took the view that attack was the best means of defence and the only consolation I had was the knowledge that I had caused his clients and their friends a little anxiety. We had our successes but I was well aware that the rewards for the vice merchants were such that they would persist in meeting the demand. Our specialist local unit was really only holding the ring, preventing the worst excesses and, not least importantly, protecting the integrity of the force.

The dangers faced at that time by active policemen in Soho are well illustrated by the events that followed the arrest by PC Saunders of Frank Mifsud for using threatening behaviour one evening in Greek Street. Mifsud, who was a powerfully-built man, resisted arrest by holding the constable by the throat, and to make him let go Saunders hit him, giving Mifsud a black eye. Mifsud was charged with threatening behaviour and with assault on police and when he appeared at Bow Street Magistrates' Court the following day he was granted a remand to get legal representation.

I learned that Mifsud was very angry at being humiliated in front of his Soho associates by PC Saunders and that he was going to 'get' him. Saunders had Club Office experience but was at the time employed on uniform beat duties in Soho, and my contact impressed on me that Mifsud's threat should be taken seriously and not regarded as an idle boast. I immediately arranged for Saunders to be employed on station duties until the hearing of the case against Mifsud, and that he should be warned to be on his guard and to keep away from Soho.

Frank Mifsud eventually appeared in court where, represented by counsel, he contested the case but was found guilty and fined for both offences. Some days after the court hearing I was shown by Chief Superintendent Starritt a complaint file that had been sent out from the Yard to him. It was recorded there that Norman Beach had gone to the Yard and complained that PC Saunders was demanding money from a young Maltese man whom, some months earlier when he had been employed on Clubs Office duties, he had dealt with for living on the earnings of prostitution. Detectives from C.1 Branch who investigated the complaint reported going to a Soho pub where the man concerned was to meet Saunders to give him the money he had allegedly demanded. I made inquiries and discovered that Saunders had indeed received a message that this man wished to see him at the public house about some information he had for him, but because of the advice he had received Saunders had ignored the message. There was no doubt in my mind that had he gone he would have been compromised and, with perhaps a criminal charge against him, the prosecution of Mifsud would have had to be abandoned. At the time I felt a cold anger and a sense of impotence at not being able to do anything about what was a criminal conspiracy to pervert the course of justice, mixed with relief that Saunders had not fallen into the trap set for him.

It was a standard instruction to my Clubs Office staff that when they were meeting informants they should always arrange to be observed by a colleague. If they were given anything like an envelope they were to open it immediately and if it contained money they were to arrest the person concerned. The value of being absolutely correct and ethical when dealing with anyone under investigation was brought home to me over a year after I had dealt with the Establishment Club in Greek Street.

This club during 1962/3 achieved some notoriety as the home of satirical entertainment after the appearance there of the American sick comedian and drug addict, Lenny Bruce. An article appeared in the *Sunday Times* on 3 February 1965 about the owners of the Establishment Club, Nicholas Luard, described as the twenty-five-year-old impresario of satire, and his partner, the actor Peter Cook. Luard was quoted as saying about a warning – the source of which was not disclosed – that he might be prosecuted for obscenity if Lenny Bruce reappeared at the Club, 'Nothing would please me more, he is worth fighting for. The police and anyone else can take note that he will be there again in April.' A few days after this article appeared a routine observation by Clubs Office staff inside the club disclosed licensing offences. It was raided just before midnight, and in April the joint licensee, a Mr Copp, was fined for supplying drink outside permitted hours.

Lenny Bruce did make an attempt to enter the country by way of Eire, having earlier been refused permission to enter through Heathrow Airport, and he was promptly returned to the USA because a gating order had been made by the Home Secretary that enabled the immigration officer to turn him back. The Establishment Club ran into difficulties and the owning company, Cook and Luard Productions Ltd, went into voluntary liquidation shortly afterwards.

The club was said to have been acquired by Raymond Nash, a close associate of Perac Rachman. An inside observation showed it was badly run, with licensing and gaming offences being committed there, and in the early hours of a Sunday morning in late September the premises were again raided. Mrs Nash was present, but not her husband. Luard told me that Peter Cook, still the joint licensee with him, was appearing on Broadway in New York, and that their company was indeed in voluntary liquidation.

Later in the week Raymond Nash kept an appointment to see me at my office. He was a swarthy, suave individual – the sort of man you would hesitate to buy a second-hand car from – and as he sat down he placed his briefcase on my desk and when I asked him if he owned or controlled the Establishment Club, he answered, 'Yes, if you want me to.' I told him that what I wanted to know was who was responsible for the club. After another ambiguous answer, I told him that I believed that we were wasting each other's time and he was shown out.

About eighteen months later, when I was deputy to the commander of the West End district, James Starritt, he told me that Sir Joseph Simpson was concerned because a Mr Ben Parkin, MP, had told him that a fellow Member, Tom Driberg, had had a tape given to him by Raymond Nash which incriminated the superintendent in charge of the Clubs Office. Today covert taping by people being interviewed is not uncommon, but such behaviour in the early Sixties was practically unheard of.

Although Superintendent (Clubs) was by then my colleague Reg Doak, I recalled that after my own interview with Nash I had been told by a Soho source that Nash had tape-recorded our conversation because he had hoped to compromise me. It occurred to me that this might be the tape Nash had given to Mr Driberg, and Jim Starritt passed on the circumstances of the interview to the Commissioner, suggesting that he should ask Mr Parkin to get Mr Driberg to play the tape to him. This was done and Sir Joseph later said that Mr Parkin had told him that far from being incriminating the tape recording he had heard reflected credit on the superintendent interviewing Nash. Presumably this was a case, in my experience not unusual, where an MP accepted a story about the police and passed it on without checking it in detail.

While I was operationally committed to organizing and carrying out a never-ending anti-vice campaign, if I was also to be effective as a senior officer at West End Central I had to keep in touch with every aspect of policing in this busy area. The period 1962/5 was to see a series of traumatic events, which began on Saturday, 10 November

1962, when an artist named Herman Woolf was knocked down by a Jaguar car as he was crossing Park Lane.

Mr Woolf was taken to St George's Hospital where, after he had been examined and certified fit to be discharged, he was arrested by PC Grant for being in possession of sufficient cannabis to make about thirty-odd cigarettes and he was taken to West End Central police station. The duty police surgeon, Dr Peters, concluded that Woolf was suffering from the effects of drugs but was fit to be detained. On Sunday afternoon he was found on the floor of the detention room in a semi-conscious condition; Dr Peters examined him again and advised his removal to hospital. A fractured skull was diagnosed and some thirteen days later, on 28 November, he died at the Atkinson Morley Hospital after two operations had failed to save his life. The verdict recorded at the inquest held on 5 December was that the cause of death was a contusion of the brain following collision with a car.

Mrs Woolf, whose marriage to Herman Woolf had been dissolved in 1946 but who had remained on friendly terms with him, did not learn about the accident until he was dead. She saw the body in the hospital mortuary the day after his death, noticed that his face appeared to be marked and bruised and suspected that he had suffered injuries at West End Central police station during the time he was in custody. She consulted Sidney Silverman, MP, a solicitor and at that time a prominent campaigner for the abolition of the death penalty, and so began an attempt to reverse the inquest verdict and blame the police for Woolf's death.

In November 1963 an application to quash the Inquisition on the Inquest, which really means to set aside the verdict, was heard in the Divisional Court of the High

Court of Justice and refused. However, so vociferous were Mr Silverman and his supporters that in December Henry Brooke, MP, the Home Secretary, appointed Mr Norman J. Skelhorn, QC, who later became the Director of Public Prosecutions, to hold an inquiry into the behaviour of the Metropolitan Police in relation to Herman Woolf.

The inquiry, held between 16 January and 6 February 1964, where some seventy-eight witnesses gave evidence, found that Woolf was not subjected to any violence or deliberately maltreated by the police. I gave evidence on the charging and feeding of anyone in custody at the police station. The medical evidence was quite conclusive that Woolf had sustained a fracture of the skull when he was knocked down in Park Lane, but Mr Silverman, whom I do not think it unfair to describe as anti-police in his views, was disinclined to accept this and created an atmosphere of putting the police on trial. I recall that John Williams, the solicitor to the Metropolitan Police who was personally instructing our counsel, John Leonard, at the inquiry, was very angry about the attitude of his professional colleague.

It has been my experience that the majority of policemen are strong and resilient characters who are able to work under pressure and adversity. Occasionally the stress is too much and there is a breakdown, but certainly ordeal by fire, which is frequently the lot of a police officer, can do much to strengthen and mould character. Detective Sergeant Joe Bell from the Woolf Inquiry comes into this category. At the time he was a comparatively young officer and was regarded as both reliable and conscientious, but he came under considerable criticism for searching Woolf's flat because he thought there might be more drugs there without first obtaining a search warrant. Sergeant Bell told Mr Woolf of his intention and there was no objection, but it was later argued that Woolf was not in a fit mental state to give his consent. This criticism, the public inquiry and the unfounded allegations that Woolf had been physically harmed while he was in custody so worried the detective sergeant's wife that she had a serious breakdown. Fortunately she eventually made a full recovery, but at the time this must have added considerably to the pressure on Sergeant Bell. However, such was the calibre of the man that he weathered the storm, did not become bitter and before he retired in the 1980s became a very able detective chief superintendent. He was a tower of strength to his juniors during the long investigation of the Deptford fire disaster in 1981 where thirteen young black people lost their lives.

Hard on the heels of the Woolf incident came the much more serious matter of the Challoner Inquiry conducted by Mr Justice James, QC. One of the detective sergeants, Harry Challoner, MM, was accused of planting a brick on a Mr Donald Rooum, who was arrested while taking part in a demonstration on 11 July 1963 outside Claridge's Hotel protesting against a visit to this country of Queen Frederika of Greece. At the Old Bailey in June 1964 Challoner was found insane and unfit to plead, while three young constables employed as aides to the CID, who had worked under his supervision and been charged with him, were convicted of conspiracy to pervert the course of justice and sent to prison. These young men had come very much under the dominant influence of Challoner's strong personality and, although what they had done was very wrong, in the particular circumstances their colleagues could not help but feel some sympathy for them.

Harry Challoner had a tough war record. He had

been parachuted into northern Italy with the Special Air Service where he was captured, tortured and sentenced to be shot. He escaped, linked up with Italian resistance fighters, and helped ambush enemy military convoys and blow up bridges and trains before regaining contact with British forces. When he returned home he was awarded the Military Medal for his gallantry. How much his wartime privations accounted for his later schizophrenia doctors found it hard to say, but the incident that apparently tipped the balance of his mind took place the day before the arrest of Mr Rooum. Inspector George Brooks, who had been on duty at Claridge's, returned to the police station with a cut and bleeding head after he had been hit by a piece of brick thrown by one of the demonstrators. I happened to see him when he came in and he was quite an ugly sight. Apparently Sergeant Challoner also saw him and vowed to avenge him.

The criminal investigation of Challoner and his young colleagues, an independent police inquiry by Mr Norman Goodchild, the Chief Constable of Wolverhampton Borough Police, and finally the James Inquiry set up by the Home Secretary, put the whole station – but particularly the CID – under very close scrutiny. I remember going one day to the Civil Service Commission building in Chesterfield Gardens, when my chief, James Starritt, was giving evidence to the inquiry. He was being questioned about a report that he had submitted before Challoner was suspended from duty and charged, drawing attention, for the information of the Yard's medical branch, to his apparently irrational behaviour and suggesting that he should be seen by the Chief Medical Officer. The examining counsel seemed to be doubting whether the report had been submitted at all or querying the date given, when the chief superintendent, who stood about six foot six inches and was built in proportion, drew himself to his full height and said, 'Sir, may I tell *you* that in the whole of my thirty-odd years of police service I have never had my integrity doubted.' The learned counsel was quick to assure him that he accepted what he had said and that he in no way intended to impugn his integrity. Honour appeared to be satisfied.

As the result of the Goodchild report the Met system of recruiting to the CID via selection from young uniformed constables employed in plain clothes and known as aides to CID was changed. A new procedure of selection as temporary detective constables with greater emphasis on training and supervision was introduced.

Another case which had its origins in Soho hit the headlines in 1962/3. This was the Stephen Ward, Christine Keeler and Mandy Rice-Davies scandal that involved the then Secretary of State for War, John Profumo, and Captain Eugene Ivanov, an assistant naval attaché at the Russian Embassy. Dr Stephen Ward, a society osteopath and procurer of girls for rich clients, was known to me as a social acquaintance of Perac Rachman and it was through Ward that Keeler, a prostitute, was installed in a Rachman flat at Bryanston Mews, Marylebone.

The fuse which was to cause the resignation of Mr Profumo on 30 May 1963 was lit in the early hours of 28 October 1962 at the All Nighter's Club in Wardour Street. Two West Indian men with criminal records from Notting Hill, 'Lucky' Gordon and John Edgecombe, both of whom had lived with Christine Keeler, had a fight about her. Lucky Gordon's face was slashed and needed seventeen stitches, and John Edgecombe disappeared before the arrival of the police.

After the slashing of Lucky Gordon, Keeler continued to live with Edgecombe but eventually left him, and in the afternoon of 14 December, only fifteen days after Rachman's death, Edgecombe went to Ward's flat at 17 Wimpole Mews where he expected to find Keeler and Rice-Davies. He discovered that both women were there but they would not let him in, so he created a scene and fired a number of shots from an automatic pistol. On this occasion he was arrested and charged with the shooting and with the wounding of Lucky Gordon at the Wardour Street club in October. In the course of the next six months, amidst a welter of rumour and speculation, Edgecombe was sentenced to imprisonment for seven years, Dr Ward was arrested, found guilty of living on the earnings of prostitution and committed suicide by an overdose of drugs before he could be sentenced, and Mr Profumo resigned.

Such were the bizarre stories of erotic sex parties, perversion and intrigue that mounting political pressure led the Prime Minister Harold Macmillan in June 1963 to appoint Lord Denning to inquire into the circumstances of Mr Profumo's resignation and particularly as to whether national security had been endangered. Lord Denning's report was published in September (Cmnd 2152) and in it he concluded that there was no evidence that national security had been affected.

The Metropolitan Police were involved in helping to assemble evidence for the Denning inquiry and these efforts were co-ordinated by the deputy to the Assistant Commissioner 'A' Department, Arthur Townsend. He allocated to me a number of inquiries, some of which were never completed because the people I wished to interview had gone abroad. One person I did talk to who was helpful and became a very useful contact in the West End was the late Percival, known as Val, Murray, proprietor of the Cabaret Club in Beak Street, which he had founded in 1920. Val Murray, who had started as a First World War entertainment organizer, ran a straight club. His hostesses cum cabaret artistes, who gave two shows nightly, were housed on the opposite side of Beak Street to the club, and it was not an uncommon sight to see them tripping across the street in their exotic costumes. His records of employees were well documented, including those of Keeler and Rice-Davies who had both worked there, and he was, because of his long association with West End club life, extremely well informed.

It was an interesting experience to be present at a final meeting convened and presided over by Lord Denning and attended by those who had helped with the inquiry at which he reviewed the evidence that had been gathered. Although he was very tactful there was one embarrassment, referred to in paragraph 85 of the report: a delay at an important point in interviewing Keeler that was caused by a failure of co-ordination between two branches of 'C' Department, C.1 Branch and the Special Branch. Commander (the rank would now be Deputy Assistant Commissioner) Reg Spooner, a senior Yard detective who at the time was terminally ill with cancer, was called to the meeting but he was unable to explain the delay. Co-ordination was an area to which I was to give considerable attention during my own period of office as Assistant Commissioner 'C' Department, but by then a mix of mainline CID and Special Branch personnel in units like the Anti-Terrorist Squad, and a degree of selective interchange, had eliminated most of the problem.

In the midst of operational matters during 1963, I was shown a newly published Government White Paper on Higher Police Training. It was proposed to inaugurate a six-month senior command course at the Police Staff

College, to help equip middle-ranking officers for chief-officer positions. Applications were invited from all police officers in the country holding the ranks of chief inspector to chief superintendent, and the Home Office received 1,500 applications. These were whittled down by regional and central interview panels, and finally a three-day extended interview procedure, to thirty successful candidates.

I went to the staff college for the extended interview from Wednesday to Friday during the first week in July. The early summer at Bramshill House was pleasant and between interviews I sat by the lakeside watching a colony of Canada geese. Despite the importance of the occasion, it was such a pleasant contrast to the pressures of the West End that I felt very relaxed and enjoyed the whole experience. Returning to West End Central on the Saturday, it was business as usual with a late-night execution of a drugs search warrant at the Huntsman Club in Berwick Street, Soho. Then began the wait for the result of the interviews.

In early November I was briefed by the Commissioner to take the Home Secretary, Henry Brooke, on an evening tour of Soho as he wished to see at first hand something of the night life there. The Challoner Enquiry, which had been set up by him, was in progress at West End Central and for this reason Mr Brooke did not want to come to the police station. With my deputy, Chief Inspector Douglas Culpin, I met the Home Secretary and the Permanent Under Secretary of State, Sir Charles Cunningham, at the Reform Club in Pall Mall.

Rumours had been circulating that the results of the command course extended interviews were out, and we had only been walking towards Soho for a few seconds when Mr Brooke told me he understood congratulations were in order. Sir Joseph Simpson had told him that I was among the thirty successful candidates. However, he said, I would have to wait until the second course in June of the following year because the Commissioner did not want too many changes in the West End and my colleague, Colin Woods, would be going on the January course. This was good news and coming from the Home Secretary himself, I felt entitled to believe it!

In the course of the tour I took Mr Brooke into strip-tease clubs in Wardour Street and Greek Street, a near-beer establishment and a Chinese gambling club in Gerrard Street. The Home Secretary was dressed in nondescript fashion, wearing a raincoat and a trilby hat, and as he wished to remain anonymous our visits to these Soho night spots were brief. Afterwards I took him to the Commissioner's office at the Yard where Sir Joseph was waiting for him, and a few seconds after we arrived Sir Charles Cunningham came in. 'Do you think anyone recognized you, Home Secretary?' he asked, to which the Home Secretary replied, 'No, I don't think so, Charles, except perhaps those inscrutable Chinese gentlemen.'

At the end of the year and after seventeen months in charge I relinquished my command of the Clubs Office. There had been frustrations but also some successes, and it had been very rewarding to work closely with a selected staff that maintained such high standards of dedication and integrity. The wealth of experience, the local knowledge and the contacts I had made were to prove invaluable later on in my service.

For the next six months I was the deputy to Chief Superintendent Starritt, who was now in command of the whole West End area. Much of my time was taken up with administrative matters, including local complaints and discipline, but both Jim Starritt and I made time to get out and about. We both believed in the adage, 'There is no fertilizer like the farmer's foot,' and made a point of patrolling on foot, especially in the late hours, in order to see and be seen as identifying with that most important person, the policeman on the streets.

The summer of 1964 came and I spent six pleasant months on the newly constituted senior command course. There were twenty-four senior officers on it, eight from the Met – including my friend and Notting Hill colleague, John Gerrard – and the remainder from various forces in England and Scotland. The company was good and professionally stimulating. Twenty-one of us eventually achieved chief officer rank and an average of fifteen of us, with our wives, have met for an annual reunion dinner for the past twenty-two years.

In 1964 Mr Roy Jenkins, during his first period as Home Secretary, introduced the Police Act, 1964. It was a far-reaching piece of legislation becoming, in fact, the statutory authority for the modern police service. It enabled the Home Secretary to put through his dramatic amalgamation programme that reduced police forces from 123 to 47. While it was a shock for many cities, boroughs and even counties to lose their own police forces, and local civic pride in many cases was wounded, the amalgamations were necessary to bring the police service into the twentieth century. Many of the old forces were too small to provide a proper career structure, or the training and experience necessary for proper efficiency. The 1964 Act, a bold and imaginative one, was long overdue.

When I returned from the staff college in January 1965, I went back to my old job as a deputy to James Starritt at West End Central police station. Somehow or other at this time I found myself on the committee of the London Region of the Police Superintendents' Associations of

England and Wales and also one of two regional representatives on the executive committee of the national association. Although I had not previously been involved in police representative organizations I was, during the next three years, to find myself as Chairman, with Kenneth Newman as Secretary, negotiating for radical changes in the status and salary of our members.

The first few months of the year went by very quickly and in the Met we were busy with our own minor reorganization to line up the boundaries of our territorial divisions with those of the newly formed Greater London boroughs. The administrative changes on the 'C' or St James's Division to deal with the acquisition of the historic Bow Street area and the transfer of the Tottenham Court Road police station territory had just been completed when I got the news that my second spell of service in the West End was nearly over and that I was on the move, this time to East London.

6
The East End

In May 1965 I was called to the Yard to see the Commissioner. He told me that I was being promoted as from 1 June and that I would have the command of the 'H' or Tower Hamlets District where my old chief from my inspector days in the West End, Charles Strath, was retiring.

Although it was one of the new London boroughs, Tower Hamlets was, in fact, a very old borough. It had been in existence since 1832, when it was formed from the parishes of Bethnal Green, Poplar and Stepney. Under the London Government Act of 1899 the three parishes became independent boroughs and enjoyed this status until their second amalgamation in 1965.

The whole area is steeped in history and notoriety. The Tower of London contrasts with the mean streets where in the late 1880s the unsolved Jack the Ripper murders of prostitutes were committed, and with Sidney Street where Winston Churchill when he was Home Secretary personally took charge at the 'Siege of Sidney Street'. Commercial and religious life was also equally varied and showed the influences of centuries of immigration. The Chinese settled in Limehouse, the Huguenots from France at Bethnal Green, the Irish influx after the famine in the nineteenth century influenced the whole area where they found work building the new docks, and the most influential of all the large-scale immigrations was that of the Jews who came to the area in the nineteenth century to escape persecution in Eastern Europe. In the 1960s the latest wave of immigrants to join the very cosmopolitan population of about a quarter of a million inhabitants came from the Indian sub-continent and settled in the Brick Lane and Commercial Road area. The docks and the Port of London, although they were beginning to show signs of decline, were still busy and brought seamen from all over the world to the area. It is sad that the borough with its great historical connection with shipping – Blackwall became the headquarters of the East India Company in 1612 and it was from there that the founders of the first permanent colony in America sailed in 1606 – no longer has any working docks. As a consequence many industries have left the area and in recent years it has become one of the most socially deprived in the country. It is to be hoped that the redevelopment schemes now under way by the Dockland Development Corporation – including a new inner-city airport on the Isle of Dogs – will bring some prosperity back to the borough.

Before his retirement, Charles Strath invited me to a lunch at which he introduced me to two of the local MPs, Peter Shore and Bill Hilton, as well as the Mayor, Tom Mitchell, and the Chief Executive, Jack Wolkind. Despite his reputation for being a somewhat taciturn individual, Mr Strath had clearly worked hard at establishing local rapport. Over the years I got to know and admire Jack Wolkind, who had formerly been the town clerk of Bethnal Green. He became the doyen of the London boroughs chief executives and only retired from his post in 1985.

London really is a collection of large villages, and close relationships between the local police, local authorities and the public can prove of immense value. I feel that the preservation and strengthening of these local identities is essential, for without them there is just one large, amorphous, centralized mass of anonymity, indifferent to local issues, and the character and social fabric of the capital city would be diminished. The senior police officer of a London borough has an important role to play in these local relationships and it is difficult to see what benefits will come from the recent decision to abolish the post of commander in the boroughs. Local authorities and their executive officers are likely to miss this senior contact who related directly to them, and the chief superintendents of the territorial divisions within the boroughs may not function so efficiently without his leadership and co-ordination.

The principal instructions given to me by Sir Joseph Simpson about my new command were, first, to use my initiative, exercise leadership and run an honest and professional unit capitalizing on the history and traditions of the East End; and, secondly, to get alongside the local authority, elected councillors and their professional officers, to identify with them and the new borough as their local police force.

The 'H' or Tower Hamlets District had a population of approximately 250,000, four territorial commands with superintendents (later chief superintendents) in charge and a total police and civil staff establishment of about a thousand people – a larger organization than many police forces before the Jenkins amalgamations. There were eight police stations in the borough, all but one, Limehouse, old and inadequate buildings.

For the next few years I had the opportunity of putting my ideas on leadership into practice with a good degree of autonomy. While I took a keen interest in day to day operational matters my style was very much to promote and develop a team approach, with my senior officers running their own commands and contributing as members of a borough management committee. At this time some of the post-war recruits were reaching middle management ranks and I was lucky enough to have a very good team. An indication of their quality is the fact that in later years no fewer than eight of them reached assistant or chief officer rank in the Met and provincial forces.

With Sir Joseph Simpson's commissionership came an encouragement to move forward to challenge old concepts and institute changes, but in a hierarchical service steeped in the tradition of obedience – especially to New Scotland Yard – development was bound to be slow and the opportunities not welcomed by everyone. When Sir John Waldron took over after the untimely death of Sir Joseph, he continued – with some reservations – this moderately iconoclastic approach, and later Sir Robert Mark had no inhibitions about making more drastic changes. However, looking back, I see them as a series of events, a kind of natural development, hastened – sometimes too slowly – by the leadership of the force. Some of the changes were organizational ones and a number of these took place in 1968 following a report on the force by PA Management Consultants. However, more important, particularly in the long term, were the changes in attitude brought about by an increased delegation of responsibility and the encouragement to develop local initiatives.

Within months of taking up my new command I had occasion to challenge authority at the Yard, which brought the Commissioner to the East End to see me. This was over the housing of four of my senior officers. They had recently been promoted and, not living within five miles of their police stations, they had been directed to occupy police-owned flats at Arbour Square, near the

Commercial Road. They were married men with children at school and living in their own houses – some only marginally more than five miles away – and they were, to put it mildly, upset when their appeal against the direction to move their homes was refused by Sir John Waldron, then the Assistant Commissioner 'A' Department at the Yard.

One of the benefits of the senior command course had been to learn something about force administration, including housing policy and the standards recommended by a Home Office post-war committee on police housing. An inspection of the police flats convinced me that they did not measure up to the specification for senior officers' accommodation as laid down by that committee. I took up the cudgels by writing to 'D' Department at the Yard, pointing out the substandard condition of the flats and saying that, in my opinion, they were not suitable as homes for my senior officers. Subsequently I received a telephone call from a 'D' Department officer of my own rank who, while informing me that the force had no flats which conformed to the committee's recommendation, inquired whether I wished my report to go forward as 'they' wouldn't like it.

A few days later, much to my surprise, I received a phone call from Sir Joseph who said he wished to come and see me and the married quarters I had written about. He came, inspected the flats, agreed with me that they were substandard and discussed the force policy on the five-mile rule. I told him I believed it was outdated because many of the flats over police stations had had to be taken into use as office accommodation to allow these older stations to function at all, and that this rule was already more honoured in the breach than by observance. The ultimate result was that the force policy was revised to give more flexibility, and my senior staff were allowed to continue living in their own houses. This episode became known in the East End as the 'Relief of Arbour Square', and the change in policy was universally welcomed.

The borough was very much a multi-racial community and despite regular Sunday morning meetings at Petticoat Lane Market by the Union Movement, often addressed by Sir Oswald Mosley, there was no public order problem. Mosley, and all that he stood for, were detested in the East End but, sensibly in my opinion, local people ignored his meetings. This tactic was far more effective than the policy of militant confrontation adopted by the hard Left in later years. Community relations in Tower Hamlets in the late 1960s were very good, with few complaints about racial prejudice and harassment.

One of the problems of the area was crimes of violence: assaults, woundings and some robbery. Although by the statistics of the late 1970/80s the number of such crimes was not high, they did cause concern. The victims, frequently seamen and patrons of public houses and late-night cafés in the Cable Street area, and the peak hours for these crimes, between 11 P.M. and 1 A.M., indicated a correlation between them and drunkenness. Manpower shortages prevented much of an increase in preventive foot patrols, but the institution of a regular mobile van patrol to arrest drunks and increased prosecution of licensees for permitting drunkenness virtually eliminated such crimes. The following year there was some comment on the steep increase in drunkenness offences when the annual statistics for the force were published. Although various reasons were advanced, no one identified 'H' District's anti-violence activity as being responsible for a major part of the increase! As a field commander it was a change to find the light of publicity did not shine quite so intensely on East End events as it did in the West End and this made life a little less stressful.

We had our share of national publicity, however, when on 9 March 1966 a man named George Cornell, an associate of the south London Richardson Brothers, who was then dabbling in striptease and porn in the West End, was shot dead in the Blind Beggar public house in the Whitechapel Road. Jim Axon, my detective superintendent, who later became the Chief Constable of Jersey, took up the murder investigation. He told me that a barmaid at the pub had more than hinted that Cornell had been shot by a local criminal, Ronnie Kray. However, she was terrified, would not make a written statement and was likely if pressed to deny that she had seen or mentioned Kray. Detective Superintendent Tommy Butler of the Flying Squad arrested Ronnie and had him put up on an identification parade at Commercial Street police station, but he was not picked out. There was no forensic evidence to link the murder with Kray, and although local gossip blamed him, no witnesses could be found who would identify the gunman. When Jim Axon had exhausted all local leads the inquiry team had to be run down and the facts were recorded and put on file at the Yard.

Although the Krays' family home was in Vallence Road in Bethnal Green, the twins were not often seen in their native East End during the late 1960s because they had graduated to Belgravia where they controlled a gambling club named Esmeralda's Barn. This club was patronized by a variety of people including show biz personalities, peers of the realm and of course crooks in dinner jackets. Ronnie Kray's twin, Reggie, it is said, enjoyed the new scene in more salubrious surroundings, but Ronnie hankered after the rough and tough East End where he was feared because of his violent nature.

Some two years after the shooting of Cornell, after members of the Yard's Serious Crime Squad led by Detective Chief Inspector Leonard 'Nipper' Read and Detective Inspector Frank Cater had arrested the Kray twins and about fifteen of their associates for murder and various crimes of violence, the barmaid and others were persuaded to come forward and give evidence. The Kray twins, who are still in prison, were sentenced to life imprisonment for the murders of Cornell and a man named Jack McVitie, and Ronnie has been certified as suffering from paranoid schizophrenia. Their elder brother, Charles, received ten years and other members of the gang were also given long sentences for the parts they played in these murders and other serious crimes.

Leonard Read, who in the late 1940s had been a sprinter in the Met Police Athletic Club team, became an assistant chief constable of his native county of Nottingham and the National Co-ordinator of Regional Crime Squads before he retired. I had first met Frank Cater when he came to Notting Hill as a detective constable from C.1 Drug Squad to assist with club raids. He was a valuable member of my senior CID team throughout my period as AC (Crime), and was Commander of the Flying Squad for the last two years of that period before his own retirement.

From time to time attempts were made by some East End criminal families, who could loosely be termed Kray disciples, to operate local protection rackets. These criminal enterprises usually involved licensed premises and quite often the licensees were either front men for the criminals or were too scared to complain and co-operate with the police. Determined investigation of cases of assault in or around the premises and strict supervision of the licensing laws kept control of the situation. The latter tactic, commonly practised by experienced policemen in the field, is particularly effective. The regular, overt appearance of a policeman checking on drunkenness and enforcing strict observance of licensing hours is as unwelcome to the clientele as it is to the management of such public houses. It usually results in a loss of trade and – satisfactorily for the police – the disappearance of the criminal element. Such problems dealt with locally by vigorous action are snuffed out fairly quickly; they only become serious when inept police leadership or, worse, corruption allows criminal gangs to develop and become a real threat before they are identified centrally.

For most of my service in the East End I had, as the chairman of the London District, been a member of the Executive Committee of the Superintendents' Association of England and Wales and I was elected president of the association for 1968. Roy Jenkins's programme of amalgamations had increased the size of provincial forces so that their chief superintendents had much larger commands than hitherto. Through a working party of the Police Advisory Board, of which Kenneth Newman and myself were members, a higher scale of pay had been negotiated. Not for the first time there was an anomaly as far as the Met was concerned, and the Home Office would not agree to the same numerical criteria being applied to the force for which the Home Secretary was the Police Authority. However, as the Met representatives, we had agreed with our provincial colleagues, in return for their support later, to accept the pay settlement although it excluded us. In due course a claim was made for regrading and for new salary scales for Met chief superintendents.

In April 1968 as the result of the recommendations of PA Management Consultants the Home Office agreed to the abolition of the existing rank of deputy commander and the allocation of more decision-making functions to chief superintendents, but there was still no progress on the grading/salary issue. Sir Joseph Simpson was paternalistic in his approach, concerned and genuinely convinced that he could get a better pay deal for his chief superintendents without any regrading. I and my colleagues were equally convinced that the matter could only be resolved by use of the Police Advisory Board which had been brought into being by the Police Act of 1964, and which required a national agreement.

The Home Office used the blotting paper technique: no answer to letters, or at best long delays. There was also an attempt at 'divide and rule' by suggesting that as the provincial grading had been settled, the Met position should be resolved between the Commissioner and the Home Office. The National Executive Association rejected this ploy and raised the issue at the PAB meeting in May when the Home Secretary, James Callaghan, was in the chair and expressed his concern about the delay and offered to mediate.

By the end of January 1969, as no progress had been made, we requested a personal interview with the Home Secretary both in his capacity as the Police Authority for the Metropolis and as Chairman of the Police Advisory Board. A few weeks later a meeting took place at the Home Office with Mr Callaghan and the Permanent Under Secretary of State, Sir Philip Allen, on one side of the table and myself with Superintendent Kenneth Newman and the association's secretary, Harry Staples, on the other side. I presented our case, expressing the concern and the discontent of the Met at the inordinate delay in resolving the issue, pointing out that he himself had expressed concern at the PAB meeting the previous May. I also mentioned the contrast between the alacrity of the implementation of PA Management Consultants' recommendations, which placed more responsibility on chief superintendents, and the delay over the regrading issue. No counter-arguments had been presented and it was our view that the Home Office was unwilling to accord the status and salary to Metropolitan officers that had been granted to those in other police forces.

Mr Callaghan, who had listened intently, closed the meeting by saying that he would urgently consider what had been said and then let us have his decision. We did not have to wait long for a reply, for on 10 April a letter was received from him approving the regrading of new superintendents to chief superintendents and the existing rank of chief superintendent to commander. The principle had been won, but it took until February of the following year before the salary scale was agreed and then, despite the delay being all on the official side, it was only effective from the previous October.

Negotiating was certainly frustrating and at times highly irritating, testing one's patience to the full. Several of my colleagues from time to time suggested that it might be advisable to let someone else take over the negotiations as my involvement would not do my career any good. However, it was not in my nature to back off from something in which I believed and I was confident that neither Sir Joseph Simpson nor his successor, Sir John Waldron, were petty or spiteful men.

In December 1968, when I had held the Tower Hamlets command for nearly four years, I was sent for by Sir John

Waldron. He told me that after over twenty-two years in the field it was about time that I came into the Yard and that I was to join the Management Services Department as deputy to my former West End colleague, Colin Woods. So the time had come to say goodbye to my colleagues and friends of Tower Hamlets, with whom I had enjoyed working, not least among them the sportsmen who had won the Met's Victor Ludorum every year that I had been in command. Sporting activity, especially competing against non-police clubs, had made quite a contribution to community relations and our tug-of-war team had the added prestige of being selected to represent England in international competitions.

In addition to resolving local senior officers' housing problems I had spent some energy pressing for improvements in operational working conditions. The Architect and Surveyor's Department at the Yard had been very helpful in carrying out amelioration work at most of the eight stations, particularly at the Isle of Dogs where a new small station to replace the existing one, adapted at the turn of the century from an old chapel, was agreed. After much discussion, Leman Street police station had finally been closed and, after demolition, was to be rebuilt as a new district headquarters station.

When I left I hoped I had carried out the instructions of Sir Joseph to capitalize on the history and traditions of the East End. In trying to do so I like to think that a little of the indomitable spirit of the area had rubbed off on me and I was mindful of the optimistic motto adopted by the new Greater London Borough of Tower Hamlets, 'From Great Things to Greater'.

7

Management Services and the USA

The Management Services Department was formed in 1968 as one of the recommendations contained in a report of the previous year by management consultants whose brief had been to 'investigate in the broadest possible way the distribution of functions and responsibilities within the Metropolitan Police'. It consisted of about twenty police officers, some civil staff personnel and six scientists who had recently been recruited. The senior of the scientists was Dr Norman Hand who over the years has been the backbone of the unit, and in 1983 became the director of the, by then, much enlarged department. By ensuring that the force made use of computer systems and other modern technology Norman's contribution to efficiency has been considerable, and since our first meeting in 1969 I have often been grateful for his professional help. One problem we had in common, but never resolved, was the control of our goodnatured but strong-willed pet beagles!

Within a few weeks of my joining the department Colin Woods was appointed the Commandant of the National Police Staff College at Bramshill. He was replaced by Deputy Assistant Commissioner John Bliss who, having set up the Regional Crime Squads organization, had been the national co-ordinator for some years before returning to his parent force. It surprised me that a man like Mr Bliss – one of the few of Trenchard's pre-war Hendon College men to make his career in the CID – was not given a senior post in 'C' Department at the Yard, for his experience could have been very valuable. Also, as a new member of Management Services, I met for the first time Detective Chief Superintendent Ronald Steventon, who a few years later was to become a great ally of mine, before retiring in 1983 as one of 'C' Department's DACs.

I had just begun to understand something about how work study, ergonomics and the application of business organization and management techniques might be used to improve police efficiency when I was awarded a Ford (Dagenham) Trust Fellowship to visit the United States from September to December 1969 to study law enforcement in that country.

The Federal Bureau of Investigation kindly agreed to act as my host and I chose to study the main federal law enforcement agencies. With the assistance of a member of the FBI, John Minnich, a Texan who was then a legal attaché at the Grosvenor Square embassy, I drew up an itinerary. This was to involve my travelling some 8,500 miles in the States which took me from Washington to Miami, along the Gulf coast via New Orleans and El Paso, to San Diego and Los Angeles, before returning through the Middle West and Toronto to New York City. On the advice of John Minnich, in order to get the feel of his country and to help in budgeting my finances, I did all my travelling by the Greyhound Express Bus Service on a $165 three-month See America ticket – at the exchange rate then prevailing, the cost was a little less than £70.

At the time of my visit the legendary Edgar J. Hoover was still the Director of the FBI. I did not meet him, but his influence was very evident at every FBI unit that I visited because there was always a large photograph of him in the office of the agent in charge, identical in size to one of the President of the United States alongside which it hung. As a guest, I refrained from passing an comment about this but on one occasion a young agent confided in me that he felt it was a bit embarrassing and unhealthy. Another example of the invisible presence of their Director occurred in the FBI office at El Paso in Texas – two time zones away from Washington – when one afternoon an agent I was with looked at his watch and said, 'I guess Edgar J. has gone home now, so we can relax.'

In 1969 the FBI, which comes under the Justice Department of the US Government, had about 7,000 agents, the majority of them based at the fifty-eight field offices situated in the major cities of the country. As part of the strong centralized control system developed under Hoover, a copy of every report or letter originating in any field office had to be sent to the Bureau Headquarters in Washington.

One of the most important cities that I visited was New Orleans where I spent some time with the Bureau of Narcotics and Dangerous Drugs. This agency had only been established in 1968 under the Justice Department from an amalgamation of the Treasury Department's Bureau of Narcotics and the Food and Drug Administration Bureau, and very recently, under its later title of the Drugs Enforcement Agency, it has been further amalgamated by coming under the control of the Director of the FBI.

While I was in New Orleans I witnessed the final stages of an operation in which twenty-three people were arrested on a bill of indictment signed by a Grand Jury alleging trafficking in heroin. A Grand Jury consists of twenty-three residents of the State who are appointed for one year. Sworn evidence, in camera if necessary, is given before them and if the jury is satisfied that there is probable cause to believe the persons named have committed the offences alleged, a bill of indictment is signed authorizing their arrest. In most cases, as in this one, to satisfy the US federal courts sworn evidence has to be given by federal agents of purchases by them of drugs, witnessed by other agents, on several occasions inside the premises concerned. The security risks of giving all your evidence to twenty-three jurymen, even in camera, while the suspects are at liberty is self-evident.

The difficulties faced by the American agents from their Supreme Court rulings on the interpretation of the Fourth Amendment to the United States Constitution made me realize how fortunate the police and the public in this country were not to have the same handicaps. The Supreme Court case of *Mapp* v. *Ohio* ruled that evidence obtained from illegal search and seizure is not admissible in any court. In American practice this meant that if in executing a search warrant for a specific item of stolen property, other property, like dangerous drugs for example, is found and seized, no evidence may be given about this. I witnessed such a situation at first hand in Los Angeles when I went with secret service agents to a house in the Watts area where a man arrested for counterfeiting dollar bills was also in possession of a quantity of cocaine. He denied any knowledge of the drug and no action against him was possible other than the forfeiture of the cocaine.

The ruling in our Court of Criminal Appeal in the case of *Regina* v. *Bass* that it is in the public interest that evidence relating to a crime other than that for which a search warrant was granted should be admissible is almost the complete opposite of the American situation. There are some lawyers in this country who advocate the adoption of the American Supreme Court judgment and other exclusionary rulings, known as the 'Suppression Doctrine', their reason being that it is necessary to protect the public from police practices. It seems to me that to adopt such a doctrine would, in fact, punish the public and encourage the criminal. It is very much better to leave the question of the admissibility of evidence in the hands of the judge than to have mandatory rules.

New Orleans is the home of one of the United States' notorious Mafia figures, Carlos Marcello, who in 1982 as the result of an FBI 'sting' operation was sentenced to a total of seventeen years' imprisonment for corruption and other offences. When I was there, Marcello, who is reputed to have made millions of dollars from the numbers game, other forms of gambling and from investments throughout the State of Louisiana, was on bail on a charge of assaulting Federal Agent Patrick Collins. Marcello, together with some other Mafia associates, had been arrested in New York in 1967 and, having been bailed, flew back to New Orleans. Pat Collins was amongst the reception committee at the airport of reporters, policemen and federal agents when Marcello lost his temper, lashed out and hit him.

I was invited by Pat Collins to his home in the French Quarter of New Orleans to meet his wife, Eileen, an English girl from Newcastle, and I was their house guest for a few days. Pat was a first-generation American citizen, born in New York, and spoke the Sicilian dialect fluently and he was something of a specialist on the Mafia and organized crime. From him I heard at first hand some of the details of the Mafia organization, whose methods included murder, kidnapping, bribery and extortion. He pointed out to me the opulent home of Marcello and some of the properties owned or controlled by him.

Although some local police officers that I met tended to suggest that the connection between organized crime and illegal betting and gambling was exaggerated, Pat

Collins was in no doubt that these activities had always been a major source of income for organized crime syndicates. Part of the answer to the problem is borne out by its history in this country – the enforcement of laws that do not accord with community norms is a difficult task and the ultimate solution is usually in the hands of the legislators. In recent years there have been moves in several states of the USA to legalize off-course betting and gambling by the granting of licences.

The problems arising from the immense size of the United States, as well as different political and judicial systems from our own, make direct comparisons between our law enforcement procedures and theirs difficult. However, our common concept of individual freedom under the rule of law means that those who are engaged in guarding that freedom have much in common. We both recognize the truth in the statement of a former American President when he said, 'A nation's laws are only as strong as the people's will to see them enforced.' Without exception during the period of my study in 1969 and in the years since then I have found the federal agents of the USA to be dedicated professional men, always most co-operative in international law enforcement.

Back in 1969 it was interesting for me to see how central government in the United States, mindful of the constitutional position and the fierce independence of the various states, cities and townships, set out to raise the standards of local police forces by providing funding for the training and education of their personnel and for those preparing for police careers. However, I could not help feeling that the multiplicity of federal, state, city and local law enforcement agencies, all with different jurisdictions and responsibilities that required enormous efforts to co-ordinate, was a handicap.

At the conclusion of my tour in 1969, I wrote, 'The complexities and the sophistication of modern life will in the future increase the need for specialization in some fields, but, as crime and criminals do not recognize demarcation lines, success is more likely to be achieved by an organization charged with responsibility for all aspects of criminal law enforcement rather than through a number of separate agencies having autonomous jurisdiction in a limited field and therefore requiring extensive co-ordinating machinery to secure a corporate effort.' I have not had cause to change my mind.

8
Back to the West End

I had hardly had time to settle down in the Management Services Department on my return from the USA when in February 1970 I was sent for by Sir John Waldron who told me that as from 1 March I was to return to the West End as the commander of the 'C' or St James's District. As always there were problems there, some, like the proliferation of porn shops, simmering away under the surface, and others like the invasion of the area around the Eros statue at Piccadilly Circus by hippies, more apparent and much more easily resolved.

There had been many complaints, including one from the Tourist Board of Great Britain, about obstruction and general nuisance caused by the hippy fraternity using the Eros concourse as a camping site. This seemingly trivial problem had begun the previous summer. It had received national and international media attention and looked like escalating. Some of the young people, including foreign students touring Europe on a shoe-string budget, had become victims of opportunist thieves who, mixing with them, had stolen their money, passports and even, on occasion, their boots and shoes as they slept.

I gathered that because a stipendiary magistrate at Bow Street court had not supported the local police by convicting a number of them who had been arrested for wilfully obstructing the highway a certain amount of apathy had developed, and constables on the beat were tending to avoid the area. A little encouragement to restore their interest, and insistence on some daily firm but polite policing of the traditional 'move along, please' variety as soon as a crowd began to form, quickly remedied the situation. I am not sure where the hippies went but it may not have been a coincidence when later in the year disturbances were reported from Amsterdam when the Dutch police dispersed a persistent similar type of assembly in Damm Square by using water cannon.

The American Embassy in Grosvenor Square was still from time to time the focal point of demonstrations, although the organizations had changed from being mainly CND to groups protesting about the Vietnam War who were now inclined to use violence. On Saturday 9 May 1970 there was a large demonstration by the British Campaign for Peace in Vietnam that nearly went wrong. About 4,000 people marched from Trafalgar Square to Grosvenor Square, and several hundred of the demonstrators broke through a police cordon in Oxford Street and instead of entering Grosvenor Square on the opposite side to the embassy, they came into it by way of North Audley Street, immediately opposite the northern corner of the embassy. They tried to break through the police cordon there, but fortunately did not succeed. The noisy struggle went on for about three hours before the breakaway marchers were forced back on to the agreed route. To add to our difficulties there was a fault on the radio channel allocated to us, with repeated interference from radio traffic about a sporting event at the Wembley Stadium. From the observation platform of the control vehicle, I frequently had to use a mounted branch inspector to send instructions to my sector commanders in the front line of the various cordons.

At the end of the afternoon, when the demonstration had run out of steam, some fifty people had been arrested and sixty-five police officers injured – two of them being kept in hospital. On the following Monday morning, I received a letter from Mr Walter Annenberg, the American Ambassador, complimenting the police on their professionalism in dealing with the demonstration and for carrying out their duty of protecting the embassy with such restraint.

The Commissioner, Sir John Waldron, was present for most of the demonstration. He was in plain clothes and on one occasion, at the height of the noise and skirmishing, I remember glancing down to see that he was nonchalantly swinging his umbrella as if he were practising a golf stroke. At no time during the operation did he interfere and he did not even speak to me until it had ended, but all of us were aware of his reassuring presence. At the debriefing exercise the following week the technical radio fault and the need to strengthen the Oxford Street cordon that had been breached were noted for attention before the next demonstration.

During his term of office Sir John had great success with his policy of using traditional methods to police events likely to cause public order problems, helped by improved mobility, communications and early intelligence. He was a firm champion of the right to peaceful public demonstration and had he lived I am sure that he would have been saddened by the escalation of violence that, in recent years, has increasingly caused his successors to apply to the Home Secretary for Orders banning certain marches and processions because serious public disorder was anticipated. Many of us felt that a reference to him after his death in David Ascoli's very good book, *The Queen's Peace*, as 'not being the stuff of which Commissioners are made' was both unfair and unkind.

It was pleasing to find at West End Central a number

of officers whose service extended back fifteen years or so to the time when I was their inspector. They were well informed on the happenings and the criminal inhabitants of their manor and, not for the first or the last time, I found their opinions an excellent sounding-board. I learned from them that some of the old Soho vice barons were still around, a few of them, regrettably, gaining in influence, and there were one or two new aspiring entrepreneurs striving to get in on this lucrative field. Their main objective now seemed to be to get into the pornographic bookshop trade rather than striptease clubs, as had been the case when I was last serving in the West End six years earlier.

The Clubs Office, under the able leadership of one of my former East End chief inspectors, now Chief Superintendent Colin Hewett, were continuing their never-ending task of controlling vice activities, and they now had the responsibility for supervising the licensed gambling casinos and liaising with the newly constituted Gaming Board of Great Britain. They were also attacking the latest organized prostitution racket – bogus escort agencies controlling a chain of call girls who were required to pay a percentage of their high fees to the agency proprietors – by prosecuting these men for living on the earnings of prostitution.

The expansion of the bookshop trade was disturbing, and the names of Silver, Mifsud and John Mason were mentioned as we discussed who held controlling interests. However, the responsibility for initiating any prosecutions under the Obscene Publications Act was the prerogative of the Obscene Publications Squad at the Yard. I considered that they could have been more effectively dealt with by my local officers and told the Assistant Commissioner 'A' Department so. However, although he agreed with me, he was not in a position to vary the policy because the Obscene Publications Squad was part of 'C' Department where there was no desire for a change. I encouraged some of my inspectors, like Ronald Hay who later became a key member of my corruption inquiry team, to prosecute under the Vagrancy and Indecent Advertisements Acts when the windows, or displays inside the shops that could be seen from the street, could be said to be indecent. While this was good for our morale it was little more than a minor irritant to the porn barons and certainly did not deter them from expanding their businesses.

The jealousy, intrigue and general double dealing among Soho criminals and their associates meant that violence, and even murder, to settle their differences was always a possibility. One such gangland killing on 7 May 1970 in a Soho night-club, the Latin Quarter, reminded us that the menace of protection rackets still existed. There was a fight in the club and one of the men involved, Alfredo Zomparelli, stabbed to death David Knight, a young brother of Ronald Knight, the husband of the actress Barbara Windsor. Ronnie and another brother, John Knight, also took part in the fight and they were among those arrested and charged with making an affray when Zomparelli was charged with murder. At the Old Bailey in July Zomparelli was found guilty of manslaughter and sentenced to three years' imprisonment. The jury trying the Knight brothers on the affray charge failed to agree a verdict and they were discharged. During the course of the murder inquiry the proprietors of the club had admitted that they had paid protection money to the man who had been killed.

The sequel to the crime took place in September 1974, when Zomparelli, having completed his prison sentence, was shot dead in the Golden Goose Amusement Arcade in Wardour Street, Soho. Revenge was high on the list of possible motives for his murder but the crime remained unsolved until 1979, when George Piggot, a one-time henchman for Perac Rachman at Notting Hill, confessed while he was serving a prison sentence for armed robbery that he and an accomplice had carried out the murder for money. Piggot, who appeared at the Old Bailey and received the statutory sentence of life imprisonment for his part in the crime, was to become one of our 'supergrasses' who will be discussed in Chapter 13.

One of the long-awaited developments to improve working conditions at West End Central was the reopening of the old Vine Street police station at Piccadilly Place. Before its closure in 1940, there had been a police station on the site since the birth of the Met in 1829 when the Parish of St James's Watch House at 10 Little Vine Street, as Piccadilly Place was known then, became a police station house. One day in June 1971 when the reopening was imminent I had just returned to my office after having a look around the renovated building when I received a telephone call from the Commissioner saying that he was calling to see me the following morning. I was naturally intrigued to know why he was coming to West End Central rather than asking me to go to the Yard, but I could think of no particular reason.

Sharp at 10 A.M. Sir John arrived, settled into an armchair and after a short conversation about the general situation in the West End, suddenly said, 'Kelland, have you ever thought about going into the CID?' Since I had been a Metropolitan police officer for twenty-five years, my answer was, 'Yes, Sir John, but not recently.' He then went on to tell me that he felt it would be good for the Met to have some interchange between senior uniformed and CID officers and because of my operational experience he wanted me to be one of the guinea pigs. I told him that I welcomed a challenge and an appointment was made for me to see Peter Brodie, the Assistant Commissioner (Crime) later in the day.

The upshot was that I was offered the post of CID Commander of No. 2 Area, which was the whole of north-west London and included Heathrow Airport. Like my commander colleagues responsible for the other three Met areas, I had an office on the fifth floor at New Scotland Yard. I replaced Commander Ernest Bond who had taken control of the newly formed Bomb Squad – the forerunner of the present Anti-Terrorist Squad – set up to investigate a series of explosive attacks by the so-called 'Angry Brigade', including one on the Barnet home of the Home Secretary, Robert Carr.

When news of my transfer and appointment was published in the next issue of the Metropolitan Police Orders, an article appeared in the *Daily Telegraph* under the headline 'Yard angry over CID to uniform switch'. It mentioned my appointment and went on to discuss 'this major change in policy'. The crime correspondent wrote, 'As I toured various divisions last night I was met with a barrage of questions about the new scheme and told repeatedly that not only had it taken CID officers by surprise but that it was against all their advice.' Well, it was nice to be told by Fleet Street of my welcome – sometimes an element of surprise is no bad thing!

I had been around too long to be alarmed by newspaper comment and certainly in the next few months I experienced no overt sign of the alleged anger. My deputy, Detective Chief Superintendent Sam Leckie, and the other detective chief superintendents under my command were all helpful and co-operative, though at a higher level relationships with some of my immediate superiors, the departmental DACs, can best be described as formal. I understood the reason for this and, being used to the independence of territorial command, was not unduly concerned. However, the feeling of mutual wariness was disquieting and I could not help thinking that the warm welcome I had had from the AC (Crime) had been somewhat muted by his deputies.

One of the senior CID officers to go in the opposite direction to a uniform post was my former Management Services colleague, Ron Steventon. He also went to No. 2 Area, to the headquarters at Paddington, as staff officer to the Area Inspector. The holder of this post was Deputy Assistant Commissioner Trevor Williams, a man with a vast experience of policing in the East End of London who was a doughty fighter for improvements in integrity and professional standards. He and Ron Steventon, whose firm principles were well known within the CID, formed an effective team with whom I enjoyed an excellent understanding which was, I like to think, to the benefit of No. 2 Area.

Apart from the worrying increase in armed robberies at banks, one of the problems peculiar to No. 2 Area was the policing of Heathrow Airport, which the Met had recently taken over from the British Airports Authority Police. The theft of valuables in transit was a particular thorn in our side and an operation had been going on to target some of the cargo loaders and their associates outside the airport who we suspected were dishonest. Using their ingenuity and no little courage, because a slight slip could have resulted in serious injury, local detectives had started a new airside approach. To prevent an alarm being given and to catch a dishonest loading crew, they would drive up to a working conveyor belt in a maintenance vehicle, one officer would jump on the moving conveyor belt and a few seconds later arrive in the aircraft hold. In this way they caught some thieves red-handed in the act of rifling baggage.

DAC Trevor Williams as a younger man had been a good fast bowler and had played in the Met cricket 1st XI with Sir John Waldron. The Commissioner had a high regard for his professionalism and his personal campaign for the need to improve internal procedures, including complaints investigation, was probably the catalyst that caused Sir John in his last full year as Commissioner to propose and obtain the approval of the Home Secretary in December 1971 for the setting up of an independent internal complaints investigation unit. After a meeting in September 1971 of a working party chaired by the Deputy Commissioner, Robert Mark, with James Starritt, then Assistant Commissioner 'A' Department, and Trevor Williams among its members, to discuss a paper submitted by Williams, they recommended the formation of a complaints investigation branch answerable directly to the Deputy Commissioner. Commander Raymond Anning (now Commissioner of the Royal Hong Kong Police) was appointed in June 1972 as the first commander of the unit, with Ronald Steventon as his deputy.

Anning and Steventon – and there were others like them I knew in the force – had long demonstrated their personal commitment to high standards of integrity. Their reputations and the fact that they were not late converts to a rolling bandwagon made their leadership as two of my 'C' Department DACs in the difficult post-porn and other corruption trials period of the late Seventies of inestimable value in maintaining morale in the CID.

In December 1971, when I had been a commander for about six years, I was promoted to Deputy Assistant

Commissioner and became one of the four Inspectors of the force responsible to the Deputy Commissioner. I was given responsibility for No. 4 (south London) Area and vacated my office on the fifth floor at New Scotland Yard, returning again to the field with an office above Brixton police station.

Within a few months of my promotion Robert Mark became the Commissioner, and on 24 April 1972 he published a Police Order outlining a number of immediate administrative changes affecting the control and supervision of the force. A particularly significant step was the transfer of the four CID area commanders from the central office at New Scotland Yard to the four geographical area offices where they were answerable to their respective deputy assistant commissioners who compromised the force Inspectorate. I was joined in No. 4 Area by Commander Wallace Virgo, who served under me until he retired some months later just before I was appointed to conduct the Humphreys pornography inquiry.

In the period between the official announcement of Mr Mark's appointment and his taking office, in conversations with my senior colleagues, Assistant Commissioners James Starritt and Colin Woods, I rode my favourite hobby-horse about the enforcement of the Obscene Publications Act being passed from the CID to become part of 'A' Department's anti-vice responsibilities. It was pleasing to find that this was one of the Commissioner's intended operational changes. The change at the Yard was to come about by a gradual phasing-out of the existing CID staff of the Obscene Publications Squad and their replacement with selected uniformed officers chosen from applicants from all over London. The enforcement of the Obscene Publications

Act in the Met's territorial divisions was to become a local responsibility forthwith and in the West End that meant it became another duty for the Clubs Office.

In late 1973 on the directions of James Starritt, who was by then the Deputy Commissioner, the phasing out of the CID officers still in the Obscene Publications Squad was expedited following a report by me during the early stages of an inquiry into allegations of corruption between pornographers and detectives – dealt with in the next chapter – that I had strong suspicions that some of the remaining detectives were involved in corrupt practices. My suspicions were later confirmed when evidence was obtained and in 1976 some of these same men were arrested and convicted of corruption offences committed during this 1973 period.

9
The Porn Inquiry

From April 1973 until late 1976, though I was still responsible for No. 4 Area and, after a transfer, for a Yard administrative command, I directed a major investigation into allegations of corrupt relationships between pornographers and Yard detectives which became known as the Humphreys Inquiry.

It may perhaps help to clarify the details of this long inquiry if I say something to begin with about the organization of the porn bookshop trade at that time, the law, the people who were involved and the role that journalists played in helping to end corrupt practices that had extended over a period of about twenty years.

From the middle 1960s to the early 1970s there took place in Soho a boom in the sale of pornographic material: obscene, illustrated, glossy magazines and video films. In earlier years there had been a handful of shops where in a back room a more or less discreet trade in poorly produced obscene books took place, but by 1970 there were at least forty shops stocking pornographic material, some of them occupying quite large premises with garish window displays that left little doubt in the minds of passers-by as to what was on sale inside.

There was quite a lot of public criticism of these sordid businesses, and the adequacy or otherwise of the Obscene Publications Act, the law that was supposed to control the worst extremes. In 1971 Lord Longford chaired a commission of inquiry into pornography and when his report was published it stimulated further interest. As a result investigative journalists of the *Sunday People* and the *News of the World* set out to expose the people who were involved in this trade. As I have said earlier, the rapid growth of the bookshops had caused concern at West End Central police station, particularly in the light of what we knew about the characters of the people who were believed to be their real owners – Bernie Silver, Frank Mifsud, Jimmy Humphreys and John Mason. However, the sole responsibility for any action against these shops, until Robert Mark became the Commissioner, rested with the Obscene Publications Squad of C.1 Branch at the Yard.

The shops were managed by front men who concealed the identities of the real owners and who were paid to accept responsibility in the event of a police raid. However, we were to learn from Humphreys and others in the course of our investigation that there was little risk of any real element of surprise in the raids because of corrupt arrangements with detectives of the Obscene Publications Squad who did know who the real owners were. Most of the bookshops had two rooms, with a partition or screen separating the front from the back of the premises. Normally girlie pin-up magazines were kept on display in the front room and the hard porn and obscene video films would be on sale in the back room, but then the proprietors found that their takings could be increased considerably if hard porn was put on sale in the front of the shop. According to pornographers who later gave their co-operation to my inquiry, there was a protocol which required the shop owners to have the approval of the squad to do this – for which they paid. I learnt from Humphreys that in 1970/71, when Inspector Ron Hay, encouraged by me, prosecuted some of the men in charge of the shops under the Indecent Advertisements Act because the material on display could be seen from the street, the shop owners complained to their Obscene Publications Squad contacts but were told that nothing could be done to help them.

Much of the obscene material sold in the shops came from Holland, the United States and from Denmark, and wholesalers and their agents from those countries looked on London as a very lucrative market. The material was smuggled into the country by various means. One common method was to pack the books and films into boxes similar to those used for other products that were being imported in container lorries and mix them with the genuine cargo. Although the Customs authorities sometimes made seizures – usually when they acted on information – it was quite impossible for them to open and examine every container lorry arriving at English ports. Some wholesalers did print books and films in this country, and had no hesitation about pirating magazines and films bought in foreign countries.

Even after 1972, when the law was energetically enforced, we were handicapped by the fact that there was no satisfactory definition of obscenity in the Obscene Publications Act, 1959. In cases committed for trial the Act allowed a defence of public good, and many and varied were the lucid arguments advanced by expert witnesses and learned counsel to convince juries that the alleged obscene books had therapeutic and other virtuous purposes.

It became apparent during my inquiry that the senior officers of the Obscene Publications Squad during the 1965/73 expansion of the Soho porn trade had become very rapacious. Humphreys, Mason and other pornographers who eventually gave evidence at the Old Bailey trials told how they had paid from £2,000 to £14,000 to open their shops and a weekly 'licence' fee of about £500. Wholesalers of obscene books and films also told us that they had paid substantial regular bribes in order to carry on their trade without interference. For instance, Big Jeff Phillips, who drove a Rolls-Royce and lived in magnificent style in a manor house with stables at High Cockett in Berkshire and in a town flat in Sloane Square, paid £200 a week as a 'licence' to supply films to Soho shops.

Phillips got his films from Denmark and from the USA through his business associate Charlie Julian of Las Vegas. He became a millionaire but in May 1975, after he had served a prison sentence during which he made a statement about his corrupt relationships with porn squad detectives, he committed suicide when he was only thirty-three because of an unrequited love affair. Had he lived he would have given evidence of the systematic bribery of detectives, lavish social entertaining of them and, in some cases, of their wives, and of arranging payments into numbered bank accounts in Switzerland.

In November 1971 the *Sunday People* published an article that anticipated the findings of Lord Longford's commission on pornography and fired the first shot in their campaign to expose pornographers and corruption in Soho. In this and subsequent articles they named Jeff Phillips, Gerry Citron, John Mason, Jimmy Humphreys, Frank Mifsud, Barry Anderson, Thomas Hawksford, Rex Swift and the American Charles Julian as the main pornographers in London and accused them of corrupt dealings with detectives. A few years later the first four of these men, after they themselves had been convicted, made statements and agreed to be Crown witnesses in the trials of the corrupt detectives.

At the time of the articles the Yard appointed a detective chief superintendent from the Fraud Squad to investigate the allegations in the *Sunday People*. Apart from Humphreys, who through his solicitor declined to be interviewed,[1] the others who had been named all denied having anything to do with pornography. Obscene Publications Squad detectives, when they were interviewed, almost without exception said that they had never met any of the alleged pornographers and had no knowledge of any of them being in the dirty bookshop business. Strange as it may seem, these explanations were accepted by the investigating officer and by his senior to whom his report was submitted. However, the file was useful to me when I came to investigate most of the same officers, because I was able to use their earlier statements to prove that they had lied.

By 1971 Jimmy Humphreys had corrupt relationships with senior detectives and, in an uneasy partnership with Bernie Silver, had become one of the porn barons of Soho. His detailed account, given to me in 1974, of how he became a dirty bookshop proprietor is a story of intrigue, conspiracy and corruption. A central figure in the negotiations – like a spider in its web – was the notorious Soho godfather, Bernie Silver.

Just before Christmas 1969, Humphreys and his wife were fellow guests with senior CID officers, including Commander Virgo, at a dinner held at the Criterion restaurant in Piccadilly. During the evening he complained to Virgo, whom he had met before, that Detective Chief Superintendent Moody, who was then in charge of the C.1 Obscene Publications Squad, would not give him a 'licence' to use his property in Soho as dirty bookshops. A few days later Bernie Silver told him that an appointment had been made for them to meet Bill Moody in a

[1] He told me later this was on the advice of a police friend.

Mayfair restaurant the following evening when they would be able to talk over his problem. Over dinner Humphreys and Silver discussed with the detective chief superintendent the opening of a bookshop in Rupert Street, though the only decision reached was that Silver and Moody would meet for lunch the following day when Silver would make some proposals. After the lunchtime meeting had taken place Silver told Humphreys that agreement had been reached about the opening of the Rupert Street shop, subject to certain conditions. These conditions were to pay £14,000 for the 'licence' and to take him in as a half-share partner – the Soho bookshop fraternity would then think that it was his shop, and this would satisfy Moody who did not want to encourage any newcomers to the trade. Humphreys reluctantly accepted the conditions, paid the money demanded and also agreed to pay £2,000 a month to keep the shop open.

This fragile partnership was not improved when early in 1971, while Silver was out of the country, Humphreys had an affair with his mistress, Dominique Ferguson, which became common knowledge in Soho. Humphreys was warned by his friends to beware because they believed that Silver would make him pay for this act of lese-majesty. He became very alarmed the following month when Dominique told him that at a Sandown Park race meeting she had overheard a conversation between Silver and a senior detective friend about 'fitting him up' – meaning, to frame him for some crime. His immediate reaction was to get in touch with Commander Drury of the Flying Squad, whom he had recently met socially, and arrange for him to lunch with Dominique and himself at the Meridiana restaurant in Chelsea, where she repeated the story of the plotting at Sandown Park. Drury promised to make some inquiries, and a few days later he told Humphreys that he had dealt with the matter and that he was not to worry. For his services Humphreys claimed he paid £1,050. Some confirmation that Drury had intervened and possibly stopped a conspiracy against Humphreys came when the detective who was said to have been at Sandown Park with Silver was eventually interviewed. He denied any knowledge of a plot against Humphreys but recalled, at about that time, Deputy Assistant Commissioner Dick Chitty, who was Drury's immediate boss, telling him that there was to be no 'fitting up' of Jimmy Humphreys.

The relationship between Drury and Humphreys had only begun early in 1971 when they met at a lunch party given by Humphreys to celebrate the promotion of a Flying Squad friend, Detective Inspector Alex Ingram. From the time of their first meeting Humphreys regularly socialized with Drury and vied with Silver as to which of them could get the best table at which to entertain their senior CID guests at such events as the charity dinner/boxing shows at the Grosvenor House Hotel staged by Jack Solomons on behalf of the World Sporting Club. Humphreys claimed that in this rivalry his friendship with Stan Flashman, known as the king of the ticket touts and who had influence with Solomons, enabled him to upstage Silver. I must say that when I examined some of the table bookings for this period with the co-operation of the boxing impresario, his boast seemed to be justified.

In February 1972 the *Sunday People* published a second series of articles exposing pornographers and again alleging corrupt dealings with detectives, and in so doing started a chain of events which eventually destroyed the insidious links that had been developed over about twenty years between the two. One article which shook and embarrassed the Yard was published on 27 February and reported Commander Kenneth Drury of the Flying Squad and his wife's recent return from Cyprus, where they had been on a luxury holiday with their host the pornographer Jimmy Humphreys.

Robert Mark was then the Deputy Commissioner and he immediately appointed Deputy Assistant Commissioner F. J. (Dick) Sheppard, MC, to investigate the association between Drury and Humphreys. When he was interviewed Drury said that he had gone to Cyprus with Humphreys, paying his share of the cost of the holiday, because he believed he would be able to help him find the long-escaped Great Train robber, Ronnie Biggs. He had not told his immediate senior officer about this plan and there was no intelligence at the Yard that pointed to Biggs being in Cyprus – he was, in fact, in Australia at the time. Although it was supported by Humphreys, this far-fetched story was not believed and on 6 March Drury was suspended from duty. He was served with disciplinary papers in April but resigned and left the force on 1 May before a disciplinary board could be held.

Shortly after his resignation Drury wrote an article which was published in the *News of the World*, justifying his relationship with Humphreys by naming him as his paid informant. This enraged Humphreys because as a criminal with some status among his associates – bestowed for having served a sentence in Dartmoor – this was the ultimate insult. He gave the newspaper an alternative story saying that far from being an informer or receiving any money from Drury, he had wined, dined and lavishly entertained him ever since their first meeting. This was indeed bad publicity for the CID and for the Met.

Two weeks before Drury's resignation became effective Robert Mark took up his appointment as Commissioner, and the favourable publicity about his plans for changes in the Met helped to restore some of the damage. His new policy of giving responsibility for enforcing the Obscene Publications Act in Soho to local uniformed officers soon sent a chill wind of change blowing through the seedy back streets. The first inspectors to lead the local vice squad were Ron Hay and John Hoddinott.

At the same time as the local offensive was launched against the dirty bookshops the new Assistant Commissioner (Crime), Colin Woods, directed the Serious Crime Squad, led by Detective Chief Superintendent Bert Wickstead, to begin an operation aimed at the Soho vice syndicates. Early in 1973 the two units combined forces for some joint operations – a happy omen after an era of distrust between Clubs Office officers and Yard Porn squad detectives. Bernie Silver, probably well informed and sensing danger, left the country and Jimmy and Rusty Humphreys went to Holland.

A few weeks earlier the Serious Crime Squad had traced a man named Peter Garfath because they had been told that during October in the Dauphine Club in Marylebone he had been attacked and injured by Humphreys and some other men to teach him a lesson for having had an affair with Mrs Humphreys. Garfath made a statement about the attack and named Humphreys as one of about six men who had assaulted him. Although they were reasonably sure that he was in Holland the squad could not apply for Humphreys to be extradited until he had been found and arrested.

On 28 January, the day after a series of raids – including the searching of the Humphreys' Dean Street flat – by the Serious Crime Squad assisted by 'C' District vice squad and the Special Patrol Group had led to a number of arrests and the seizure of tons of pornographic material. Rusty Humphreys returned home, concerned about Jimmy's young son by another woman, who was being cared for by her maid Rosie at their flat. She was arrested and later bailed after she had been charged with conspiring to pervert the course of justice and conspiring to cause grievous bodily harm to Peter Garfath, her former lover. Later at the Old Bailey she was acquitted of these charges.

My own first involvement with the saga began on 19 February when James Starritt, the Deputy Commissioner, asked me to make some inquiries after he had received a letter written to him from Holland by Jimmy Humphreys. In the letter Humphreys claimed that he had not attacked Peter Garfath but that he was being framed for this crime by Detective Chief Inspector John Bland and certain criminals who frequented the Leigham Court Hotel in Streatham as a backlash to the resignation of ex-Commander Drury. He said that he had written to Mr Starritt because he could trust him not to reveal the contents of his letter to a Soho millionaire who was able to acquire copies of confidential police documents – we concluded this was a reference to Bernie Silver – and that if we put an entry in the personal column of *The Times*, 'Roger, Ronnie Corbett' it would be a signal for him to write again. I reported that a warrant had been issued for the arrest of Humphreys for attempted murder and causing grievous bodily harm to Peter Garfath and that there was no reason to believe he was being framed for these charges. No entry was placed in *The Times* and the Deputy Commissioner did not hear again from Humphreys.

The next development came on 18 April when Rusty Humphreys complained to A.10 Branch about her fugitive husband's corrupt relationships with senior detectives, details of which, she claimed, were recorded in his personal diaries taken by the Serious Crime Squad from their Soho flat at the time of her own arrest some three months earlier. Jim Starritt was immediately informed and the next day I received the official file notifying me that he had appointed me, under Section 49 of the Police Act, 1964, to investigate Mrs Humphreys's complaint. With typical thoughtfulness he had enclosed with the file a personal note saying that he was sorry he would not be able to discuss the case with me until he returned from a holiday that began the following morning.

My first reaction on reading Mrs Humphreys's statement was one of scepticism. Surely, if these diaries were as explicit as she claimed, they would have been passed on to the Deputy Commissioner at some point during the past three months? The explanation that was given for this oversight was the pressure of work on the senior officers of the squad dealing with her case, but I have always found this difficult to accept. Within hours of receiving the official file I went to Tintagel House on the Albert Embankment, then the HQ of the Serious Crime Squad, and collected the diaries from Detective Chief Inspector John Bland. They were a 1971 pocket diary and a 1972 Letts desk diary, both with entries in them in Humphreys's handwriting. Examination of them enabled me to identify about twenty-one detectives – ranging in rank from detective inspector to commander – and many of the entries related to appointments at well-known restaurants. A number of Jimmy Humphreys's porn associates such as Silver, Phillips and Citron were also mentioned as well as one or two other criminal and social contacts. Early in May Mrs Humphreys gave me an alphabetical index book belonging to her husband listing individuals, many by christian name only, and telephone numbers. A check on these showed that they included the office and home numbers of various senior detectives.

Mrs Humphreys helped me, as far as she was able, to interpret the diaries, but some of the entries had to await the assistance of Jimmy Humphreys himself. Although I believed that the diaries were genuine contemporary records, I realized that by themselves, even when they had been confirmed by their author, they would have little value as evidence. Independent corroboration was essential, and this became my first objective.

At the beginning of the inquiry I had the part-time help of Detective Chief Superintendent Arthur Howard and Detective Sergeant Norman Stagg of A.10 Branch. I also employed Chief Inspector John Smith from Lewisham, whom I had known as an inspector at West End Central, to make some inquiries in the West End, where he was able to get verification of some of the restaurant appointments. I soon lost his services though, when, after being recommended by me, he was appointed as the first uniformed officer to command the Yard's newly constituted Obscene Publications Squad. In this capacity he continued to help me throughout the long inquiry.

While it was obvious from the beginning that many people, both detectives and criminals, would have to be interviewed, the timing of these interviews would be very important. It seemed that most of them would have to wait until after Humphreys had been seen, unless other facts were discovered which made earlier questioning essential. Meanwhile inquiries to corroborate the diary entries continued, and early in July I received information that a man named Lionel Gallwey, a former employee of Big Jeff Phillips who was serving a sentence in Maidstone

Prison, might be prepared to talk about the Soho pornography scene. I went to see him and he made a statement that described trading in obscene films with Humphreys and others and how his employer paid £500 – although Phillips later said it was £200 – a week for his 'licence' from the Obscene Publications Squad. He claimed that these payments had been made via Humphreys and that on some occasions when he had taken the money to his Dean Street flat Drury had been there. Gallwey was a witness at Drury's trial and the statement he made was also useful in persuading Phillips, at that time in custody awaiting trial for Obscene Publications Act offences, also to make a statement about his relationships with detectives.

Two of the telephone numbers recorded in the index book kept by Humphreys were of Gloucestershire hotels. One of them had been used by Drury as a base when he had carried out a murder inquiry in the county, and at the other a London publican had paid for accommodation for a party attending a Cheltenham race meeting. Included in the party was a detective superintendent acquaintance of Jimmy Humphreys whose name was shown in his diaries. While there was no evidence here of any criminal offence there were certainly disciplinary matters that needed investigation, but before these inquiries had been completed the officer tendered his resignation and left the force.

On 15 June came the news that Humphreys had been arrested by Dutch police and was being held in an Amsterdam prison pending deportation proceedings. These proceedings looked as if they would take a long time, and I told Mrs Humphreys, who travelled to see him every week, to ask her husband whether he would agree to see me if I went to Holland. Early in September she came to see me with her legal adviser and he told me that, subject to an assurance that he would not be prosecuted for confessing involvement in corruption, Humphreys was willing to be seen and to co-operate with my inquiry.

In mid-October, after consulting the Director of Public Prosecutions' representative and reaching agreement with the Dutch legal authorities, I went to Holland with Arthur Howard and at the Amsterdam prison in the presence of his legal adviser had a long interview with Humphreys. This was our first meeting and I was interested to find that he very much conformed to the mental picture I already had of him. He was well groomed, which fitted his reputation for being fastidious about his personal appearance, softly spoken and mentally alert: he showed himself very adept at talking around any topic he did not wish to discuss. He asked some probing questions himself, including what had happened about his letter to the Deputy Commissioner, and he was clearly watching my reactions. It was easy to see why some policemen regarded him as a plausible, cunning and devious criminal possessed of very few scruples.

When we left the prison I felt that on the whole we had made a fairly good start. On the basis that we would have a question-and-answer session the following day which would be tape recorded, no notes were taken at this meeting and I believed this encouraged Humphreys to talk more freely. I was therefore quite surprised when we arrived at the prison on the following morning to be told by his legal adviser that Humphreys was refusing to be interviewed again and that he had been unable to persuade him to change his mind. This was disappointing, but the situation – which did not change until after his extradition and conviction at the Old Bailey in May 1974

– had to be accepted. In our long interview the previous day he had given a lot of useful information. I had made notes on it after returning to our hotel, and I now had a number of new leads to follow.

At this stage I was already sure that I was dealing with a well-established and sophisticated system of corruption between Soho pornographers and former members of the Obscene Publications Squad, and that Humphreys had additional links with some former members of the Flying Squad. My terms of reference were to investigate the complaint by Mrs Humphreys. However, I felt strongly that although there were no other formal complaints it was essential, if this large-scale corruption was to be dealt with, for my inquiry to be widened to include the activities and relationships of detectives with any pornographer, not just Humphreys. The time had come for decisions about future strategy and, if my plans were approved, to select some additional inquiry staff.

I discussed the whole situation at length with James Starritt and he gave my proposals his approval and support. I acquired some office space accommodation at the Yard on the floor occupied by A.10 Branch, and recruited Inspector Ron Hay and Sergeant Jim Sutherland from West End Central as investigators, and Sergeant Jim Bilby from Southwark as our collator and office manager. A card index system was set up to log and cross-reference the mass of data and intelligence, much of it yet to be gathered; and former complaint files, case papers and other records were examined to identify individuals and patterns of activity. Dossiers were opened on suspects to build up a picture of their involvement with pornographers and with each other, and they included details of housing, cars, holiday addresses and any other relevant intelligence. We were well into psychological profiling.

We were told by informants in the porn trade that word had gone around in Soho for heads to be kept down and mouths shut until my inquiry petered out, like others before it. I felt that at this stage there was little or no likelihood of any confessions from pornographers – or from corrupt detectives – so I decided on the unusual strategy in a complaint inquiry of making one pornographer a target for a criminal prosecution. The chances of success would be improved because this would be quite unexpected.

The pornographer we selected, Ronald Eric – known as John – Mason, a man in his middle fifties, once a stage hand at the London Palladium, was an important figure in the porn world with extensive contacts with former members of the Obscene Publications Squad. He had been in the business since the early 1950s, and was believed to own at least five shops, though he preserved his anonymity by leasing them through a nominal company, S.J.D. Properties Ltd, to individual front men. He had not been in trouble with the law since 1957 when he was jailed for a year at the Old Bailey for obscene publications offences at a bookshop in Walkers Court in Soho. Our information was that Mason, who was keeping a low profile and staying away from Soho, was very worried about the possibility of being sent to prison again. We suspected that if he was arrested and charged he would probably talk.

Mason's current address was not shown on his record file nor recorded on any of the Yard indices, but Jimmy Humphreys, during our talk in Amsterdam, had told me that he lived at Weybridge quite near to his main police contact, Detective Chief Superintendent Bill Moody, a former head of the Obscene Publications Squad who was now stationed at Hammersmith. It was quickly established that Mason owned a large detached house named 'Manaton' on St George's Hill in Weybridge and that he also had a town flat in Audley Street in Mayfair.

Not long after, we got direct evidence of a personal relationship with Detective Chief Inspector George Fenwick, a one-time member of the porn squad who was then stationed at Kingston. Sunday is normally a rest day for the majority of CID officers and, perhaps for this reason, criminals seem to be less wary on this day and often spend it in socializing. A sergeant working in the A.10 administration office was quite a keen photographer, and as he lived not far away from Weybridge I asked him if on a Sunday morning he would discreetly photograph Mason's house and make a note of any cars he saw there. He photographed two cars standing in the driveway of the house, one of them Mason's Mercedes and the other, a Triumph, owned by Fenwick who, according to the records at Kingston police station, was the duty senior CID officer on that Sunday. Because of our operation against Mason it was not prudent to question Fenwick just then, but further information was soon to be received that would mean he had to be interviewed.

Just before Christmas 1973 an opportunity occurred to question Billy Jeal, whom Jimmy Humphreys, when I saw him in Amsterdam, had named as a middleman, that is a collector from other pornographers of corrupt payments for police. On a list of recent convictions of pornographers by the West End Central vice squad he was shown as having been fined £100 at Bow Street Magistrates' Court. Looking at his criminal record file, I noticed from his history that he was living rent free at a Croydon address. This was unusual so I had the rateable

LEFT: PC 548 'A' Kelland, 1946
BELOW: 'Ask a policeman,' 1949

ABOVE: Winning the 5,000 metres for the Met against the Belgian police in Brussels, 1949
RIGHT: In the Fifties Soho's crumbling buildings were used by greedy landlords who operated behind agents to rent out flatlets to prostitutes at astronomic rents.

The Porn Trial: Jimmy Humphreys *(left)* is brought back to England to stand trial for the beating up of Peter Garfath, January 1974

ABOVE: Rusty Humphreys in her Soho flat
BELOW: Ex-Commander Drury at his trial in 1977

ABOVE: With David McNee on the Grunwick picket line, June 1977
BELOW: With Peter Cutting (*second left*), Chief Investigating Officer of HM Customs and Excise, and John Smith, head of the Drugs Squad (*far right*), after the Press Conference to announce the success of Operation Cyril

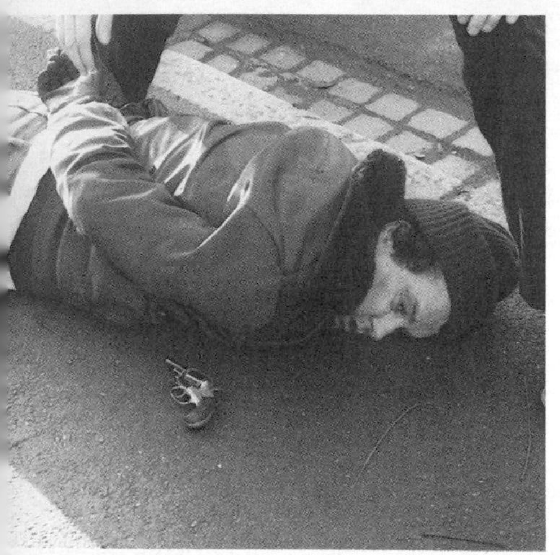

ABOVE: Armed robbery: photograph taken by a police officer at the raid on the Bank of Cyprus, 1977

LEFT: The arrest of Billy Tobin after an attempted armed robbery in Dulwich, 1981

BELOW: The driver of the van used by Tobin and his associates had been bound and gagged. He was released minutes after their arrest

RIGHT: Terrorism: the poison capsule used to murder Georgi Markov in 1978 (*greatly enlarged*)

BELOW: With Mrs Thatcher and Sir David McNee at the Yard in 1980 when she was shown a collection of terrorist weapons

ABOVE: The scene minutes after the Harrods bombing, 1983
BELOW LEFT: This poster was used to alert the public after the escape of Gerry Tuite from Brixton Prison in 1980
BELOW RIGHT: The supergrasses: George Piggott presented me with this collage of varnished eggshells which he had worked on in police custody before the trial in 1980 for the Zomparelli murder

THIS MAN
MUST BE CAUGHT

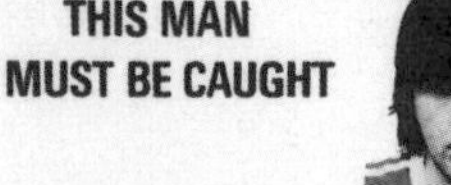

He will disguise his
appearance and adopt
convincing false identities.

occupier of the property checked and was told that it was a George Chandler. Closer examination of Jeal's file showed that many years earlier a Detective Constable Chandler of C.1 Obscene Publications Squad had arrested him for a pornography offence at a Soho bookshop. I also knew that Chandler had served as a detective inspector at West End Central in the early 1970s. Jeal was interviewed but, while he admitted he was the tenant of a house owned by Inspector Chandler, whom he had known for many years, he denied any corrupt relationships with any police officers. The conduct of Inspector Chandler in having a business transaction with a man he knew to be a convicted criminal meant that he had a case to answer of acting in a manner likely to bring discredit on the force under the police disciplinary code. He was suspended from duty and served with disciplinary papers but retired on grounds of ill-health without the case being heard. The publicity over this matter was bad for the image of the Met but helpful in that it showed our inquiry was wide-ranging and had teeth.

With some twenty-seven years' police service, my contacts with serving officers of all ranks, especially those who had worked in the West End, were extensive. Information and general assistance was volunteered because of personal and service relationships in a way which I doubt would have been the case with a senior officer from outside the Met. One example of this happened on a Saturday in March 1974 when a sergeant who had been a constable at West End Central while I was serving there as an inspector telephoned me at home to say he thought I might be interested to know that he had heard that Detective Chief Inspector Fenwick had bought a car hire business near Coulsdon railway station. Subsequent inquiries established that Fenwick, with Detective Inspector Cyril Jones and ex-Detective Constable Chamberlain – all of whom had served in the Obscene Publications Squad together – had acquired this business and a similar one at Tolworth, both of them being operated through a third party. The serving detectives were interviewed but they declined to answer any questions. However, the circumstances – regulations forbid serving police officers to have business interests without official approval – and the absence of any explanation about the businesses or the association with Mason, justified their suspension from duty. This put more pressure on them and on their associates. During the interview with Fenwick he was asked about his meeting with Mason at the St George's Hill house in Weybridge, and thus he was now alerted to our interest in the pornographer.

December 1973 was an eventful month. Just before Christmas the extradition of Humphreys from Holland was finally accomplished and at the end of that month Silver, who had returned to London from the Continent, was located by the Serious Crime Squad and arrested. Silver was remanded in custody charged with living on the earnings of prostitution; almost a repeat of the 1955 situation when he was acquitted, except that now his scale of flat farming was much greater. He was also charged with the murder of Tommy 'Scarface' Smithson, an East End strong-arm man who had been shot in a house in Paddington in 1956. At the time, a Maltese, Philip Ellal, had been arrested for the crime and after being found guilty of murder was sentenced to be hanged. However, he was reprieved and served eleven years of his life imprisonment. On release he went to live in America where in 1973, in the course of inquiring into

Soho vice syndicates, the Serious Crime Squad interviewed him. He told them he had been hired by Silver and Mifsud to shoot Smithson. Ellal gave evidence at the Old Bailey and Silver was found guilty and sentenced to life imprisonment for the murder but, on appeal, the conviction was quashed. At a separate trial, the jury found Mifsud not guilty of murder. The extradition of Humphreys, the arrest of the Soho godfather, Silver, and the activities of the porn squads of West End Central and the Yard were causing consternation amongst the vice merchants and their associates; Inspector Hay skilfully made use of the situation as he gathered evidence about John Mason and his business interests.

In April 1974, after information had been given to local police by a farmer about pornographic books stored in a farm outbuilding at Esher, the Serious Crime Squad arrested Gerald Citron and seized forty tons of obscene material. Citron, a porn wholesaler, was committed for trial at the Old Bailey and over the Easter weekend his solicitor, John Blackburn Gittings, telephoned me at home to say that, on his advice, his client wished to make a statement about past corrupt dealings with porn squad officers. Citron gave me a full account of his activities and named Fenwick who was already suspended, Detective Inspector O'Hanlon who had served with Fenwick as a sergeant on the old Obscene Publications Squad and now after promotion during 1973 was serving with the Central Drugs Squad, their mutual friend ex-Detective Constable Chamberlain and three other former members of the old Obscene Publications Squad. In due course the serving detectives were suspended from duty. At interviews, after being cautioned, they had all exercised their right not to answer any questions. A few weeks after he was interviewed by me Citron pleaded guilty at the Old Bailey and the judge, after being told that he was assisting in a major corruption inquiry, fined him £50,000 or twelve months' imprisonment, giving him six months to pay the fine.

It transpired that Citron was only interested in saving his own skin and staying out of prison. He failed to turn up as a prosecution witness, disappearing to the United States where he was finally traced working as a Rolls-Royce car salesman in Los Angeles. Some years later, after he had exhausted all the appeal channels, the American authorities deported him, but when he arrived in the United Kingdom he promptly disappeared again, and his £50,000 fine is still unpaid.

An amusing incident occurred while this Repton public school boy and graduate of Manchester University was awaiting trial. He was with his solicitor and wearing his Old Reptonian tie when an elderly man, also wearing the tie, got into conversation with them and asked Citron what he was doing. 'Oh,' he replied, 'me, I'm in publishing.'

On 25 April 1974 Jimmy Humphreys was found guilty at the Old Bailey of causing grievous bodily harm to Peter Garfath and sentenced to eight years' imprisonment. A few days later his solicitor let me know that he was now willing to see me and help my inquiry. On 15 May at Wandsworth Prison there took place the first of some fifty meetings which were to be spread over the next three years between Humphreys and me, or senior members of my team.

Initially, Humphreys was very much preoccupied with an application to appeal against his conviction and it was not until the following April that this was refused. He was not exactly easy to get along with. He had a false idea of his own importance which had been fostered by the media and other attention, and he considered the authorities should have done a deal with him, as had happened with a bank robber, Bertie Smalls, who had recently received an indemnity for turning Queen's evidence. Humphreys, concerned about his status in the criminal world, would not be drawn into saying anything detrimental about his former criminal associates, or even admit, if he could avoid it, that they had been his associates. Even when he was talking about his dealings with detectives, he attempted to pick and choose between those he liked and those he felt had let him down. This culminated in his refusing to give evidence at the committal proceedings of the first porn trial at the Old Bailey of Fenwick, O'Hanlon and four others at the end of 1976. However, with much patience, persistence and understanding, a certain rapport was established and a succession of detailed statements were taken from Humphreys.

After he had agreed to help, the growth in the number of our lines of inquiry, all of them needing urgent attention, made it necessary to ask for additional staff. At this same time Detective Chief Superintendent Arthur Howard, who had been working with me for over a year, was asked to take charge of the Heathrow Airport CID, and I was anxious not to delay his new appointment. Fate made a fortunate intervention one day in late May as I was taking a lunchtime walk around St James's Park when I bumped into my old colleague, Ronald Steventon. He was now a commander and was just completing an assignment as a member of a project team that was evaluating an American video file system for the Yard's Criminal Record Office. As we walked together, he told me that he did not know what his next post would be and asked, 'Have you got a job for me?' He was being serious and it occurred to me that the help of a man of his rank, whose professionalism and integrity I held in high regard, was just what I needed to press on with the next vital stage of the inquiry.

Later that day I discussed this with the Deputy Commissioner and, as always, Jim Starritt gave me his full backing, arranging for Steventon to begin duty on 10 June. He also agreed that Chief Superintendent Donald Williams, who was in command at City Road police station in Islington, should join me on the same day. I did not know him personally but he had been well recommended by colleagues, including Ron Steventon whose judgement I respected, and he proved to be a true professional who was both fearless and resolute. Finally, to complete the small team which now numbered seven, Sergeant Keith Oliver from 'J' District was chosen by Williams as his assistant. Much progress was made during the next six months and the number of interviews carried out, statements taken and inquiries made by the team was phenomenal.

Inspector Hay and Sergeant Sutherland had already uncovered a great deal of evidence against John Mason which confirmed the assertion of Humphreys that he was a close associate of Detective Chief Superintendent Moody. In March 1974 Moody was stationed at Hammersmith and had given two months' notice of his intention to retire. This was subsequently withdrawn when as the result of a fall he was injured and placed on the sick list.

A check on the history of a red Lancia which Moody owned and had used when he was engaged during 1970–72 on *The Times* inquiry[2] showed that the previous

[2] An investigation lasting two and a half years into corruption involving three Met detectives, an inspector and two sergeants, instigated by *Times* reporters and overseen by Frank Williamson, an Inspector of Constabulary. Two of the detectives were convicted and jailed, and one jumped his bail but gave himself up some seven years later when he too was convicted and jailed.

owner had been George Vinn, a convicted pornographer and an associate of Mason. Vinn, when interviewed, gave a story about advertising the car for sale on a local newsagent's board and Moody coming along and buying it – Inspector Hay did not think it was convincing.

One day, having made sure that George Vinn was out on business, Hay and Sutherland called to see Mrs Patricia Vinn and found her very helpful indeed. At that time she was not very pleased with her husband, and she thoroughly disliked Bill Moody whom she knew quite well from having met him socially at Mason's house. She gave a lot of useful information and said that the car had been given to Moody by her husband in 1969 for his help in seeing that he did not get a prison sentence when he was charged with possessing obscene films at Mason's Dean Street shop. Mason was much later to give evidence at the Old Bailey at Moody's trial that he returned from Spain after Vinn's arrest and gave the detective chief superintendent £14,000 for his help. Armed with Mrs Vinn's statement and other information, I prepared a questionnaire, and on 14 June at New Scotland Yard I interviewed Detective Chief Superintendent Moody under caution.

Unlike the majority of officers he did not exercise his right to remain silent, but answered all my questions. He was obviously not aware of the conversation with Mrs Vinn and how much we knew about the Lancia and his association with John Mason, and he lied about both. The interview was a long one, with Commander Steventon recording the answers of the questionnaire before Moody signed it and certified their accuracy. Extra time was taken because Moody, wearing a surgical collar as the result of his fall at Hammersmith police station, occasionally got up and walked around the office. Whilst he did this, ostensibly to ease the pain in his neck, I realized that these walk-abouts seemed to coincide with questions he found particularly difficult, and that they gave him more time to think before answering. Immediately after the interview I consulted with the Deputy Commissioner and he gave directions that Moody was to be taken to Hammersmith and suspended from duty by his local commander.

With such a small and dedicated inquiry team, internal security was not a problem, but we had continually to remind ourselves to be careful and ensure that all statements and data remained under lock and key under the control of Sergeant Bilby, the office manager. Dirty tricks were always a possibility and I was concerned when I was told by a Soho informant that private inquiry agents were asking questions about me in the West End. It seems that they, or whoever had hired them, thought that anyone who had served there, as I had, for a total of ten years must have been compromised in some way and be a target for blackmail. I reported this to the Deputy Commissioner and also took the precaution of instructing my bank manager to let me know immediately if any cheques or cash, other than my salary, were paid into my account. While, like my colleagues, I found the duty of investigating fellow officers distasteful I had remained fairly matter-of-fact about it but now I found myself taking note of any strange cars parked near my home and being generally wary, even when I was off duty.

On 19 December Bernie Silver, who had been arrested a year earlier, appeared at the Old Bailey, together with six members, all Maltese, of his Soho vice syndicate. They were all convicted and he was sentenced to six years' imprisonment and fined £30,000 for living on the earnings of prostitution. Although Silver had not complained or talked about his association with police – and knowing him I did not believe that he would – in order to keep up the psychological pressure and to demonstrate support for the Serious Crime Squad, the Deputy Commissioner and I attended the Old Bailey for the sentencing.

After the seizure of Humphreys's diaries and my conversation with him in the Amsterdam prison when he made allegations against Drury, it was clear that the investigation, concluded in May 1972, about the holiday he had had with the ex-Commander of the Flying Squad in Cyprus would have to be reopened and linked with the inquiries into the new complaints. Humphreys was very bitter about Drury's reference to him in a newspaper article as a paid informer, and insisted that from May 1971 until Drury's retirement he had been making regular payments to him of £100 a week. However, at the end of the investigation the case against Drury very much depended on whether the jury would believe Humphreys. I was reminded, by a parliamentary question in April 1974, about this aspect of my inquiry and how in a large organization a lack of communication – in this case probably attributable to strict security – can sometimes lead to wrong information being given. Arthur Lewis, MP, asked why the Home Secretary would not set up an investigation by someone unconnected with the police into all matters concerning relationships between Drury and Humphreys. The Home Office Minister of State, Dr Shirley Summerskill, replied that she had no reason to think that any further investigation now would serve any useful purpose. Fortunately, this inaccurate answer did not cause any embarrassment – or lead to an official inquiry.

The case of Piet Mulder, a Dutchman living in Germany and working for an Amsterdam wholesale pornographer, serves to illustrate the devious character of Jimmy Humphreys. There were references in his 1972 diary to Mulder and to telephoning the Yard about him on the day before our records showed that this man had been arrested, but when he was asked to explain this Humphreys was vague and unhelpful. According to the official records Mulder had been arrested in London on 5 July in possession of a van full of pornographic books. Having been charged and after appearing at the local magistrates' court, he was bailed, with two friends of Humphreys standing as sureties for him, but he jumped bail and left the country and returned to Holland via Dublin. There was a discrepancy between the number of boxes of porn recorded as seized and the number in the property store, and when the sureties were seen they said that they had each been reimbursed by Humphreys their £2,000 bail money that had been made forfeit by the court.

Mulder was found at an address in Germany, and Detective Chief Inspector Hay interviewed him there with the assistance of the German police, arranged through Interpol. The German Federal representative insisted, although Mulder spoke good English, that the interview should be conducted in German and the answers from Mulder translated into English by an interpreter. Hay was not happy about the interview and the answers he was getting through the interpreter, but he did have some conversation with Mulder in English, stressing that the Yard wanted his help with our inquiry and asking him to telephone us when he was next in Holland.

The questions that were being asked clearly intrigued Mulder because his Dutch solicitor contacted us and offered his co-operation. I went with Hay to Amsterdam since the local police said they had no objections to Mulder being interviewed by us at his solicitor's office. There we got a full account of what had happened to him in England. He had flown to Heathrow from Holland on Sunday 2 July and the following day, after spending the night at the Hilton Hotel in Park Lane, he hired a van and went to an M1 motorway service station where, by arrangement, he took delivery from a Danish international lorry driver of fifty-five boxes of pornographic magazines. Having stored the van and the boxes in a private lock-up garage in north London belonging to a female pornographer who lived in Mayfair, he returned to the Hilton where he telephoned Humphreys and made an appointment to see him the following evening. This was the date of the entry in Humphreys's diary of the phone call to the porn squad about Mulder.

On Wednesday evening he met Jimmy Humphreys at his Dean Street flat, and they went with Rusty Humphreys, Charlie Julian and another American to the Royal Garden Hotel in Kensington where over dinner he arranged for the delivery of the magazines ordered by Humphreys, without disclosing where they were stored. The procedure agreed was for Mulder to go to Humphreys's Dean Street flat at 8.30 the next morning when someone would drive him to the store and collect the pornographic material. Mulder said that he now believed that detectives, tipped off by Humphreys, had followed him to the store because the next morning just after he had left the Daimler car in which he had been driven from Dean Street and had walked a short distance to the garage, he was arrested. He also confirmed that there had been some thirty more boxes in his van than there were in the police store, each containing 450 magazines with a retail value of £5 a copy. We learned from him that his Dutch employer had reimbursed Humphreys for the £4,000 he had paid to the two people who stood bail for him.

It became clear to us – and, I am sure, to Mulder – that there had been a conspiracy between Humphreys and the Obscene Publications Squad to arrest him and steal part of his load of pornographic books, which were no doubt sold in Humphreys's shop bringing in £67,500 of clear profit. When this was put to Humphreys he became angry and, I believe to save his face, he made a statement that he had not wished to talk about Mulder because what had happened was that he and Mulder together had conspired to cheat Mulder's employer by arranging with Detective Inspector O'Hanlon to have the load seized. Humphreys later complained that as a result of our inquisitiveness Mulder had contacted Rusty to tell her he had stopped paying the £200 a month which had been his share of a pornographic mail-order business to this country which was being run from Holland in partnership with Humphreys. Our Customs and Excise colleagues had given me great co-operation, especially Sam Charles, the deputy chief investigating officer, and they were made aware of the facts and took steps to deal with this foreign mail-order business. Although in the light of our inquiries the DPP authorized the withdrawal of the warrant for Mulder's arrest, he still refused to come to London as a witness.

I learned from Humphreys, and from Big Jeff Phillips before he committed suicide, that so close was the relationship between certain detectives and the West End pornographers 'licensed' by them that any foreigner or other stranger showing a commercial interest in the trade was certain to receive official attention. Perhaps the best example of this took place in 1970 and involved the

Sunday People, whose investigative journalists had consistently endeavoured to expose the corruption that surrounded the Soho vice trade.

At the end of 1970 two *Sunday People* reporters had been carrying out an investigation in Soho and had devised a plan for two of their agents claiming to be from the Middle East to purchase some 1,200 or so pornographic films for £15,000 from a man named Stuart Crispie, an agent of Big Jeff Phillips. The reporters had established that Phillips was associating with Detective Sergeant Tilley and Detective Constable Brown – both of whom were prosecuted in one of the porn trials – and they planned to take photographs and confront Phillips when he delivered the films.

Their plan misfired for two reasons, firstly because Phillips reported his potential customers to his Obscene Publications Squad contacts, who checked on the tenancy of the flat occupied by the men and found it was rented to Odhams Press. Secondly, the two reporters, who knew Humphreys as a strip-club owner, sounded him out about what he knew about dirty bookshop owners paying bribes to the police, and he reported this to another of his contacts, Commander Virgo at the Yard. All the Soho pornographers were made aware that the two Middle East buyers were press agents and a counter attack on the reporters' operation was devised.

When a meeting took place at the Hilton Hotel at which it was hoped Phillips would deliver the films, his employee attacked one of the reporters saying he knew he was a reporter trying to set him up, and a photographer working for Jeff Phillips took pictures of the press men. Later, when the reporters asked Humphreys if he knew how their plan was discovered, he told them that Phillips had checked on the tenancy of their agents' flat. He also told them, in an attempt to divert their attention away from Soho, about a violent attack on a north of England porn bookshop proprietor and arranged for them to meet his American pornographer friend, Charlie Julian, who gave them a story about the American porn scene. Humphreys claimed that he gave Julian £500 for his help and that the reporters gave him £300 for the interview.

Quite naturally the *Sunday People*, having originally exposed the Humphreys and Commander Drury holiday in Cyprus and other aspects of pornography in Soho, was interested in my inquiry. I was aware that the newspaper continued to keep in touch with Mrs Humphreys and, through her, Jimmy Humphreys complained to them about the activities of myself and my team – particularly when he was feeling disgruntled. Investigative journalists from the *News of the World* were also making inquiries and publishing articles about the Soho vice barons. While I appreciated the principle of protecting their sources of information, I thought there might be details known to the journalists of these papers which could be helpful and could be passed on to us without breaching their ethical code. Laurie Manifold, assistant editor of the *Sunday People*, readily agreed to come to the Yard to see me, and after talking it through agreed – subject to protecting his sources – to co-operate, while Trevor Kempson of the *News of the World* raised no objections to helping out too. These meetings, I believe, helped to establish some rapport and, I like to think, convinced these experienced representatives of Fleet Street that we were serious about carrying out a searching and exhaustive investigation with the possibility of criminal proceedings at the end of it. Their co-operation then and later, although not vital, was most helpful. I pay tribute to their willingness to give such help as they could without at any stage ever demanding –

or even hinting – that assistance would only be given on a quid pro quo basis. Later on when I was AC (Crime) I found that in monitoring the health of the delicate area of police/criminal contacts, especially in the West End, the occasional viewpoint of some reliable, experienced reporter was very useful. Robert Mark's personal example and policy of a free and open relationship with the press certainly paid dividends as far as I was concerned.

On 2 December 1974, with the authority of the Deputy Commissioner, I submitted to the DPP the first interim report outlining the extent and direction of the inquiry – including the targeting of John Mason. I gave brief details of forty detectives who had come to our notice either as the result of allegations by Humphreys or through our inquiries. Of these, six had been suspended from duty, eighteen had resigned – eleven prematurely – and twenty-two were still serving. Every club and restaurant recorded in Humphreys's diaries had been visited and in some instances confirmation of reservations on the dates recorded was obtained – in fact, I could not point to one entry that could be proved false. At that stage 240 people had been interviewed and 3,500 pages of statements and questionnaires taken.

Early in January 1975 a report was sent to the Director of Public Prosecutions recommending the prosecution of John Mason, and in February he authorized an arrest warrant being applied for in respect of six offences under the Obscene Publications Act. However, the bird had flown, having been warned, as we learned from him after his eventual arrest, by Moody and Fenwick just before Christmas to leave the country. He went to Belgium, Switzerland, Germany, Spain, France, Jersey and finally Guernsey, where he was located and arrested in November by the now Detective Chief Inspector Hay.

Mason told how earlier in the year, in June, while he had been shopping with his wife in St Peter's Port, he had been surprised to meet Moody, who had said he was on a boating trip with some of his former colleagues. We subsequently learned from ex-Detective Constable Culver, a former member of the Obscene Publications Squad who will be mentioned later in this chapter, that Moody had gone to Guernsey on the boat of a detective chief inspector of the Criminal Intelligence Branch. Culver also told us that Moody had asked this officer to give evidence for him at his trial. These were matters that this senior detective had a duty to report, and he was dealt with under the discipline code, being sentenced to be reduced in rank to inspector. Two months later he retired from the force on an ill-health pension.

Early in 1975 Sir Norman Skelhorn, QC, the Director of Public Prosecutions, appointed Treasury Counsel Mr John Matthew, Mr David Tudor-Price and Mr Michael Neligan to deal with the corruption inquiry in its entirety. From time to time, as further reports were forwarded, conferences were held and advice given by these counsel who in 1976 and 1977 were to conduct the series of prosecutions arising from the inquiry.

In order to keep up the pressure on Silver's camp after his sentence to six years' imprisonment and his pending trial for the murder of Tommy 'Scarface' Smithson, I had a meeting with his common-law wife, Dominique Ferguson, and arranged for her to visit him in Wandsworth Prison. This was to sound out whether he was prepared to help in the inquiry. She reported that he would be prepared to help after the murder trial had been concluded. As I mentioned earlier, he was convicted and sentenced to life imprisonment for the killing in July 1975, but he appealed and in October the following year the conviction was quashed. Silver was interviewed in prison on six separate occasions, but apart from verbally confirming what Humphreys had said about their police contacts, he would not be drawn about the officers and ex-officers whom he regarded as his friends. Inspired newspaper comment immediately after his conviction that he had decided to help the inquiry caused anxiety in some quarters, but I was told that his close friend ex-Detective Sergeant Walter Sandison, now dead but then the landlord of the White Horse public house in Newburgh Street, Soho, gave reassurance after a prison visit by relaying a message that Bernie had said his friends were not to worry.

Having interviewed most of the Soho bookshop people, we turned our attention to the mail-order business proprietors. This was a worthwhile line of inquiry as many of them were not as hardened as the bookshop fraternity and some of them had no criminal convictions at all, which increased their value as potential witnesses.

The mail-order businesses were usually carried on from temporary accommodation addresses. Their biggest worry was that someone who received their unsolicited advertising sheets would complain to the police and thus bring their activities to light. Examination of old case files showed that the majority of cases reported to the DPP had resulted in cautions or no further action because of insufficient evidence. In some cases summonses had been issued but later withdrawn because they could not be served since false names or false addresses had been recorded. By contrast, in every case where a caution or no further action had been approved, the people reported were all shown as having been seen and informed. Humphreys claimed to have been told by his Obscene

Publications Squad contacts of cases where the accommodation addresses had been raided by them before the mail-order proprietor could collect the post. As a result thousands of pounds in cash and postal orders had come their way and had never been officially accounted for.

The new Obscene Publications Squad got to work on the mail-order businesses, locating the accommodation addresses, identifying the people concerned, and prosecuting them. When they were questioned by my team they admitted that in the past they had made regular payments to members of the Obscene Publications Squad for permission to carry on their trade without interference. Some of them also disclosed that on occasion they had bought mail-order customer address lists from squad members who had seized them in raids on their competitors.

Throughout 1975 much information and intelligence had been collated and the inquiry gathered momentum. Eleven officers had been suspended from duty by this time and some had been allowed to resign whilst so suspended. Three officers had appeared before disciplinary boards, being either dismissed or required to resign, and in one of those cases Humphreys had been brought from Gartree Prison to the Yard to give evidence. In all the discipline cases the Director of Public Prosecutions had decided that there was insufficient evidence for criminal proceedings.

We had suffered a couple of setbacks in losing two important potential witnesses, Big Jeff Phillips, who committed suicide, and Bernard Mansfield, a mail-order pornographer who died of a heart attack. This was compensated for when John Mason agreed to co-operate as a witness after his arrest. Since it is never beneficial to the end result, or fair to the suspects, to enter into public debate on the detailed progress of a criminal inquiry of this nature, inevitably there was extensive media speculation and some criticism of the delay and apparent lack of action by the inquiry team.

There was no shortage of parliamentary questions either, mostly written ones from that prolific question raiser, Arthur Lewis, MP for Newham North West. He was joined by Robin Corbett, MP for Hemel Hempstead, who befriended Mrs Humphreys and got a fair amount of copy in the Sunday papers. His theme was that there should be an independent investigation into Humphreys's allegations, not one conducted by a senior Met officer who had served in the West End. One parliamentary question we viewed with some disgust came from John Stonehouse, who at that time was himself awaiting trial for fraud after he had been brought back from Australia having failed in his attempt to fake his own death by drowning in Miami.

By the end of the year, in addition to a number of disciplinary case files, a total of 21 reports (640 pages), 737 statements (3,242 pages), 99 questionnaires (3,160 pages), and 5,511 copies of documents had been sent to the Director of Public Prosecutions. This volume of work by our small team is some indication of the efforts that had been made and of the support we had received from the A.10 civil staff typists – especially a blind audio typist named Maureen – and from the document reproduction unit. We now knew that, although there was still much to be done, it was only a matter of weeks before arrests would be made.

During May, Raymond Anning, the first A.10 commander, was promoted to Deputy Assistant Commissioner in 'C' Department, and Commander Ronald Steventon took his place but continued to help with my inquiry. In December I myself had been transferred from my No. 4 Area Inspector's post and appointed Deputy Assistant Commissioner 'A' Department, though I still continued with the porn corruption inquiry. In my new post I was responsible for complaints, the betting, gaming and licensing policy and the new Obscene Publications Squad. It was an interesting and influential post and one where I was able to introduce some innovations in the light of the experience gained in the corruption inquiry. Both Ron Steventon and I were based at the Yard and were readily available to our hardworking senior investigators, Chief Superintendent Williams and Chief Inspector Hay. Our frequent late-evening discussions were to last for yet another year.

On Tuesday, 24 February 1976, I was told that the Solicitor-General had decided that proceedings should go ahead in respect of twelve serving or former detective officers who had been named in the reports submitted during 1975. Three days later, with Informations prepared by the DPP specifying the alleged offences, Commander Steventon obtained twelve arrest warrants from Bow Street Metropolitan Magistrates' Court. The Commissioner and the new Deputy Commissioner, Colin Woods, who had succeeded the retired Sir James Starritt, were informed that the warrants would be executed on the following morning.

Late in the evening of Friday, 27 February 1976, Williams, Hay and ten other detective superintendents or detective chief inspectors selected from A.10 Branch by Ron Steventon assembled in my office to be briefed. There was a tense atmosphere as they were each given a dossier containing the arrest warrant and details of the person they were to arrest. I did not mention any individuals by name but told them to arrest the person named on their respective warrants as near as possible to 7.30 the next morning and then bring him to Cannon Row police station where the charging and bailing procedure would take place. They were told not to speak about their assignments with anyone. However, security was breached. Without exception, when the arresting officers arrived at the addresses they had been given, reporters and in some cases television camera crews were already there, while several of Saturday morning's national newspapers carried headlines anticipating twelve arrests that day.

Shortly after eight o'clock I arrived at Cannon Row, the police station where I had begun as a constable nearly thirty years earlier, and Steventon told me that nine arrests had been made, including the three most senior officers, Drury, Virgo and Moody, but in the remaining three cases the people concerned had not been at home when the A.10 officers called. However, they were soon located and by 1 P.M. all twelve men had been charged, fingerprinted and bailed, each in his own recognizance of £5,000, to appear at Bow Street Metropolitan Magistrates' Court on Monday, 2 March 1976. They were all charged on varying dates between January 1960 and December 1974 (eight months after the inquiry began) with conspiring to receive money and other considerations corruptly from persons trading in pornography. Such a scandal involving so many senior detectives – two ex-commanders, one ex-detective chief superintendent, one ex-detective chief inspector, four detective inspectors, two ex-detective inspectors and two ex-detective constables – had not occurred since the notorious Trial of the Detectives' case in 1877.

The Met and its friends were shocked and saddened at the news. The great majority of policemen had no idea that corruption on such a scale had taken place and, even now, were reluctant to accept the situation, wondering if the evidence of the convicted criminals they had read about in the press was reliable. The only satisfaction that I and my small investigating team had was that we strongly believed, for the eventual benefit of the force, the crow of corruption had to be publicly nailed to the barn door to convince, and remind, everyone of the need for positive action and eternal vigilance to combat this particular evil. On the Monday, after we had been to Bow Street court and all those arrested were remanded on bail, Sir Robert Mark saw Commander Steventon, Chief Superintendent Williams, Chief Inspector Hay and myself and thanked us for our efforts.

The twelve arrests, although a major success, were by no means the end of the inquiry. There were a number of outstanding suspects to be pursued and much to be done in preparing the cases for trial. Now the proceedings had started, orders under the Bankers' Books Evidence Act could be obtained to examine the bank accounts of those charged. We did not expect to find out much from this source as we believed the people concerned were too worldly wise to pass money received corruptly through their personal accounts, but this could not be taken for granted. Nothing conclusive was found, but an exercise on Drury's bank statements with a graph showing cheques drawn for cash – presumably spending-money – for the year before he was associating with Humphreys and the year when Humphreys claimed he was giving him £100 a month showed considerably fewer withdrawals in the latter year.

In any major criminal inquiry there is nothing like some arrests to give it impetus and encourage witnesses to be co-operative. For a long time I had been studying the files of officers who had belonged to the Obscene Publications Squad during the crucial periods, looking at their recorded involvement – or lack of involvement – with pornographers and trying to find someone prepared to talk about the system of distributing corrupt monies which I was convinced must have existed. The analysis eventually focused attention on a detective inspector of C.11 Criminal Intelligence Branch. This officer had worked for my colleague DAC David Powis when he was investigating a complex corruption inquiry, and I know he thought highly of him. David told me that he was a staunch Scots Presbyterian, an excellent detective and a good family man. In his opinion the detective inspector was likely to have a very troubled conscience if he had been involved in any wrongdoing. It seemed to me that this man had a lot in common with the Scot on my team, Detective Chief Inspector Hay, and I decided that now was the psychological time to have him interviewed. David Powis agreed to speak to him to let him know that, on my behalf, Hay wished to have a confidential talk with him, and arrangements were made for them to meet away from the Yard where they would not be seen by fellow officers.

Hay duly reported back to me that the detective inspector had told him all about the system and that he was prepared to make a statement and give evidence. The rest is history.

Detective Inspector Anthony Kilkerr courageously stood up to be counted and told how, as a young detective sergeant, after only two weeks with the Obscene Publications Squad, he was compromised by the operational head, Detective Chief Inspector George Fenwick. It was on a Friday evening and the regular weekly drinks party was taking place in the squad's general office when the detective chief inspector told him to come to his office. They had no sooner entered the room when, after closing the door, Fenwick tried to press some bank notes into his hand, saying, 'Here you are, this is for you.'

Kilkerr refused to accept the money and asked what it was all about. He was told not to be so bloody silly as it was the safest money he would ever get and Fenwick added, as he pushed the money into the breast pocket of the detective sergeant's jacket, 'It's the share out.' He walked out of the office leaving Kilkerr standing there in a state of shock. When he returned to the general office Fenwick was drinking with the other members of the squad and, feeling confused and embarrassed, he decided to go home. He described his anguish as he left the Yard and walked to St James's Park underground station where he took the bank notes from his pocket and without looking at them threw them away.

Having been compromised he felt trapped, with no alternative but to accept the system until he could get a transfer away from the squad. When Fenwick and five other former members of the porn squad stood trial and were convicted at the Old Bailey, Detective Inspector Kilkerr spent three days in the witness box giving evidence and being cross-examined by one or other of the six defending counsel. No one who heard him could have failed to sympathize with the mental torment he had been through, or to admire his courage in helping to expose the web of corruption into which he had been unwillingly drawn. It pleased me to hear from him that in addition to the support he got from myself and the members of my inquiry team, he had received letters and messages of encouragement from many officers with whom he had formerly served.

Although this was the breakthrough that I had been

looking for, I was concerned that in isolation Kilkerr might be vulnerable and possible to discredit. I asked him if any of his colleagues of that time felt as he did about the matter, and he named a detective sergeant. This officer was sent for and after speaking privately with Kilkerr he, too, agreed to help the inquiry. Later four more officers, a detective inspector and three detective sergeants, also made voluntary statements. All described similar experiences of being given envelopes containing money, varying between £10 and £20, by their supervisors, usually on Fridays at the weekly social gathering of the squad. None of them was ever told – or heard – from whom or from where the money came. Considering the very large sums the pornographers who made statements during the inquiry said they regularly paid to senior members of the Obscene Publications Squad, it is a reasonable assumption that the weekly distribution to junior detectives of what were comparatively small amounts was aimed at implicating them and so securing their silence. Full complicity in the system, by being a collector, a banker, or rendering some other nefarious service, probably brought greater financial reward.

There was no evidence that these six officers had had any personal relationships with pornographers or that they had carried out any unlawful acts. They frankly admitted that they guessed where the money was coming from but felt they had been compromised by their superiors. Although they had guilty consciences they could see no way out of the situation because they thought no one in authority wanted to know what was going on. The Director of Public Prosecutions decided to treat these officers as Crown witnesses, and in due course they gave evidence at committal proceedings and later at two separate trials at the Old Bailey.

In the next months three more former members of the porn squad, an ex-detective inspector and two serving detective sergeants, were arrested and committed for trial with the others arrested in February. The evidence of the police witnesses who had been members of the Obscene Publications Squad was a bombshell for their former colleagues and, although reporting restrictions were not lifted, details of their testimony soon circulated and caused quite a stir throughout the Met.

I was anxious to monitor what was going on and to ensure that as far as possible these witnesses were not subjected to any form of intimidation. Shortly after they had given evidence at the committal proceedings at Lambeth Magistrates' Court, an attack on their credibility came from two national newspapers. On 3 and 4 August 1976 the headlines read, 'Anger as "Bribe" Cops Stay At Work' and 'Angry Police Snub Detectives Who Accepted Bribes'; the articles under the headlines said that they were being ignored by their colleagues and that some officers had applied for transfers to get away from them. The newspapers reported that they had given evidence at a magistrates' court against colleagues facing bribery charges and that reporting restrictions had not been lifted. As indeed reporting restrictions had not been lifted, it seemed to me these articles amounted to contempt of court. I caused the following statement to be issued by the Yard's press office: 'The reports in today's *Daily Telegraph* and *Daily Mirror* regarding the alleged reaction of colleagues who are witnesses in a current corruption case have been drawn to the attention of the Director of Public Prosecutions, who is conducting the prosecution. No officers have applied for a transfer.'

Although this official statement was published and there was no further press comment, I was incensed by the misleading attack on the men who were showing such enormous moral courage. In order to present as many true facts as possible to serving police officers – and journalists – I enlisted the aid of an old colleague from my East End days, ex-Sergeant Howard Perry, KPM, BEM, who was now enjoying his retirement as deputy editor of the weekly magazine, the *Police Review*. I gave Howard the 'Story behind the Story' which was edited and printed in the next issue of the magazine. I can do no better than quote the article which both informed the police service and gave some support and encouragement to our key witnesses.

TALKING POINTS

Story behind the Story

On 3 August a *Daily Telegraph* headline read ANGRY POLICE SNUB DETECTIVES WHO ACCEPTED BRIBES and the *Daily Mirror* asked ANGER AS 'BRIBE' COPS STAY AT WORK. Both newspapers alleged that two Metropolitan CID officers who were witnesses for the prosecution in a corruption case had themselves confessed to accepting bribes; that normally they would have been suspended from duty but because they were not they had been ostracized – 'sent to Coventry' – by their colleagues. The papers also claimed that officers on a division where one of the men was serving had applied for transfers in order to get away from him, and that the Police Federation was angry that there had been no suspension from duty. And Les Male, chairman of the Police Federation, was quoted in both papers as saying that his organization was very unhappy about the case. As the newspapers well know from their court reporters' notes, however, neither of the officers has confessed to taking money from pornographers.

New Scotland Yard put out a statement the following day denying that any officer had applied for a transfer and pointing out that the articles in the newspaper had been drawn to the attention of the Director of Public Prosecutions. The reference to the DPP clearly indicated a possible infringement of Section 3 of the Criminal Justice Act 1967 since the newspapers mentioned a bribery case going for trial where, at the committal hearings, restrictions on reporting had not been lifted. Only specified factual details may be published in these cases and from the viewpoint of publicity the evidence remains *sub judice* until the trial.

It is manifestly unfair therefore to make a comment about a police officer, or in fact any witness, when because of the CJ Act, full details on which a balanced judgement could be made cannot be given. And as Crown witnesses themselves, the officers are also precluded from making any public statements on the matter.

Our inquiries show that the officers have *not* been ostracized by their colleagues, that no transfers have been applied for or taken place – facts which the *Daily Telegraph* could have verified from Scotland Yard, from the officers' divisions, or from the officers themselves before printing the allegations, but they did not. Not exactly fair play! Neither did either paper contact the Metropolitan Police branch board offices at Limehouse at any time. Had they done so they would probably have been told, as was *Police Review*, by Insp. Peter Latham, secretary of the inspectors' branch board: 'I have received no representation from my members on this matter and neither have any of my colleagues so far as I know. I have however made some inquiries since the allegations were made by the newspapers and found nothing to support the stories of "sending to Coventry", bad feelings, and requests for transfers.'

Some policemen have suggested that deliberately inaccurate reporting such as this was an attempt to run a story without infringing the CJ Act. *Police Review* is not only precluded from commenting on the case by the Act but also because we believe in the good old maxim of English law – that a man is presumed innocent until proved guilty. But this must also surely apply to these two officers who now find themselves branded as guilty of corruption on no evidence and, at this stage anyway, unable to defend themselves?

The evidence they gave at the committal proceedings is not a secret to newspaper reporters nor to many Metropolitan officers. But, we have been assured, far from being angry with their two colleagues, they have shown much understanding and appreciation of their courage in giving evidence. As one officer put it: 'Thank goodness there are some men who are prepared to stand up and break the wall of silence.'

It has also been pointed out to us that the story broke two months after the evidence had been given in open court, and that it was prompted by a 'note' containing an extract from the committal proceedings addressed to certain national crime reporters on 2 August. We have been unable to confirm this or, if this was the case, to do more than guess at the reasons behind the circulation.

The case is *sub judice* and the law of the land will prevail. In the meantime it is reasonable to accept that Sir Robert Mark and his senior colleages are not noted for their softness on corruption in the service. And if it were not enough that the British public has learned in the past few years to rely on the Metropolitan Police Commissioner's judgement in these matters, it is as well to remember that all cases of corruption are dealt with by the Attorney-General, the highest legal authority in the land without whose fiat no prosecution can commence.

This then is the story behind the story – or part of it. Crime reporters for their own professional purposes need to cultivate some police officers in the more glamorous operational posts as indeed many police officers too need to have their contacts to do their jobs properly. It behoves all responsible journalists however to think twice before unwittingly undermining the good work done by the Metropolitan Police under Sir Robert's leadership to improve the standards of integrity among its members.

Parliamentary question – 5 August

Detectives: Mr Ridsdale (Harwich) asked the Home Secretary if he will call for a report as to why detectives who received corrupt payments with regard to pornography have been granted immunity from criminal and disciplinary proceedings. *Dr Summerskill*: No. I understand that the circumstances which I think the member has in mind are not as suggested in the question. As the relevant case is, however, *sub judice*, it would be improper for the Home Secretary to intervene or comment in the matter.

From *Police Review*, 13 August 1976

In April 1976 John Mason appeared at Knightsbridge Crown Court and after pleading guilty to five counts of possessing obscene publications for gain was fined £5,000 for each offence or six months' imprisonment on each. He paid the £25,000 fine and we continued to keep in touch with him in order to ensure his attendance as a witness in the forthcoming trials.

John Mason's witness statements covered a period of over twenty years of corrupt associations as he built up his pornographic empire. Too much time had elapsed to find the corroborative evidence necessary to prosecute his earliest police contacts, but this was not important as these men had retired and some were dead. One of them, an ex-detective superintendent, from the date of his retirement until his death in 1972 had been paid £10 and expenses to come to London once a week to proof-read and to give advice on manuscripts submitted by contributors for publication in a soft-porn magazine produced by Mason. The institutionalized nature of these corrupt police/pornographer relationships is well illustrated by the fact that on the death of this ex-superintendent who in 1960 had first introduced Bill Moody, then a detective sergeant, to Mason, his proof-reading role was taken on by Detective Chief Inspector Fenwick, who was then stationed at Kingston but was known to the pornographer since this time as the operational head of the Obscene Publications Squad.

One of the milestones, Mason recalled, was the occasion in 1971 when his monthly routine payments to his Porn Squad contact, Moody, which had begun in 1955 at £60, first went through the £1,000 barrier. Just as incredible was his account of how he was supplied with a CID necktie to wear when he was taken to the Obscene Publications Squad's store in the basement of Holborn police station to select, from confiscated obscene materials awaiting destruction, items to be delivered to him later after he had paid sums which varied between £500 and £1,000 for them. Mason was not without a sense of humour and while making a statement about a detective inspector he said, 'I remember him well because he always ate his asparagus with a knife and fork!'

During May and June at special hearings at Lambeth Magistrates' Court the twelve detectives, or former detectives, arrested in February were committed in three separate groups to stand trial at the Old Bailey. It was decided to have old-style committals where the witnesses attend, give their evidence on oath and are liable to cross-examination, rather than serve copies of the written statements of witnesses on the defence. This was done to test the witnesses thoroughly and to see how they stood up to cross-examination. With the exception of Humphreys, who refused to give evidence against the group that included Fenwick, Jones, O'Hanlon and three others, the witnesses all came up to proof. The value of the extensive inquiries to find additional evidence and corroboration of Humphreys's allegations was demonstrated when he refused to testify at this committal or at the subsequent trial, which was the first in the series of three trials.

Before the second trial at the Old Bailey we played on his vanity by making sure it reached his ears that people were saying that Humphreys had lost his 'bottle' and that John Mason was a more important witness than he was. He gave evidence in the trial of the second group, but again became difficult before the third trial, where he was the key witness against ex-Commander Drury, who was one of the three defendants. Ron Steventon arranged for Laurie Manifold of the *Sunday People*, whom Humphreys trusted, to see him in his cell beneath the court. Assured by Mr Manifold that his complaint of being wrongly convicted of wounding his wife's former lover was being investigated by police – which it was – he agreed to testify. If he had maintained his refusal, then the case against Drury must have collapsed.

The first trial ended just before Christmas, on 22 December 1976, with five of the six defendants being found guilty of the charge of conspiracy and also separate substantive counts of specific acts of corruption with named pornographers. One detective inspector, who had been arrested in July and joined with the others to stand trial, was sentenced to four years' imprisonment; the others received sentences varying between seven and ten years. One detective inspector was found not guilty but was ordered to pay £2,000 costs. He remained suspended from duty and resigned before disciplinary proceedings could be taken.

Towards the end of November, when this trial had been in progress for about two weeks, some additional evidence came to hand in a disturbing manner. A steward on a cross-channel ferry was arrested in possession of travellers' cheques which had been stolen from a west London hotel. When questioned he said he had been given them by his brother in London, ex-Detective Constable Ernest Culver. Culver had served in the Obscene Publications Squad in the late 1960s and had voluntarily retired from the Met in 1970, taking up employment as a hotel security officer. When he was arrested he said that the travellers' cheques had been given to him by a former colleague, Detective Chief Inspector Ridley of

Kensington, specifically to be cashed by his brother on the cross-Channel ferry. Inquiries by A.10 investigators revealed that Ridley had dealt with some cheques that had been recovered after a theft from a Kensington hotel, and since he was unable to explain satisfactorily some discrepancies in the official records he was suspended from duty. Culver also claimed that he was willing to give information about corruption in the Obscene Publications Squad when he served in the unit and, consequently, he was again seen by Detective Chief Inspector Hay, who had interviewed him once before in 1975.

Culver gave a graphic account of corruption as a member of the porn squad, and of his personal involvement with the operational head of the squad, Bill Moody, in collecting money from pornographers. He described how some time in late 1964, just after Moody had been appointed to the squad, they went on a lunchtime drinking session to the Pill Box public house near Waterloo station. He was told that he would have to help collect bribes from bookshops and pornographers in the West End which, Moody said, he was going to 'properly organize'. From that time until two years later, when he was transferred, Culver was Moody's messenger and runner. He regularly took monthly payments to Moody of about £200, usually given to him in public houses by any of three 'middlemen', individuals in the porn trade trusted to collect from their associates. On Moody's instructions, Culver sometimes met Mason at the White House restaurant near Regent's Park or the George and Dragon public house in Soho to collect his monthly 'licence' money. He claimed that for his role in this organized corruption scheme his detective inspector paid him £15 a week. One of John Mason's right-hand men, his chauffeur Ron Davey, was known as 'Ron the Dustman' because of his former occupation, and from this their favourite pub, the George and Dragon, was dubbed by Culver and his colleagues 'God and the Dustman', 'God', of course, being Mason!

Culver recalled on one occasion going with Moody to a large house near Hastings and meeting Jimmy and Rusty Humphreys. At this time Humphreys was the chairman of Hastings United Football Club and kept a number of racing greyhounds at his country home. They discussed the possibility of Humphreys converting a strip club owned by him in Soho into a bookshop. Moody told him it would probably cost him £4,000 for the 'licence' but that he could not authorize it and would have to report back to someone at the Yard. According to Culver, this was the incident which convinced him of the need to get out of the corruption in which he had become trapped. Although he got a transfer out of the Obscene Publications Squad in 1966 his experiences still depressed him and this was the main reason why he resigned from the force four years later. After his resignation he had a nervous breakdown and spent a month in a hospital receiving treatment. He went on to tell us that ever since his previous interview with Hay, when he had nearly confessed, he had been very worried about his personal position. When he heard of Mason's arrest he was frightened and his anxiety increased when shortly afterwards Fenwick and a suspended detective inspector came without warning to the hotel where he worked to talk to him. In the course of conversation he was asked if he knew of anyone who would take up a contract on Mason – that is, to murder him for money. They told him that they would all, including him, get about ten years' imprisonment unless something was done about John Mason and that if everyone involved put up £500 it would pay for the contract. He flatly refused to have anything to do with the plot and they left, telling him to keep his mouth shut.

Culver's statement was passed to the DPP and it was decided not to introduce him as a witness at the current trial – where Fenwick was one of the defendants – but to use him in the second trial when Moody would be in the dock. In October 1977, after he had appeared as a Crown witness at the Old Bailey, Culver was sentenced to six months' imprisonment, suspended for two years, for handling the stolen travellers' cheques. The Director of Public Prosecutions decided there was insufficient evidence to prosecute ex-Detective Chief Inspector Ridley, who had resigned while still suspended from duty. We were to hear more about him in the next few years and in May 1982, after stolen metal worth £200,000 – including several tons of printing plates used to produce the *Daily Telegraph* and the *Daily Express* – was found in a raid on a Deptford scrap yard, Ridley and two associates were convicted of conspiracy to handle stolen metal and he was jailed for twelve months.

The second porn trial lasted over two months and was the longest of the three. Humphreys gave his evidence well and stood up to rigorous cross-examination. Ex-Detective Chief Superintendent Lambert was a witness. He had worked with Frank Williamson, one of Her Majesty's Inspectors of Constabulary, on *The Times* corruption inquiry in 1970 before being taken off the investigation and replaced by Detective Chief Superintendent Moody. In January 1976, before any arrests had been made, Fred Lambert, whom I had known since he was a detective constable and I was a uniformed constable at Rochester Row in the late 1940s, agreed to make a statement about his knowledge of C.1 Obscene Publications Squad. After his removal from the 1970 corruption inquiry he had supervised some of the paper work of the porn squad and finding it inadequate sent some of the reports that were intended for the DPP back for further details to be included. Again his responsibilities were changed, and shortly afterwards he retired on medical grounds. In cross-examination by defending counsel his credibility as a senior detective was attacked, and his removal from Frank Williamson's inquiry team was used as a basis for raising doubt. After discussion with prosecution counsel on how to rebut this, it was decided to ask the former Inspector of Constabulary if he was prepared to attend the Old Bailey as a witness to Lambert's efficiency at the relevant time. Mr Williamson, who since his retirement had made no secret about his disquiet at the lack of co-operation he received from the Met in *The Times* inquiry, willingly agreed to give evidence, in the course of which he expressed his satisfaction with Mr Lambert but dissatisfaction with the efforts of Moody.

This second porn trial ended on 13 May with all six defendants being found guilty and sentenced to terms of imprisonment varying between four and twelve years. The conviction of ex-Commander Virgo was quashed on 15 March 1978, when in the Court of Appeal Lord Justice Lane and two other judges allowed his appeal on the grounds that the trial judge, Mr Justice Mars-Jones, had failed to direct the jury properly on a point relating to corroboration. However, in the course of his judgment Lord Lane complimented the trial judge saying, 'It is only fair to say that the judge's direction to the jury was a tremendous *tour de force*. It involved an enormous amount of homework and no one could have produced a summing-up of such length and complexity in such a clear and masterly way without a great deal of preparation and care' (*The Times* Law Report,15 August 1978).

No. 1 Court at the Old Bailey in May was at times pretty hot and stuffy. One evening when we were going over the day's proceedings and preparing for the next day, it was implied by one of my juniors that Mr Justice Mars-Jones had had his eye on me in the afternoon because I had dozed off. I told this young man that, as he would discover when he reached my age, the closing of the eyes sometimes helps concentration and, I added, if anyone can sleep in No. 1 Court at the Old Bailey then he must have a clear conscience! I was very proud of my team when at the end of the trial Mr Mars-Jones called upon us to stand while he complimented us on the work that had been done.

The third and final trial involved ex-Commander Drury, ex-Detective Inspector Ingram and Detective Inspector Legge, and it opened on 14 June. Although Ingram and Legge had the common factors of serving on the Flying Squad under Drury and both had held the rank of detective inspector, their relationships with Humphreys had been very different.

As I mentioned earlier, it was at a party to celebrate Ingram's promotion in March 1971 that he introduced Jimmy Humphreys, whom he had known for about six years while serving at West End Central and on the Flying Squad, to Drury who was just about to become the commander of the Flying Squad. Ingram after his promotion became a detective inspector in south London but continued to keep in touch and socialize with Humphreys up to the time when he ceased all association with detectives after the publicity about his Cyprus holiday with Drury. Because he was mentioned in Humphreys's diaries we had begun to make inquiries about Ingram when in August 1974 he had voluntarily retired without qualifying for a pension.

When Humphreys was interviewed he made no specific complaints about Ingram, but from our inquiries we traced two of his former employees who had carried out some minor building work at Ingram's home. And in tracing the history of cars which Humphreys had owned we came across a Singer Vogue estate which in 1972 had been registered in the name of Mrs Ingram, the previous registered owner having been Humphreys. When these facts were put to Humphreys he agreed that he had paid the wages of his men while they had done some work at Ingram's house and that he had given him the motor car in September 1971 to show his appreciation of past services.

By contrast Legge, when he was a young detective sergeant on the Flying Squad, had been pressed by his commander to join him and other members of the squad at social functions hosted by Humphreys. On occasions when he had excused himself he had been rebuked. In May 1971 Legge confided in his commander that he was having some serious domestic difficulties and Drury's advice was that he should get away for a holiday. Shortly afterwards it was suggested that he should take advantage of an offer from Humphreys and stay at an apartment owned by him in Ibiza. Entries in Humphreys's diaries led to a check of the Flying Squad leave records which confirmed that Legge had gone to Ibiza.

Long before Humphreys was extradited from Holland, Detective Inspector Legge became the only detective investigated in the inquiry to make a voluntary statement. He explained his relationship with Humphreys and the circumstances behind the holiday in Ibiza, but he denied having at any time solicited or received any money from him. However, in view of the holiday, he was suspended from duty pending the completion of inquiries. After

Humphreys was extradited a statement was taken from him about the diary entries relating to Legge and he more or less confirmed the account given earlier by the detective inspector. He was very insistent that Legge was one of the very few who had never wanted or accepted a penny from him and the only personal favour he had ever had was the use of the Ibiza apartment. A report was sent to the Director of Public Prosecutions who in due course replied that he did not intend to institute proceedings against Legge, though there was still the disciplinary position to be dealt with. However, before a decision had been reached about this the law officers of the Crown had reconsidered the position and decided that proceedings would be taken after all, so Legge was now standing trial. After Humphreys had given evidence to the effect that he had never given him any money and his counsel had made a submission that his client had no case to answer, the trial judge directed that Legge be found not guilty and he was discharged. He resigned from the force a few weeks later.

I felt that but for his domestic problem this detective would probably not have gone on the ill-fated holiday, and that taking into account the pressures he had been under he had done well to resist the temptation to join in the corrupt relationships so willingly entered into by Humphreys. In my view justice was done by his acquittal.

On 7 July the jury found Drury guilty on five counts of corruption and Ingram guilty on two counts. They were sentenced to eight years' and four years' imprisonment respectively and ordered to pay £2,000 and £1,000 towards the costs of their legal aid.

The following reply by the Home Secretary, Merlyn Rees, published in *Hansard* on 20 July 1977 in reply to a request from Arthur Lewis, MP, for information about the corruption investigation, is a concise statistical summary of three years' work:

I understand from the Commissioner of Police of the Metropolis that the investigation into allegations made by James Humphreys and others embraced the activities of 74 officers or former officers of ranks from constable to commander. Full reports of all the investigations were submitted for the independent scrutiny and advice of the Director of Public Prosecutions, who decided after consulting senior Treasury counsel that nine former officers and six suspended officers should be prosecuted. I understand that no further prosecutions are contemplated.

The Commissioner informs me that of the 74 officers or former officers investigated, 12 have resigned, and 28 have retired with a pension entitlement in accordance with the Police Pensions Regulations. These officers left the force voluntarily: they were not advised or encouraged to reach a decision to leave. In addition, eight officers have been found guilty in disciplinary proceedings and dismissed or required to resign, in one case for offences unconnected with the above mentioned allegations; and disciplinary proceedings against another officer are pending.

The figures in the last paragraph include 13 officers or former officers sentenced to imprisonment at the recent trials, six of whom retired with pensions. I have the question of these pensions under consideration.

I would like to pay tribute to Sir Robert Mark and all those officers who helped deal with this matter, and in particular to the team of investigators, to whose skill and unstinting perseverance in pursuing the allegations the force and the public are greatly indebted.

The compliment which I value most came in November 1977 from David Tudor-Price, a senior Treasury counsel, who was made a High Court judge in 1984 and died in February 1986 in Swansea while on the Wales and Chester Circuit. In his final advice he wrote:

Finally, as I think this is likely to be the last advice that I will be required to give in this very long inquiry, I would wish to express my admiration to Mr Kelland, Mr Steventon and Mr Williams for the way in which everything in connection with this matter has been done. The quality of the twenty-eight reports and the painstaking thoroughness of the whole inquiry, which has been approached with complete impartiality, has been marvellous. A most unpleasant task has been magnificently done.

I may say that to work for such a long time in close association with senior members of the Director of Public Prosecutions' staff and with Mr Tudor-Price and his Treasury counsel colleagues was a privilege. Their encouragement and professional advice were invaluable in bringing the inquiry to a successful conclusion.

On 25 August 1977, after serving two years and four months of his eight years' sentence, James William Humphreys was released from Maidstone Prison by the exercise of the Royal prerogative. For the next two years he sent a Christmas card to me at the Yard, but this seasonal greeting ceased after 1982 when he was circulated by Interpol as being wanted in Eire for involvement in the manufacture of amphetamine drugs. I understand that he has left the United Kingdom and is once again a fugitive from justice.

10

Appointment by Royal Warrant

Nineteen seventy-six had been an eventful year, but from my own personal point of view it was also one of uncertainty and very much a prelude to 1977, which saw an almost complete change in the hierarchy of the Met. Not only did Mr David McNee, the Chief Constable of Strathclyde, succeed Sir Robert Mark as Commissioner but we had a new deputy commissioner and changes in three out of the four asssistant commissioners. The most senior civil staff post, the historic office of Receiver, also changed hands. So by the end of 1977 Mr McNee was presiding over an almost entirely new Policy Committee – the 'Cabinet' of the force – though some continuity was maintained by the fact that all the new appointments except his own came from promotion within the organization.

There was naturally much speculation early in 1976 when the retirement of Sir Robert Mark was widely rumoured for the following March. This speculation was finally ended in October when, after an erroneous report in the *Sunday Times* that the then Deputy Commissioner, Colin Woods, was to succeed Sir Robert, there came the official announcement that Mr McNee was the Commissioner of Police designate. The Assistant Commissioner 'A' Department, John Mastel, was due to retire in December 1976 and, as his deputy, I had a personal interest in who was going to succeed him. Again there was the usual crop of rumours but clearly much indecision because John Mastel retired before his successor was appointed.

Early in the year, in the weeks immediately after the arrest and remand on bail of the twelve serving or former detectives on corruption charges, I became uneasy. There seemed to me a risk that in the hurly burly of politics and pending senior changes the lessons to be learned from the three-year inquiry might not be taken fully on board. My senior colleague and friend for some twenty years, Sir James Starritt, his distinguished career fittingly marked by the award of a KCVO, had retired and I missed having him to confide in and regretted the absence of his forceful influence on the Policy Committee and the Home Office. I was mindful of the Knapp Commission report on corruption in New York, which had pointed out that during the early part of a reform period internal controllers may be highly committed and incorruptible, but it also documented the extent to which such commitment may fade away.

During April, before any of the three corruption trials and before our continuing inquiries had resulted in the arrest of three more detectives, I submitted to the Deputy Commissioner a lengthy paper giving a personal viewpoint on police corruption. I tried to be objective, quoting either personal experiences and intelligence gathered or information from close colleagues whom I could vouch for during my thirty years of police service. In the paper I said that, until Sir Robert Mark's term of office as the Commissioner, the saying of Talleyrand about the Bourbons, 'They have learnt nothing and forgotten nothing,' aptly summarized the attitude of the Metropolitan Police towards the problem of CID corruption. The implied message in the paper, which I know was passed to the Commissioner and a copy sent to the Home Office, was one of anxiety about the future. I knew that I was running the risk of appearing unnecessarily obsessive about the situation and, indeed, in later years I am well aware that this accusation was occasionally levelled at me. However, as an AC, this did not worry me; if being concerned and taking action to protect the integrity of the force and individual officers was judged to be obsessive behaviour then I was happy to be found guilty.

While I knew that sometimes it is politic to make haste slowly, it seemed to me that there had been undue delay in implementing some of Sir Robert's proposals made in 1972 when he became Commissioner, in particular the measures for interchange between CID and uniformed officers. It was not until 1976 that a scheme for a limited amount of interchange at sergeant and inspector level had been agreed with the staff associations, while the only senior officer to be affected had been the first commander of the A.10 Complaints Investigation Bureau, Raymond Anning, on his promotion to Deputy Assistant Commissioner. It was essential in my view for the good health and reputation of the Met to have more integration between the two operational departments, and I was not impressed by the argument that such a policy would necessarily lead to a loss of efficiency.

Now that I was responsible for the reconstituted Obscene Publications Squad, I introduced some changes to improve communication and accountability. The porn squad inquiry had demonstrated the truth of a theory expounded in the USA, that corruption thrives best in a poorly run department where lines of authority are vague and supervision is minimal. The new porn squad, headed by a chief inspector, was functioning very well, but the line of command to me – a deputy assistant commissioner four ranks up – was through the civil staff head of both A.1 Licensing Branches and the Complaints Bureau secretariat. With the best will in the world, it is not practicable for even the most experienced member of the civil staff – with no police powers or executive authority – effectively to supervise operational policemen. My immediate deputy, a commander, was made responsible for overseeing the operations of the squad and for keeping me informed about their activities.

It is important in a service like the police with a hierarchical rank structure for the most senior departmental officers to have regular contacts with key middle-management officers so that, without disrupting the chain of command principle, they establish a good working relationship. This defeats the 'three wise monkeys' syndrome of see no evil, speak no evil, hear no evil, from which these officers are sometimes inclined to believe their seniors suffer.

Another innovation had been to authorize the commander of 'C' District at West End Central, David Helm, to establish a small vice intelligence unit. One of the officers in this unit was Constable Frank Pulley who, after service at Notting Hill, A.8 Public Order Branch and the Special Patrol Group, was now back at his original station. In the autumn of 1976, through Commander Helm, I received a long report from Pulley setting out allegations from a female informant that a man known as Charles Taylor, the owner of the Leigham Court Hotel at Streatham, was a major fraudsman, involved in what was known as the dollar premium fraud,[1] and was being

[1] The dollar premium fraud: The Exchange Control Act in force at this time meant that anyone wanting to purchase a foreign investment was restricted to doing so only by using currency from other British residents, which restricted the supply of investment currency. This produced a premium over and above the price that would have been

'minded' by corrupt detectives. I knew something about Taylor from inquiries I had made in 1973 when Jimmy Humphreys had written from Holland to Jim Starritt, alleging a conspiracy between Detective Chief Inspector Bland of the Serious Crime Squad and criminals who had frequented Taylor's hotel to frame him for the assault of his wife's former lover, Peter Garfath. After some surveillance on Taylor by the West End Central intelligence unit I reported the matter to the Deputy Commissioner who agreed that he should be made a target for investigation by a team led by Commander Bert Wickstead, then deputy to the Inspector of No. 3 Area and so directly responsible to the Deputy Commissioner. Wickstead selected some staff from his own area, but to protect the security of the operation – he was being asked by a 'C' Department DAC to account for the employment of the detectives he had chosen – they were temporarily transferred to A.10 Branch.

The information that Taylor was associating with other active fraudsmen proved correct. He was eventually arrested in connection with a conspiracy to produce

---

charged had it been possible to buy directly from foreigners. This was the dollar premium, and in practice this was around fifty per cent of the pound's value. The fraud involved selling a foreign security on which it was claimed the dollar premium had been paid, when it had not. The Bank of England kept a strict watch on these transactions which made it almost impossible for an individual to carry out this type of fraud successfully, but groups of people had worked out a system requiring false documents and an elaborate conspiracy to defraud the Treasury. Perhaps the most notorious case in 1977 concerned a stockbroker, Lewis Altman, involved in a £2-million currency fraud, who was fined £200,000 for attempting to pass off currency as investment currency to get dollar premium rebates from the Treasury. Judah Binstock, a financier and associate of Sir Eric Miller who committed suicide, was also charged with this fraud but he left the country and did not stand trial.

counterfeit gold half-sovereigns and also charged with others with a dollar premium fraud. He died in 1977 of a heart attack on his way home from the Old Bailey where he was standing trial, before the case was concluded. As the result of a statement he made after his arrest about long-standing associations with some senior CID officers, the Chief Constable of Kent, Mr Barry Pain, at the request of the Deputy Commissioner agreed to carry out an investigation into the implications of these assocations under Section 49 of the Police Act.

The situation in December 1976 then was that a storm cloud seemed to be again gathering over the force, and I felt very much at a personal crossroads. Although the retirement of John Mastel was imminent, there was no firm news about his replacement. From senior colleagues in provincial police forces I heard rumours about potential candidates from outside the Met, and in one or two cases felt that they were so unqualified that I doubted whether I would wish to continue to serve if they were appointed. In Sir Robert's Mark's autobiography, *In the Office of Constable*, he says that he decided to take no part in choosing senior colleagues for his successor and suggested to Sir Robert Armstrong, then Permanent Under Secretary of State at the Home Office, that he should use the Deputy Commissioner as a medium for obtaining opinions about candidates from within the force.

John Mastel retired at the end of the year and handed over to me, and I was acting AC in January when the DC, Colin Woods, told me that I was one of five candidates who were being considered for the appointment. Two of them were Met colleagues, DACs John Gerrard and Wilford Gibson, and the others Ernest Bright, Assistant Commissioner in the City of London Police, and Fred Cutting, the Chief Constable of Northampton County

Police. The appointment of the Commissioner and the five assistant commissioners, one of whom is designated the Deputy Commissioner, of the Metropolitan Police is by way of Royal Warrant from the Sovereign on the recommendation of the Home Secretary, and unlike other chief officers' posts the vacancies are never advertised. Administrative delay in selecting and announcing senior appointments is never good for morale, and it seems that this is recognized by most police authorities. However, the one responsible for the Metropolitan Police, the Home Secretary, is, as he was on this occasion, sometimes remiss.

I received a letter from Sir Robert Armstrong confirming what Colin Woods had told me and asking me to go to the Home Office on 28 January for interview by a group whose views the Home Secretary would find it helpful to have in making a recommendation to the Queen. The group was composed of Sir Robert as Chairman, the Commissioner-designate, the Deputy Commissioner, HM Chief Inspector of Constabulary and an assistant under secretary of state at the Home Office. The interview took place in a relaxed atmosphere and covered a wide range of subjects, including my views on the organization and administration of the Met. I recall telling the committee I found it something of a paradox that after a public order disturbance, a terrorist incident or a major criminal operation, it was usual to hold a comprehensive debriefing to see if any lessons could be learnt, but that nothing of the sort was done after a major internal corruption inquiry. A few weeks later, after he had taken office as Commissioner, David McNee reminded me about this and we had a long debriefing discussion.

The route from constable to assistant commissioner,

through eight different ranks, is a long and tortuous one so it was very satisfying to be told that as the result of the recommendation of the Home Secretary, Merlyn Rees, Her Majesty had appointed me an assistant commissioner of the Metropolitan Police as from 1 February 1977. A few days after the publication in *The Times* of my appointment, I received the Royal Warrant itself, signed in the absence of Her Majesty by the Queen Mother and Princess Anne.

John Gerrard and Wilford Gibson gave me their generous congratulations. I was particularly pleased that before the end of the year, owing to unexpected vacancies, they were both appointed assistant commissioners without having to undergo any further interview procedures. I believe that David McNee chose wisely in securing these appointments, for their wide experience and professionalism contributed much to the efficiency and harmony of the Met during his five-year tenure as Commissioner.

David McNee took over as Commissioner in March 1977 and rapidly established a good working relationship with his assistant commissioners. Before his arrival some articles had appeared in the press suggesting that he was something of a teetotal, bible-punching martinet known as 'The Hammer' – journalistic licence had been given full rein. Although not well known south of the Border, there were senior Met officers who had attended the same senior command course as David McNee at the Police Staff College, and as a member of the Council of the Police Athletic Association I had enjoyed his warm hospitality when Strathclyde had hosted national events in Glasgow. I knew that he was good company and certainly not a teetotaller.

He began to get to grips with some of the outstanding

problems that needed urgent attention. One of these was the domestic issue raised by the Chief Constable of Kent's investigation into the association between a convicted fraudsman, Alfred (known as Charles) Taylor and senior officers of the force. The Director of Public Prosecutions had decided that there was insufficient evidence for criminal proceedings but no decisions had been made about disciplinary action. Since I had been personally involved in the events leading up to the criminal inquiry by Bert Wickstead, and with briefing Barry Pain and his deputy, Frank Jordan, the Commissioner questioned me closely about the circumstances and the background of this inquiry. The outcome was that Detective Superintendent Bland, who had been suspended from duty nine months earlier when details of his association with Taylor came to the notice of Mr Pain, resigned before disciplinary proceedings could be taken. In addition, a 'C' Department deputy assistant commissioner whose relationship with Taylor had also been investigated resigned at short notice and left the force.

Another problem, daily growing more troublesome, was the industrial dispute at Grunwick Processing Ltd, in Chapter Road, Neasden. This dispute had begun in August 1976 when seven Asian workers – who were soon joined by about a hundred of their colleagues – walked out of the small photo-processing laboratory complaining about their working conditions and poor pay. The owner, Mr George Ward, an Anglo-Indian, kept his business open by continuing to employ non-union Asian workers.

The strike escalated from a local to a national issue when the union APEX, the Association of Professional, Executive and Computer Staffs, took up the case and their secretary, Roy Grantham, addressed the September TUC conference seeking general support from the trade union movement. The dispute thus became something of a *cause célèbre*, and at different times various MPs joined the picket lines and militant groups like the Socialist Workers' Party helped to swell the numbers who daily gathered near the entrance to the laboratory. It became known that an extra-large mass picket, reinforced by miners led by Mr Arthur Scargill, who was then the President of the Yorkshire Branch of the National Union of Mineworkers, was going to take place on 23 June 1977 and would try to close the laboratory as they had done the Saltley Gas Works in Birmingham some five years earlier.

The detailed planning to prevent public disorder and to enable the employees of the company who wished to go to work to do so was dealt with by 'A' Department under the direction of Deputy Assistant Commissioner (Operations) Wilford Gibson. In the Met we had often talked about Saltley and the lessons to be learned. As far as the Grunwick situation was concerned we felt we had the experienced manpower – particularly our supervisory officers – the organization and the tactics to meet the threat of force by mass pickets.

Perhaps the mythology of Saltley had given Mr Scargill and his supporters a false sense of power, but the demonstration on 23 June resulted, within minutes of their arrival, in the arrest of Arthur Scargill, his NUM journalist colleague, Maurice Jones, and sixty others. There were, of course, the usual allegations of police brutality, and Maurice Jones, after being bailed, disappeared to East Germany where it was said he was seeking asylum. Arthur Scargill was eventually acquitted of the public order charge on the plea that his actions were involuntary because he was pushed from behind. Maurice Jones, after a visit from Scargill, returned from his short, self-imposed exile, and was convicted and fined £50 for the public order offence with which he had been charged. His appeal to the Crown Court against the conviction was dismissed.

The dispute dragged on from June to late November and put a heavy strain on our manpower, but once again the Met showed its expertise in dealing with public order problems. Mob rule had been prevented and the myth of Saltley severely dented.

I recall that the Commissioner and I at one point went with Merlyn Rees, the Home Secretary, on a visit to the Grunwick area so that he could see for himself the problems of policing the dispute. As we walked along a street of terraced houses some of the residents were standing in their front gardens, and Mr Rees spoke to one elderly man in his shirt sleeves, introducing himself and holding out his hand. The man angrily refused to shake hands, saying that before he retired he had been a trade unionist and an official of his union for fifty years, but the behaviour of the so-called pickets in his street was disgraceful. The Home Secretary tried to placate him but without success. At the end of the visit when he was giving a short press conference he was asked about the incident with the incensed resident and replied, 'That old man is what trade unionism is all about.' From my personal contact with Mr Rees when he was Home Secretary and later when he was shadow minister in the Opposition, I believed his visit to the scene, where some of his parliamentary colleagues had supported the picketing, was typical of his moral courage and sense of duty.

Within days of David McNee becoming the Commissioner disturbing evidence that suggested the recycling of a large quantity of Moroccan 'Cain' cannabis to criminals by members of the Central Drug Squad was put before Commander Steventon, head of A.10 Branch. Some 1,200 lbs of the drug had been seized by the squad in February 1976 and was recorded as having been destroyed by burning after the prosecution was concluded, but scientific examination had established that it was some of this same consignment that had been seized by N. 5 Regional Crime Squad officers when they made an arrest in Essex on 23 March 1977.

Inquiries by A.10 began, and during June a detective sergeant and a constable were suspended from duty while the investigation continued into the suspected complicity of more senior members of the Drug Squad. Eventually the investigators concluded that the cannabis had been removed from the black plastic bags in which it was stored and some other substance substituted before the bags were burned. The independent witness to the destruction had never examined the contents of the bags, presuming they contained cannabis as shown on the labels attached to them. Clear-plastic storage bags should have been used.

This very serious matter meant that only four years after six of its members had appeared at the Old Bailey and three of them had been convicted and jailed for perjury,[2] the C.1 Drugs Squad was again under a cloud of suspicion.

[2] In 1971 HM Customs and Excise officers complained about the relationship between the Yard's Drug Squad and a major cannabis importer they had arrested. This resulted in an inquiry by a team of Lancashire detectives led by Assistant Chief Constable Harold Prescott, but insufficient evidence was found to justify any criminal proceedings. However, a Met CID officer, Commander George Clarkson, assisted by Chief Inspector Ernie Faulkner and Detective Chief Superintendent Gordon Mees, investigated breaches of the disciplinary regulations. They uncovered evidence of criminal offences which resulted in the detective chief inspector who had been in charge of the squad, a

Almost at the same time came the news of the appointment of Sir Colin Woods – he had received a KCVO in the Birthday Honours list – as Her Majesty's Chief Inspector of Constabulary. The Commissioner told me that Pat Kavanagh, AC 'B' Department, was to be his deputy, and in the consequent departmental changes he wanted me to move from 'A' to 'C' Department as from 1 August. We discussed some of the CID personnel and organizational changes that we both agreed were necessary and Mr McNee consented to DAC David Powis, then in 'B' Department, joining me to fill the vacancy caused by the recent early retirement of a 'C' Department DAC.

Although the appointment as AC 'A' Department had fulfilled an ambition, I looked forward to the challenge of being responsible for the CID at a particularly crucial point in its history. While I was aware that there would be a few who would not welcome my return to the fifth floor at the Yard, I had sufficient knowledge of and confidence in most of the senior and middle-ranking

---

detective sergeant, one ex-detective sergeant – after extradition from Australia – and two detective constables being arrested. They were all charged with conspiring to pervert the course of justice and all except the detective chief inspector were charged with perjury.

In November 1973 at the Old Bailey all were acquitted on the conspiracy charge as were two of the five charged with perjury. Three were convicted of perjury, the ex-detective sergeant being sentenced to four years' imprisonment, and the other detective sergeant and a detective constable were each jailed for eighteen months.

The three acquitted detectives remained suspended pending the hearing of separate disciplinary charges. During the following year a detective constable resigned, the detective chief inspector retired on medical grounds – in each case before any disciplinary proceedings could be taken – and the remaining detective constable, after being found guilty by a disciplinary board of various offences against the discipline code, was reprimanded.

detectives not to feel any misgivings about the change of role.

As I took up my post the Drugs Squad crisis worsened, and I was told that the detective chief inspector in charge and a detective inspector had both been suspended from duty. Some months later the detective sergeant who had been suspended earlier was convicted and sentenced to a term of imprisonment for selling cannabis to the criminal arrested by N. 5 Regional Crime Squad officers. The detective chief inspector formerly in charge of the squad, two detective inspectors and a detective constable were later all found guilty by disciplinary boards of offences arising out of this case and, with the exception of one of the detective inspectors who was reduced in rank to constable, they were all required to resign. They all appealed unsuccessfully to the Commissioner against the findings and punishments of the disciplinary boards and then exercised their right of appeal to the Home Secretary, although two of them subsequently abandoned their appeals.

At an early conference with all senior detectives – detective chief superintendents and above – I stressed that foremost among the problems to be tackled was the restoration of the confidence of our colleagues in other forces and HM Customs and Excise, and I pointed out the damage caused by the current Drugs Squad scandal. I told them that their expertise and co-operation were needed to ensure that all criminal investigation was carried out with high ethical standards, and that if anyone could not go along with this, then it was preferable for them to make their own arrangements to leave the CID as soon as possible. Before the meeting closed I had the feeling that the conference was with me and that I would have their willing support.

During the previous five years I had been the honorary secretary of the London Region of the Association of Chief Police Officers and, in this capacity, a member of the Executive Committee of our association. The holding of this office after being active with the Superintendents' Association of England and Wales had given me a wide circle of colleagues and friends in police forces outside London. Largely as the result of Sir Robert Mark's leadership the Met was getting a pretty good press. However, I was aware from my ACPO colleagues that there was some unease still about co-operation with us in drugs matters and criminal intelligence, and the reservations about drugs were shared by my Customs and Excise friends. I was grateful to have these frank views and I knew I would receive help in rebuilding bridges.

I felt that in order to restore the credibility of the CID both within the Met and with the police service generally certain key changes had to be made. I took the point of view expressed in the biblical text and quoted in one of his wartime speeches by Winston Churchill, 'He who is not for us is against us.' Thank goodness the overwhelming majority were in the 'for us' category and senior relationships were comfortable and constructive. However, it was necessary at times to be fairly ruthless.

The current serious problems made the C.1 Drugs Squad the first priority. A quick examination disclosed that like the old Obscene Publications Squad the line of command was weak and vague: too much responsibility rested with the detective chief inspector who was the *de facto* head of the squad. A C.1 detective chief superintendent was nominally responsible for the squad but he was often deployed on major inquiries, sometimes away from London, and not available to direct and supervise regularly. The importance of this area of criminal work, with its obvious dangers and temptations, made it essential to have a detective chief superintendent whose sole responsibility was to command the Drugs Squad. Bearing in mind the need to establish confidence quickly, particularly with the Customs and Excise, Superintendent John Smith, awaiting promotion at this time and well known to the Customs people as the head of the new porn squad, was transferred to C.1 Branch to become the operational head of the Drugs Squad. The squad was reorganized to include fifty per cent each of CID and selected uniformed officers with plain-clothes experience and the new terms of reference issued made it clear that the squad's main object was to concentrate on major drug traffickers, dealers and illegal manufacturers. In addition, the dangerous-drugs storage and destruction procedures were examined, and revised systems were introduced to ensure stricter control.

Thanks to the calibre of the officers chosen to lead and work on the squad, as well as the interest shown by the most senior ranks, it went from strength to strength after that with not even a whisper of suspicion about its integrity in the seven years up to the time of my retirement.

In the field of criminal intelligence the police service was moving towards the setting up of units in geographical regions to serve both local forces in the respective regions and the regional crime squads. London was the natural centre for the densely populated south-east region and it was important that the Met should take a lead in this development. Much good work had been done by C.11 Criminal Intelligence Branch, but the conviction and disciplining of one or two of its members, or ex-members, in the course of the Humphreys inquiry had caused some of our provincial colleagues to have misgivings. Also, our recent Drugs Squad troubles had exacerbated the old 'give a dog a bad name' syndrome, providing fertile ground for gossip and innuendo which needed to be counteracted.

At this time the Metropolitan Police was inviting chief superintendents from other forces to apply for vacancies in the rank of commander. Detective Chief Superintendent Ronald Harvey of Hertfordshire Constabulary was well known to me and to most senior CID officers. He had been working closely with Commander Bert Wickstead and A.10 Branch in a complex murder inquiry, he enjoyed the highest reputation and seemed an ideal candidate. I discussed him with the Commissioner, pointing out his excellent professional qualities and how I thought he was well suited to take over our Criminal Intelligence Branch from my colleague of the early days of the Humphreys inquiry, Commander Arthur Howard, whom I wanted to take charge of C.1 Branch and its various specialist squads.

Ronald Harvey responded to the advertisement, was accepted and appointed as the commander of C.11 Branch where his reputation and ability soon quelled any rumours and restored confidence between the Met and other police forces. He went on to give sterling service in modernizing our criminal intelligence systems in close co-operation with police forces of the south-east region who seconded detectives to work with C.11 Branch. Before he left to spend the last three years of his service seconded as an assistant to Her Majesty's Chief Inspector of Constabulary, he had also helped to develop a larger and better trained surveillance unit which the central specialist squads increasingly relied upon to play a key role in their operations.

There were one or two detectives holding fairly senior

rank whose reputations did not commend them and whom I felt the CID could well do without. One, some years earlier when he was a sergeant, had gone on holiday to Ireland with Bernie Silver and his White Horse public house licensee friend, but despite this had become a detective superintendent on the Flying Squad. The Commissioner, hearing about the man's history, had transferred him from this key post. He was later insubordinate to his detective chief superintendent and I arranged for him to be transferred to a uniformed post in south London where he could be more easily supervised. Almost immediately afterwards a detective handling a cheque fraud case reported that this superintendent wanted to meet him in a Fleet Street pub to discuss helping to get a man that the detective had arrested off the cheque fraud charge. Commander John Cass, head of the Complaints Investigation Bureau, briefed the detective to keep the appointment and arranged for him to be fitted with a radio microphone. At the meeting, after attempting to corrupt the detective by offering him a bribe, the superintendent became suspicious and, putting his arm around the officer, felt the concealed radio microphone. A struggle began as he tried to get hold of it, which was stopped when Commander Cass intervened and arrested him. The superintendent was subsequently convicted of attempted bribery and sentenced to imprisonment.

At about the same time, another detective on my short list, a superintendent, was trapped by Commander Cass for conspiring with and directing two of his constables to attempt the blackmail of the wife of Adnam Khashoggi, the millionaire international arms dealer, over an insurance claim she had made about jewellery she said had been lost in air transit but subsequently found. This was a difficult case as far as the senior detective was concerned because he was keeping in the background and operating through the two constables. John Cass involved himself personally in this case and persuaded Mrs Kashoggi to go to Heathrow police station and to insist on seeing the detective superintendent. She gave him a prepared note which, if he did not report having received it, would clearly mean he was involved in the conspiracy. As we anticipated, he did not report the matter and he was later arrested with the two constables. All three were subsequently charged, convicted and jailed.

Commander Cass was a career CID officer and had served with me in the East End as a detective chief inspector in the 1960s. It is a measure of his quality, and that of others like him, that despite the corruption malaise they retained the confidence of the force to the extent that all the commanders of the Complaints Investigation Bureau with the exception of the first one, Raymond Anning, have been career CID officers.

After this preliminary reorganization I set out to ensure that in the important and sensitive West End district there would be harmony and effective team work between the CID and their colleagues in uniform. A keen and intelligent detective with a good reputation to take charge of the CID at the 'C' or St James's District was essential to the strategy. Detective Chief Superintendent William Hucklesby – who became well known as the Commander of the Anti-Terrorist Branch and whom I had first met as a detective sergeant at Commercial Street in the East End – was transferred from Croydon and did a superb job.

To make certain there was no doubt about the policy in the West End, I had an entry made in the Assistant

Commissioner 'C' Department's Confidential Instructions naming the White Horse public house and the landlord, ex-Detective Sergeant Sandison. This effectively put the public house, which had been the hub of the Silver vice syndicate for many years, out of bounds. Although the Instructions are confidential, a copy was held at every police station, and I was quite sure that Sandison and his Soho friends would get to know about it – that was part of the plan. To reinforce this message, the commander of 'C' District, then Colin Hewett who was later to become the DAC of Special Branch and is now the co-ordinator of the newly formed National Drugs Intelligence Unit, insisted that any of his personnel who had any dealings with the pub or its landlord must immediately report the fact. We were no longer prepared to accept the time-worn excuse that it was necessary to socialize with such Soho characters to get information.

The AC 'C's Confidential Instructions were a bone of contention with certain London solicitors who complained that they were listed as persons to be dealt with warily. The policy had always been to refuse to confirm, deny or discuss with complainants the contents of an internal confidential document, but this, of course, caused the parties concerned much frustration and resulted in a lot of unnecessary correspondence. After consulting with the head of our legal department, I decided that, as all solicitors were entitled to their legal rights and that the few with dubious reputations would be known to the local officers anyway, the Confidential Instructions list would be cancelled. This put a stop to an outdated practice which ran the risk of being abused and harming our relations with the legal profession.

In these early days when it was accepted that some

changes were inevitable it was vital to have active supporters in certain key positions. A vacancy occurred for a detective chief superintendent as second in command of the Flying Squad, and Detective Chief Superintendent Jim Sewell from Kingston, an outstanding investigating officer, was transferred to fill this post. Although he had never served on the Flying Squad before, I knew Jim as a strong character and a good leader. He eventually commanded the squad and led it well before being promoted as DAC in charge of the Complaints Investigation Bureau, from which post he retired in 1984 to take up a commercial appointment.

Another matter of great importance at this time was the preparation of evidence for the Lord Edmund Davies Committee of Inquiry. This Committee had been set up by the Home Secretary, Merlyn Rees, because of continuous pressure by the Police Federation of England and Wales about their pay, which they claimed was the reason why police forces were continuously under strength, the Met by some 5,000 officers. The ultimate result was a substantial increase in pay and an agreement on a formula for the future, including for the first time a realistic differential for London (£1,000 per annum), which not only eliminated premature retirements but raised morale and attracted an adequate number of well-qualified recruits.

In the late autumn of 1977, when a number of transfers of senior detectives had taken place – some of them of strategic and symbolic importance, others of a routine nature – and I had just returned from my first Interpol World Assembly held in Stockholm, I was a guest at the Fleet Street Crime Writers Association annual dinner. In the bar after dinner I was berated by a reporter, who perhaps had been imbibing a bit too freely, who accused me of moving detectives around so much that no one knew where they could be found. I listened to him patiently and then told him that, as I did not propose to tell him how to run his newspaper, I did not see why he should tell me how to do my job. The language on both sides was a little more colourful than this implies, but the message was given and received and we remained on good terms afterwards.

Throughout this early period and, indeed, throughout his period of office, I received the full support and encouragement of the Commissioner. Having been himself an operational detective in Glasgow for some sixteen years, he often asked searching and detailed questions about particular operational inquiries. Not only did this keep him well informed but it sharpened my reflexes and ensured that I kept myself well briefed by my senior departmental officers.

David McNee and my police colleagues on the Policy Committee were agreed that in the interests of building a more corporate identity and in developing the potential of senior officers we needed more interchange between 'A' and 'C' Departments. Within the year, eight of the twenty-four territorial districts had detective chief superintendents in post who had been specially selected and transferred from uniform duties. At the same time some senior CID officers had also been selected and given uniformed posts as divisional and district commanders. The Commissioner also directed that all personnel attached to a division, both uniformed and CID, would be answerable directly to their divisional chief superintendent. These changes, after a few initial teething problems, brought about an improved team spirit and greater accountability.

Another organizational change decided upon by David

McNee was to give the four area DACs operational responsibility for their areas and to discontinue their inspectorial role. The Inspectorate of the Force was reorganized with DAC Ray Anning, who was my deputy, becoming the Inspector of the Force. David Powis became my deputy and Ron Steventon, then commander of the Complaints Investigation Bureau, was promoted and joined me in 'C' Department. To complete the changes in the CID hierarchy Sam Leckie moved from training to DAC (Technical Support) and a little later on, when Bob Bryan the head of Special Branch retired, DAC Colin Hewett, who had never previously served in this branch, took his place.

I felt that I had an excellent team at the top whose positive leadership, coupled with the organizational and senior operational command changes, would give 'C' Department the impetus to tackle the problems facing us. Organized and violent crime – particularly armed robbery – was increasing, the drug menace was growing and terrorist activity was an ever-present threat: quite a daunting list. My priorities were to encourage flexibility and co-operation in order to make the most efficient use of manpower, which was unlikely to increase, and to develop intelligence and surveillance capabilities, the factors likely to make the biggest impact on combating serious crime. In the remaining chapters I will attempt to paint a picture of the specialist operations we directed from the Yard to deal with particular categories of criminal activity.

11
Drugs — Danger and Death

One of the most disturbing developments of the last decade has been the gradual escalation in drugs trafficking and the misuse of dangerous drugs with all the consequent social and medical problems. Back in the 1960s the most frequent drug abuse involved amphetamine preparations commonly referred to as 'pep pills' and, for the first time, the regular illegal possession and use of cannabis. These are the so-called soft drugs, harmful, but less dangerous than the more lethal heroin and cocaine.

At that time the main problems from heroin arose from over prescribing by a small number of London doctors for private patients, some of whom sold their surplus supplies and so created additional addicts. However, the total number of addicts remained comparatively small until the late 1970s when there was a rapid growth in their ranks.

The Dangerous Drugs Act, 1967, which came into force in 1968, restricted doctors from supplying heroin or cocaine and required them to notify the Home Office of any addicts, who then became officially registered. At the same time drug addiction clinics were introduced where the addicts could seek and receive treatment. As the restrictions on pharmaceutical heroin took effect so increased illicit supplies of the drug began to be smuggled into the country. Initially, scientific analysis identified Chinese heroin from Hong Kong as the most common type in circulation, but effective action there virtually eliminated its manufacture and this supply dried up. Since then the source, in ever increasing quantities, has shifted from Thailand – the Golden Triangle – to Iran and Pakistan.

For some years the major portion of the resources of Interpol has been allocated to the Drugs Division for its work in helping member countries to combat drug trafficking. In September 1973 the Home Office and the police service, recognizing the growing problem in Britain and realizing that good intelligence was vital to successful investigation, set up the Central Drugs and Illegal Immigrants Intelligence Unit (CDIIIU). At this time there was some large-scale illegal immigration, with people from the Asian sub-continent being brought to Europe and then smuggled across the Channel to land on south-coast beaches. This activity was short-lived and, contrary to the original perception, there was no direct evidence of a link between illegal immigration and the importation of drugs. Consequently the small number of staff employed on immigration matters was gradually absorbed into the drugs section and by the 1980s the unit had become solely a drugs intelligence agency. The CDIIIU, headed by a Met detective chief superintendent and staffed by detectives from all UK police forces – although Scotland later withdrew – was paid for from the Central Services Fund and answerable to a steering committee of representatives from the Home Office, the Association of Chief Police Officers and HM Customs and Excise. As AC (Crime) I was a member of the steering committee, responsible to them for the operational functioning of the unit whose efficiency, shortly after I took up this post, was much improved by the computerization of all recorded intelligence.[1]

[1] In November 1985 the Home Secretary, Leon Brittan, announced in Parliament that the unit was now the National Drugs Intelligence Unit, with DAC Colin Hewett moving from the position of head of the

Unfortunately, in 1978, because of rumours linking it with the recent recycling of cannabis by members of the Yard's Drugs Squad, the Central Drugs Intelligence Unit was not enjoying the full confidence of provincial detectives. I was told that these unjustified rumours were being connected with earlier suspicions about the role in a drugs intelligence matter of ex-Detective Inspector Charles O'Hanlon, one of those recently jailed for corrupt associations with Soho pornographers.

The background to this was that in February 1974, after being taken off the old Obscene Publications Squad, O'Hanlon had, on promotion to detective inspector, been posted to the C.1 Drugs Squad. In April, with a colleague from the CDIU, he had been to Canada to interview a man there who was willing to give information about drug trafficking in the United Kingdom but, only four days after his return, he was interviewed by me about his association with the pornographer Gerald Citron and suspended from duty. The man in Canada had given information, including the names of the four principals, about a syndicate manufacturing the drug LSD. Apparently this intelligence was not acted on, perhaps because of embarrassment about O'Hanlon's suspension, but it was supplied about two years later from the unit's records to a detective inspector from the Thames Valley force who was following up arrests at a Reading pop festival for possession of LSD and sought the unit's help.

As the result of this officer's inquiries 'Operation Julie',

Met's Special Branch to become the national co-ordinator with the status of a senior chief constable. He could not be given the rank of assistant commissioner because the Metropolitan Police Acts of 1856 and 1933 only authorize the appointment of the existing five officers holding this rank.

a brilliant investigation lasting over eighteen months, had been concluded in March 1978 with the conviction of nineteen people for conspiracy and the illegal manufacture of LSD. The operation had uncovered illicit laboratories in a remote cottage in mid-Wales and in a house in a London suburb, Hampton Wick, where it was estimated enough of the drug for about six million tablets had been produced. Because of the suspicions about some of the detectives working in it the CDIU had been kept rather at arm's length.

My initial inquiries produced nothing to suggest to me that there was any justification for suspecting the integrity of the unit. However, it was essential for its efficiency to make sure of the position and then to attempt to dispel the rumours and suspicions. To find out if there was any evidence of improper conduct in connection with Operation Julie I spoke to my ACPO colleagues who had been responsible for supervising the operation, Assistant Chief Constables Bob Smith of Thames Valley, Leslie Pearce of Avon and Somerset and Harry Hull of Wiltshire. They all assured me, as did the Home Office, that they had received no complaints at all about the CDIIIU. These inquiries, and discussion of the matter at the unit's steering committee, cleared the air and confidence began to improve. The unit was now led by Detective Chief Superintendent Algy Hemmingway, a man with an excellent reputation, and what was needed to set the seal of approval on it was a successful major operation initiated by their intelligence.

Such an operation, code-named 'Operation Cyril', was launched in October 1978 when Interpol in Paris passed us information received from Portugal that a yacht converted from a fishing vessel, registered at Fraserburgh and named *Guiding Lights*, might be used to smuggle drugs or arms. A search of CDIU records disclosed that two crew members named Goodship and McHugh had been arrested in 1976 for possessing twenty pounds of cannabis resin. The trail got considerably warmer in November when a 'supergrass' in police custody gave some information about a London-based syndicate importing cannabis and distributing it through a national network. In March 1979 another informant gave details of a bank account in the City of London into which the proceeds of drug sales amounting to £3,500,000 had been paid, and he said the head of the syndicate was named 'Ron'.

Further inquiries were made and in May members of C.11 surveillance section joined the team of detectives from the CDIU and the Central Drugs Squad. 'Ron' was identified as Ronald Taylor, and he was seen to arrive at a bank in his Rolls-Royce accompanied by his henchman, a one-legged ex-jockey named James Thomas Jones, and pay in large sums of money – on one occasion £100,000. Patient surveillance led to the identification of five more members of the syndicate including Robert Mills, suspected for some years of being involved in drug smuggling, who drove a Mercedes registered in the name of his common-law wife and who, with Ron Taylor, seemed to be in control. We learned that the gang had purchased pick-up trucks and a Land Rover, using false names and addresses, to carry drugs from Cornwall to London.

Suddenly the smugglers sold the vehicles. We believed they might have done this because they thought they were under surveillance and we stopped all observations for three weeks. We later learned that the decision was a wise one, because the syndicate kept careful watch during the next few weeks and as nothing aroused their suspicions they convinced themselves they had over-reacted. They then continued their activities using hired vehicles.

The policy of hiring vehicles brought the investigators a lucky break. In August Taylor was overheard talking about one of his team having an accident in Fulham and not being able to stop because he was carrying a load of drugs, but that all was well because the accident had been reported at Brixton after the load had been delivered. The accident report was checked and showed that the driver had given a false name and address, but inquiry at the hire company revealed that he had given his address as Chapel Cottage, Pelynt, Cornwall. Operation Cyril officers – including members of the Customs and Excise who had joined the team – visited Pelynt and found that 'Chapel Cottage' was derelict. They made discreet local inquiries and quickly discovered that the owner was Roderick Eagleton of Rotterdam Cottage in Talland Bay. Eagleton was known to the CDIU as an associate of Trevor Goodship, a crew member of the yacht *Guiding Lights*.

Talland Bay is on the south coast of Cornwall between Looe and Polperro, a coastline renowned for smuggling. Rotterdam Cottage was almost at the water's edge and a short distance away on the other side of the cove was the Talland Bay Café which was kept by Eagleton. We were later to discover that under the floor of the café kitchen he had constructed a smuggler's hide in which to conceal illegal drugs.

Early in September, about a year after the receipt of the original intelligence from Interpol, information was received that a boatload of cannabis was expected. Taylor was followed to a store at Penge, and since it seemed likely that this was used for drugs, a video camera was set up there to monitor the premises. This proved most useful because Taylor was filmed loading cannabis from the store into a van. In another surveillance operation three men, including Trevor Goodship, were seen meeting at Heathrow airport and joining a flight to Faro in Portugal.

I agreed that a detective inspector should go to Portugal immediately to find the mooring of *Guiding Lights*, to watch the vessel leaving port and then telephone the information back. On Saturday, 8 September, the vessel was located at Vilamoura and at 10 P.M. it left the harbour. The CDIU at Scotland Yard was alerted and a prepared plan went into operation. About forty men from the Drugs Squad, the CDIU, C.11 Surveillance Unit and HM Customs and Excise under the command of Detective Chief Superintendent John Smith were briefed to travel to Cornwall to await the arrival of *Guiding Lights* at Talland Bay. The Customs officers estimated that the vessel's journey would take about a week.

Two detectives engaged on the operation were caravan owners and they took their caravans to Talland Bay where they were used as observation posts without causing suspicion. Others booked into local hotels as fishing parties, and a local resident very public-spiritedly gave tremendous co-operation by allowing his bungalow, which overlooked Talland Bay, to be used as the main base for our radio and telephone communications. In various parts of the country where members of the drug syndicate had been located detectives were on standby in readiness to make arrests and search a number of addresses as soon as the word was given, and a surveillance team was maintaining observation on Taylor and his close associates. At sea the Customs revenue cutters *Vigilant* and *Swift* were taking up position and at midnight on 16 September they were about twenty-four miles off shore from Talland Bay.

On Sunday, 16 September, Ron Taylor and a man

named Lake travelled by rail from Paddington to Plymouth where they were met by Eagleton and another man driving a Land Rover. Taylor was very wary so no attempt was made to follow him and his companions when they drove off in the Land Rover, which was just as well because, from static observation points, they were seen on several occasions to stop and double back on their route.

It was 2.30 A.M. on Monday, 17 September, when *Guiding Lights* sailed into the trap and dropped anchor about half a mile off shore in Talland Bay, showing normal navigation lights. The only sound that broke the silence of the night was the noisy outboard motors of the inflatable belonging to the smugglers leaving the shore and of another motor boat coming from *Guiding Lights.* It took about two and a half hours for the cargo of cannabis to be brought ashore and then *Guiding Lights* weighed anchor and headed out to sea.

At about 5.30 A.M. the investigating officers, who were in position all around Rotterdam Cottage and the café, moved in, arresting Taylor, Eagleton, Lake and Timmins, seizing two and a half tons of cannabis resin in Christmas wrapping paper and £4,000 in cash. The street value of this consignment of drugs was, at that time, about £2,250,000. At sea the Customs revenue cutters led by the *Vigilant* closed in on *Guiding Lights*, then officers boarded the yacht and escorted her to Plymouth. It was established that since 1974 she had made over twenty runs, carrying cannabis between Morocco and the UK without at any time putting into port while she had drugs on board.

When the news came of the success of the operation at Talland Bay, police and Customs officers who had been standing by in London and elsewhere moved in on the other suspects. Some twenty-five addresses were searched and eight men arrested. Eventually, on 19 September at Rochester Row police station, sixteen people were charged with conspiracy to contravene the Misuse of Drugs Act, 1971, and they appeared in court the following day. However, so complex were the international ramifications of this syndicate, necessitating inquiries in Gibraltar, Switzerland, Portugal, France and Ireland, that over a year elapsed before the defendants were committed for trial.

Inquiries at banks under the Bankers' Books Evidence Act revealed that over £3½ million had been transferred from the account held by Taylor in Gracechurch Street to the Gallionos Bank in Gibraltar. The manager of the bank, a Mr Ambrose Vinalies, and a man named Edward Victory were both extradited and subsequently convicted for their part in the conspiracy. Vinalies's role was to finance Victory, who had a local reputation as a smuggler and negotiated purchases of drugs in Morocco. He then arranged for an Arab dhow to transport his cargo to a point off Cape Spartel, near Tangier, where the rendezvous with *Guiding Lights* took place.

After his arrest in Cornwall, Ronald Taylor and his associates were brought to London. Taylor was taken to his home, Little Siggers at Eastcote in Middlesex, where it was known that he had a safe, so that the house could be searched. At some stage Detective Chief Superintendent John Smith asked him what was in the safe, and Taylor replied, 'Oh, about a quarter of a million,' adding *sotto voce*, 'You can have it if you like!' As the detective chief superintendent did not reply, he did not pursue this thinly veiled hint at bribery. From the safe some £250,000 in bank notes was seized and a set of keys was found which proved to be for the garage store at Penge. Taylor was taken to this store and when the doors were unlocked another two tons of cannabis resin were found.

After one of the main conspirators, Taylor's partner Robert Mills, was arrested it was discovered that he had three different bank accounts into which large amounts of cash had regularly been paid. He described himself as a bookmaker and he was certainly a heavy betting man for an account with a well-known turf accountant showed that in the two years from August 1977 to September 1979, he had lost over £90,000.

In the late afternoon of Monday, 17 September, I had the pleasure of holding a short joint press conference at the Yard with Peter Cutting, Chief Investigation Officer of HM Customs and Excise, to announce the success of Operation Cyril. Afterwards we were able to congratulate personally the investigation team on their outstanding work and I sent a letter to thank the owners of the bungalow for their marvellous co-operation in allowing their home to be used as the local operational base.

It is necessary in the interests of good morale for senior officers to defend their men when they are unfairly attacked, particularly when the attack is on their integrity. Just before Operation Cyril hit the headlines there had been two 'knocking' articles in the press. One in a London evening paper headed 'How top drug crooks keep out of jail' suggested there was dissension on tactics between the Yard's Central Drugs Squad and Customs investigators and said that unnamed Drugs Squad men felt it wrong that they should be pulling in different directions. This article, in my view, was not only erroneous but, especially at this particular time, positively mischievous. The second press story, in a national Sunday newspaper, alleged that the West Country 'Julie' drug syndicate had successfully bribed London officers to avoid arrest. I issued correcting statements but because these statements were not regarded as news, they were not printed.

I decided therefore to use the Met's own newspaper, *The Job*, as the defence medium. This fortnightly paper is widely circulated throughout London, it reaches many police forces at home and overseas and it is read in Fleet Street. The following is an extract from the article which was published there:

Mr Kelland said: 'I think the majority of newspapers give us a very fair deal, but there is a minority which does not always do so. We do have a Press Bureau information service, and if the reporters took the trouble to check their facts with the Bureau these misreportings would not occur. Understandably, because our statements were not regarded as news they were not printed but I consider that through *The Job* the officers of our Force should be able to learn the facts.'

One of the articles to which Mr Kelland referred suggested that a lack of co-operation between the Force and the Customs and Excise allowed drug traffickers to 'go free'.

Mr Kelland issued a statement – with which Mr Peter Cutting, Chief Investigating Officer of HM Customs, associated himself – pointing out that 'All parties are agreed that co-operation has never been better.'

At the same time the Central Drugs Squad, led by Detective Chief Superintendent John Smith, were poised to launch 'Operation Cyril', a joint operation with the Customs which succeeded after four months of liaison.

Mr Kelland said: 'At no time has any allegation been received that the "Julie" drugs syndicate bribed any members of any police force. Additionally no comment or complaint of any kind has been received by the Metropolitan Police from any senior officer concerned in the "Julie" operation suggesting or indicating in any way that the persons arrested in this operation had bribed or even been in contact with Metropolitan Police officers.

'The newspaper concerned still maintains that its informant, or informants, who wish to remain anonymous, insist that New Scotland Yard was informed about corruption. What the reporter did not tell his readers was that he had spoken to senior police officers in West Country Forces – who are prepared to be named and who had responsibility for the "Julie" operation – who told him they could not confirm his report about alleged corruption. The Chief Investigating Officer of the Customs Service also communicated with the newspaper telling them there was nothing in their records about corrupt police officers in connection with "Julie".

'On these facts one would suppose that the balance of evidence was against the alleged anonymous informants but perhaps that is another story.'

The Job's article was widely discussed in police circles and I understand it did not pass unnoticed in Fleet Street, for in the aftermath of the publicity about Operation Cyril the general public reaction was favourable.

In September 1981, when fourteen men appeared at the Old Bailey, prosecuting counsel, whose opening speech lasted three days, told the court that between 1975 and 1979 the gang had made an estimated £40 million by drug smuggling. The trial lasted two months and all but one defendant, Roger Howton, were convicted. Judge Richard Lowery sentenced the gang to terms of imprisonment varying between ten years and eighteen months, and imposed fines totalling £675,000. He commented, however, on the fact that he had no powers to take money from any of the defendants' bank accounts, remarking that Parliament had not contemplated a case on this scale when the various statutes were enacted.

Ronald Taylor, one of the principal members of the syndicate, was given bail despite strong police objections and, as we feared, he disappeared and failed to stand trial. This man, who was probably a millionaire, had a penchant for expensive motor cars, especially Rolls-Royces and Jaguars, the makes of the two cars owned by him and seized by police when he was arrested. Although he had been disqualified from driving for twenty years in 1962 for causing two deaths by dangerous driving, Taylor had continued to drive by adopting the name Ronald Turner and obtaining a licence by deception in that name. He was heard of in Spain but could not be extradited because the United Kingdom did not have an extradition treaty with that country. That situation has now been rectified but the legislation is not retrospective.

It seems that Taylor took a chance and returned to the United Kingdom some time in 1985, for in September 1985 he was arrested in the West End for a major offence and he gave the name of Gargan. When the fingerprints taken from him arrived at the National Identification Bureau at the Yard his identity as Ronald Taylor was established. In June 1986 he pleaded guilty at the Old Bailey to the Operation Cyril charges and was sentenced to six and a half years' imprisonment plus a fine of £243,400, which was the amount of the money seized by the police when he was arrested.

There was yet another twist in the prosecution of the Operation Cyril drug smuggling syndicate which illustrates the dangers to which detectives employed on this type of work are exposed. In late March 1980 a City of London detective constable reported that a former colleague of his, Keith Parfitt, then a restaurateur at Crystal Palace, had asked him to get the home addresses of two members of the Met Drug Squad. Parfitt said that people he knew had been arrested by the Drug Squad and they wanted to get something on the two detectives before their trial. He added that the men who wanted the addresses had unlimited supplies of money and would pay well.

The City of London detective was introduced to Detective Chief Superintendent John Hoddinott, whom I had selected to replace John Smith when he had completed his stint as leader of the Drugs Squad, and Detective Chief Inspector Colin Coxall. Acting under their instructions he convinced his former colleague he was willing to do what was asked. Eventually the investigators identified Roger Howton, on bail awaiting trial, as Parfitt's wealthy contact. The address of an unoccupied flat owned by the Metropolitan Police was supplied to Parfitt and he was told that the detective who was supposed to be living there was on holiday. He gave the City of London officer £300 for this information and urged him to steal some documents relating to the drugs case from the Drugs Squad office at the Yard. Forensic examination of the bank notes revealed Howton's fingerprints on some of them.

A watch was maintained on the unoccupied police flat and a few days after the £300 had been paid two men were arrested while attempting to break into it. They were closely questioned, but there was no evidence to link them with the Howton/Parfitt conspiracy, and they were charged and dealt with in the normal way for the attempted burglary. Their interrogation, however, made it essential to move quickly against Howton and Parfitt and both were arrested while the burglars were still in police custody.

Parfitt, faced with a recording of his conversations with his former City of London detective colleague, made a statement under caution, confessing all and implicating Howton. Both men were charged with conspiracy to pervert the course of justice and with conspiracy to steal documents from Scotland Yard. Their trial took place after the Operation Cyril prosecution, at which Howton was the only defendant acquitted. At the second trial he was found guilty and sentenced to two years' imprisonment, while his co-defendant, Parfitt, was jailed for eighteen months.

Operation Cyril put the seal on a new era of Scotland Yard/Customs and Excise relationships and also gave the CDIU a great deal of national and international kudos. The cost in manpower and other resources of such an operation and prosecution is enormous and it was, to say the least, disappointing for everyone concerned to see a professional drug trafficker like Taylor escape from justice by jumping bail, even though he was rearrested later. This sense of disappointment was not improved when Robert Mills, who was probably the mastermind of the syndicate, after serving two of his ten years' sentence, escaped from a prison working party and vanished.

The success of Operation Cyril and the subsequent inquiries is an example of what can be achieved in a major international drug investigation by dedicated and experienced investigators as members of a multi-agency team. The value of police/Customs co-operation is self-evident, as is the fact that this can only be effective when absolute mutual confidence exists. Both Peter Cutting, who was Chief Investigating Officer of the Customs and Excise during my tenure of office as AC (Crime), and I shared this view and made it a major priority of our respective organizations. It is sometimes argued that it would be more efficient for a single agency to investigate drug offences and in theory a case can be made out for this. In practice, bearing in mind the constitutional position of forty-three autonomous police forces in England and Wales, and the Customs and Excise as a national agency with different terms of reference, especially regarding smuggling, there is much to be said for our present system. The dual responsibility provides a useful element of protection for both agencies, for inevitably they monitor each other's conduct in the course of drug investigation activities. In fact, in this dangerous area it goes some way towards answering Juvenal's perennial question, '*Quis custodiet ipsos custodes*?' I am also mindful of a discussion I had with John Warner, a very experienced drug investigator who was for many years the European Regional Director for the USA Drugs Enforcement Agency, when he said, 'Your system works and suits the British constitution. Reinforce it if necessary, but don't interfere with the structure and go down the road of a single federal agency.' However, there is the point that police/Customs co-operation might be easier and more effectively co-ordinated if both services were answerable to one government department instead of at present to the Home Office and Treasury respectively.

Although there is an established market and large profits to be made from the illegal smuggling of cannabis, which has attracted the attention of some of London's professional criminals, it was, and is, the trafficking in hard drugs, especially heroin and cocaine, which gives society the greatest cause for concern. Unlike cannabis, where the sheer bulk presents problems to the trafficker, heroin and cocaine even in minute quantities represent vast sums of money. A kilo of heroin purchased on the North Pakistan/Afghanistan border in 1984 cost about £3,000 to £4,000, and in London it would have had a street value of £750 an ounce. Major traffickers paid their couriers about £3,000 for taking the risk of smuggling heroin into European countries, which still left them with a very fat profit margin. Prices will, of course, fluctuate according to the supply and demand position, and one school of thought infers that a decrease in price indicates increasing amounts of heroin available. However, it might also be argued that it shows that there is a limited market for the drug. Certainly the purity of the heroin seized in this country compared with that in the USA implies that the dealers and pushers here – unlike their American counterparts – do not 'cut' or adulterate the drug to make it go further and increase their profits.

A common method of smuggling is for the courier to swallow rubber contraceptive sheaths, filled with heroin or cocaine which can be recovered when they pass out through the bowel. There have been one or two tragic accidents where the courier has died when a sheath filled with drugs has burst inside his stomach.

The difficulty of reducing the hard drug problem by elimination at source was brought home to me in 1980 when I went to a South-East Asia Drugs Conference at Chaing Mai in Thailand with other European Interpol delegates, jointly chairing the Conference with Major General Chavalit Yodmani of the Royal Thailand Police. During the course of the conference we were taken by helicopter to the area known as the Golden Triangle to see crop replacement programmes near the Thailand boundary with Laos and Burma.

The hill-tribe farmers in this area have for many years grown the opium poppy as a cash crop financed by lowland middlemen who lend them money for seed. Quite aside from any economic motivation, opium production is a part of their traditional culture and opium is frequently used amongst these hill tribes as an analgesic and as a remedy for a variety of illnesses. They have little conception of the suffering that opium causes after it is converted to morphine or heroin.

It takes about ten kilos of opium to make one kilo of heroin and quite apart from the replacement crop programme, largely financed by United Nations grants, the Thais had given priority to destroying the primitive laboratories used to produce heroin. This had resulted in the drug producers moving over the border into Burma and continuing the manufacturing process there. The Thailand authorities who had organized our visit were, therefore, delighted that the Burmese ambassador to their country had accepted an invitation and was a member of our party.

The alternative crops included coffee, potatoes, peaches and apples, and they had raised the economic standards of the hill tribes, which was a very real inducement to them to give up growing the opium poppy or, at least, to reduce the amount grown. But the remoteness of the region and the difficult terrain, with most parts only accessible by helicopter and mule, and only a very few by four-wheel-drive vehicles, were obstacles both to economic development and to the enforcement of laws about opium quotas. The resident United Nations representative, a much respected and dedicated American, pointed out that in addition to teaching the hill tribesmen new farming skills it was necessary to organize a market infrastructure for them to ensure that they were able to sell their new crops at a fair price. Despite all the difficulties, though, there was some optimism about the progress that was being made.

The Thai authorities and the UN representative were also concerned with the social consequences – not unknown in the Western world – where better communications and educational facilities for the hill people meant that young members were leaving their villages and swelling the slum populations of big cities like Bangkok. While we from the Western world were naturally interested in the elimination of the source of heroin, the Thais, understandably, were trying to set up an integrated highland development programme which would be beneficial to a whole section of their population.

The main source of heroin in the past few years has been Pakistan. Clearly agricultural crop replacement programmes are not a viable proposition in the tribal regions of north Pakistan around the Khyber Pass, where it is estimated the local population is swollen by some three million refugees from Afghanistan. The fact that this is a troubled, remote area where the tribesmen carry arms makes it difficult for the Pakistan government to exercise its authority.

Genuine international co-operation between law enforcement agencies and carefully monitored economic assistance are both essential in the fight against the menace of drug abuse. Perhaps more expenditure on practical help and fewer United Nations conferences, with the usual platitudinous resolutions expressing concern, would be helpful. However, I suspect the latter ritual is a necessary concomitant to achieving the former.

Early in 1984 HM Customs and Excise agreed to establish a resident agent in Pakistan to liaise with the authorities there and co-ordinate drugs intelligence. At the same time, at the instigation of the Home Secretary, I visited Holland and made arrangements with the British ambassador for the first-ever overseas posting of a Metropolitan detective as a member of the staff of a British embassy, with the status of legal attaché. Amsterdam had become very much a European centre for drug trafficking and both the USA and Sweden already had liaison officers working there with the Dutch equivalent to our CDIU. The role of our officer was to liaise with the national intelligence agency, the police and the Customs authorities, as well as with the representatives of the other countries accredited to The Hague, and report to the CDIU intelligence gathered about drug trafficking that involved the United Kingdom and British subjects. This initiative was welcomed by the Dutch authorities and a selected detective chief inspector from the CDIU was soon established at The Hague.

The most important recent development to combat drug abuse, the Drug Traffic Offences Bill, will probably be passed by Parliament in 1986. For the first time this legislation confers powers and obligations on Crown Courts, after a conviction, to order the confiscation of the proceeds of the drug trafficking as well as authority to restrain a defendant from disposing of property and assets before the trial ends. The Bill lays down that on conviction the court assumes that the whole of the offender's property, together with any assets passing through his hands during the past five years, represents the proceeds of his drug trafficking. The onus of proof in connection with a confiscatory order, therefore, shifts from the prosecution to the defence – a reversal of the normal rule of law – and the offender will have to prove which of his assets were lawfully acquired. It is proposed that the Crown Courts will be obliged to impose a monetary fine up to the total proceeds of the crime and that the maximum penalty for an offence under the Act should be fourteen years' imprisonment.

Couriers and dealers will no doubt be caught, but the Mr Bigs of the drug trafficking world, who may well live outside the jurisdiction of our courts, will take good care that their financial sources are well hidden. The new legislation will be very welcome, but if it is to work efficiently more international co-operation and considerably increased police and Customs resources will be needed.

When all is said and done, though, enforcement of the law, important though it is, will not alone solve the drug problem. The long-term aim of all governments must be to eliminate the market by educating people – particularly the young – about the dangers of drug abuse.

12
The Flying Squad and Robbery

In 1977, nearly a century after its formation with a strength of about 250 men, the Yard's CID had grown to a total of 3,500 male and female detectives, as well as a civilian support staff of 1,500. Although this is a formidable number – larger than the total establishment of all but four of the other police forces – expressed as a percentage of the total establishment of the Met in 1984 the CID amounted to 12.9 per cent. This placed the CID complement of the force thirtieth in the league table of the forty-three police forces in England and Wales. It is interesting that at the top of the table, with totals respectively of 25.5 per cent and 23.4 per cent, were Thames Valley and Greater Manchester, while at the bottom were two rural counties, Cumbria and Hertfordshire with 10 per cent and 8.1 per cent.

There were thirteen separate detective branches at New Scotland Yard,[1] and the best known, by its popular title of the Flying Squad, was C.8 Branch. The squad was formed in 1918 just after the end of the First World War. Twelve divisional detectives were called from their police stations to the Yard and told they were to become a mobile team of detectives with authority to operate anywhere in London to deal with the immediate post-war crime wave. Their transport was a covered wagon hired from the Great Western Railway, but the following year their mobility was much improved when they were provided with two ex-Royal Flying Corps Crossley motor

[1] See Appendix II.

tenders capable of a top speed of 40 mph. They were dubbed the Flying Squad after an article in the *Daily Mail* in September 1920 by a crime reporter named W. G. T. Crook, who referred to them as 'a flying squad of picked detectives'. As criminals in London became more mobile and organized, the Flying Squad was increased and by the middle 1970s it had grown to over one hundred men, all based at the Yard.

Over the years the squad and its exploits had received much publicity from crime reporters and from novelists and television producers. Their glamorous image and general free-ranging role did not, in the late 1970s, particularly endear them to their colleagues at police stations, who were all carrying heavy individual case loads. In addition, the early retirement of their former commander, Kenneth Drury, followed by his arrest and conviction for corruption in 1977 as a result of his relation ship with the notorious Jimmy Humphreys – coming on top of *The Times* inquiry convictions – had been a blow for the Flying Squad. The new Commissioner had the future of this long-standing crime-fighting unit very much under scrutiny.

When he took command of the Met, David McNee had discussions with his assistant commissioners on various policy matters. A decision was taken that as the force was some 5,000 officers under strength – all in the rank of constable – there would be no increases in manpower for the CID. The thin blue line had to be strengthened, and the emphasis was to be on getting more policemen on the street. The Commissioner also decided against a scheme, first recommended by PA Management Consultants in 1967, to reorganize the Met from the existing four to eight geographical areas. This would have included the decentralization of some of the Yard's operational functions, and one option involved the breaking up of the Flying Squad. David McNee took the view that the considerable upheaval of such a major reorganization, and the probable increase in personnel employed on administrative duties, would do nothing to ease the chronic manpower shortage or improve the quality of policing in London.

Facing a steady rise in reported crime, particularly robberies by organized gangs of professional criminals, with no prospects of an increase in manpower, it was important to examine closely the use of existing resources. As part of a management exercise the Commissioner asked his assistant commissioners to produce for his consideration long- and short-term objectives for their departments. A long-term objective approved for 'C' Department was, 'To establish a climate whereby the efforts of both detectives and uniformed officers to prevent and detect crime are properly co-ordinated and subject to effective operational control' – in other words, to develop a professional team approach to policing.

After a review of the Flying Squad's aims and organization, which included discussions with their senior officers, David Powis, who was by now my deputy, came up with a plan which proved most effective. During July 1978 the major part of the Flying Squad was redeployed to form a central robbery squad. The intelligence and co-ordinating unit was based at New Scotland Yard but the operational units were strategically located at four police stations in different geographical areas of London. For the first time responsibility for the investigation of reported cases of organized robbery was vested in the officers of the squad rather than in those of the territorial divisions concerned.

Their *raison d'être* from now on was to be the prevention and detection of robbery. Some of their other traditional roles such as the pickpocket squad, which dated back to the by then extinct racecourse-gang days, were not a good use of experienced detectives, and these were discontinued. The officers were instructed, with the sanction of removal from the squad if they failed, to pass any information on such subjects as drugs or hotel thieves to other specialist squads, and not to spend time in pursuing suspects for these types of crime.

The Flying Squad welcomed their new role and immediately got together with C.11, the Criminal Intelligence Branch, to work out a strategy. As we had anticipated, the scheme was also welcomed by the hard-pressed divisional detectives, and being based at police stations brought the twin benefits for the squad of more local information and improved relations with their colleagues. The use of a network analysis system to show the connections between various criminals and to plot their movements, which criss-crossed London, showed how futile it would have been to have tackled the problem other than on a central basis.

C.11 Branch, led by Commander Ron Harvey, was making a major contribution but, of course, like all intelligence work, this could not be publicized. Both the squad and C.11 had manpower problems, especially when staff were tied up giving evidence in long trials, and their commanders were continually looking for increases in their complement which could not be provided because of the ceiling on the CID establishment. However, as in most organizations, there were ways of helping key operational branches without actually breaching the Commissioner's ruling. The original terms of reference for the Special Patrol Group were to be a mobile force to deal with outbreaks of crime, so I sought help from Wilford Gibson, Assistant Commissioner 'A' Department. He made one of the SPG's four units available on a monthly rotating basis to work with the Flying Squad. They were keen and well-motivated policemen with a particular interest in crime who quickly became effective members of the anti-robbery team.

Surveillance work is very expensive in terms of manpower and C.11 were having to accept such assignments on a priority basis. To help them take on more work I asked each of the area DACs to make a dozen constables available for on-the-job training in surveillance work by C.11. I gave an undertaking that they would normally be employed on operations within their own police area and, with this proviso, the men were provided. This meant that a few years later, when recruiting had improved and a small increase in CID manpower was agreed, there were forty-eight trained officers ready for immediate transfer to the C.11 surveillance unit.

One most welcome side effect of the whole reorganization was the recovery of a large quantity of weapons used in connection with robbery, and identification of certain individuals who had been acting as armourers – that is, obtaining, storing and supplying firearms – for the robbers. During 1979 64 firearms, including 34 of that most terrifying of weapons, the sawn-off shotgun, 19 handguns and eight rifles, plus a large quantity of ammunition and other weapons, were recovered.

Concern about the operation of the Bail Act and the liberal granting of bail to people charged with robbery caused us to carry out some research. In 1979 almost 30 per cent of those on bail for robbery had more than one case already outstanding. The police opposed bail in 902 out of 1,678 cases of people arrested for robbery but 365

(40 per cent) nevertheless succeeded in obtaining it. Of that number, 96 were already on bail at the time of arrest.

We knew from our criminal intelligence sources that it was a repeated pattern of conduct for robbers on bail and facing heavy sentences to become involved in further robberies to pay for an expensive defence – which so often required cash on the nail – and to provide for their families in the event of a long term of imprisonment. They took the view that even if they were arrested for robbery while on bail, for all practical purposes the time actually served in prison was unlikely to be lengthened because any additional sentence would probably be concurrent. As well as writing to the Home Office about this disturbing trend in an attempt to demonstrate to magistrates the dangers likely to result from granting bail to those charged with armed robbery, I had instructions given that detectives were to take the seized weapons to the courts and to show them when they were opposing bail. This, together with publicity in the press about the abuse of bail, helped to stiffen the bench.

I can well understand how incredulous the normally unarmed detectives were at the furore and criticism from some quarters when it became known that in facing armed robbery they had on occasions armed themselves with wooden pick-axe handles instead of relying on their small twelve-inch police truncheons. One humorist said to me, 'Tell them, sir, we carry them to practise Morris dancing, because we're good at that – it keeps us on our toes.' This particular weapon in the Flying Squad armoury was not withdrawn, and bureaucracy was satisfied by detailed records of their issue, carrying and use.

There is nothing like operational success to raise morale, but it is always necessary for senior management to be aware of the pressures and ensure that the price of success is not too high. Elitism and pride in belonging to a specialist unit are fine as long as they are kept in perspective and are not allowed to develop into arrogance. Leadership at all levels is the key to keeping control in this area, plus the certainty among all the members that they are part of a team and success comes from team work. It was implicitly understood that any breach of strict ethical standards would, at the least, result in early removal from specialist duties, and this was a very powerful sanction.

This policy went into action after the arrest of the notorious criminal George Davis and others while they were robbing the Bank of Cyprus at Seven Sisters Road in Holloway, at about 9.45 A.M. on 23 September 1977.

It will be recalled that before this arrest an extremely well-organized – and well-publicized – campaign under the slogan, 'George Davis is innocent OK' had been going on for more than a year. Davis in March 1975 had been convicted of a robbery at the London Electricity Board building at Ilford and sentenced to consecutive sentences of seventeen years' and three years' imprisonment. Two other men charged with him were acquitted and the jury failed to agree in respect of a fourth defendant. On appeal, Davis's imprisonment was changed from being consecutive to concurrent.

Mrs Rose Davis, his wife, and friends alleged that there had been a miscarriage of justice and they obtained enormous attention when, to publicize their cause, they dug up the Headingly Test Match wicket. The campaign slogan was painted on walls, railway and road bridges all over London, and many people pontificated about the innocence of George Davis. A senior officer from outside the Met, Detective Superintendent Jack Moulder of the

Hertfordshire Constabulary, was appointed to inquire into complaints by Davis that he had been wrongfully arrested and convicted. In May 1976, while the independent inquiry was still going on, the Home Secretary made an order releasing him from prison.

During September 1977 we received information that George Davis, his associate Michael Ishmael, on whom the jury had failed to agree a verdict at the Ilford LEB robbery trial, and others were planning to rob a cash security van during a delivery of money to the Bank of Cyprus. It was anticipated that the gang would attack a Securicor van scheduled to arrive at 9.45 A.M. on 23 September. Robbery Squad officers were all in position some hours before the delivery van was expected, ready to ambush the robbers, and an upstairs room in a building that gave a clear view of the bank was being used as the observation and control point.

The van arrived on time and the crew had just begun to make deliveries when a red transit van drew up and four men, one waving a sawn-off shotgun, jumped out. A detective sergeant manning the control point gave the signal, 'Attack', over the radio and his colleagues closed in on the robbers. One of them, who was masked and carrying a sawn-off shotgun, threatened to shoot the detective who approached him. He then grabbed an eighty-two-year-old man who happened to be passing and held him as a shield as armed officers came towards him.

Another member of the public, a Mr Albert Carney aged about fifty, who had already called out to the security guards that the robbers were armed, was standing nearby holding two shopping bags. As the robber, with his hostage, backed in his direction, Mr Carney dropped his shopping bags and threw his arms around the body of the gunman, which made him let go of his hostage. At this point a police officer ran forward, felling the gunman with a blow from his truncheon, and Mr Carney let him fall to the ground where he was handcuffed. Within minutes the four armed men who had arrived in the transit van and two others, the drivers of the van and another vehicle, had been arrested by the squad officers.

Mr Carney later received the Queen's Commendation for brave conduct and he was also commended at the Old Bailey by Mr Justice Thesiger when he sentenced the six robbers, who included Davis and Ishmael, to periods of imprisonment varying between twelve and sixteen years.

When we heard at the Yard of the success of the operation outside the Bank of Cyprus and the arrest of Davis, we were naturally delighted. However, the following day on the front page of the *Daily Express* there was a picture of a masked robber standing on the pavement outside the bank with a sawn-off shotgun in his hands. Inquiries were made about this picture and I was assured that it had been taken by someone who was passing the bank when the raid was taking place. On the Sunday following the attempted robbery, the photograph, which had been syndicated, also appeared in the *Sunday Times*. This newspaper had done some research and drew the conclusion that the photograph had been taken from the room used as our observation and control point.

On Monday morning I had a conference with David Powis and Ron Steventon about this development. Apart from the serious breach of confidence, if a detective had supplied the photograph to a newspaper we were concerned that something like this might give the defence an opening to discredit police evidence and perhaps jeopardize the prosecution of the robbers. I had arrangements made for one of our senior photographers to visit Seven Sisters Road and take some photographs from various angles, including some from the room used as the police control point. The photographs were developed and after comparing them with the newspaper picture our photographer was positive that the published picture must have been taken from the control point. The inescapable conclusion was that the photograph had been taken by a detective and passed to a newspaper reporter. I was not pleased.

By this time it was Friday, and in the late afternoon I held a meeting in my office attended by DACs Powis, Steventon and the commander of C.8/12 Branches, Donald Neesham. We reviewed the Cyprus Bank operation and identified a detective inspector and a detective sergeant who had been in the control room at the time of the raid.

Commander Neesham shared our concern and said he would personally look into the matter. I told him that if the detective, or detectives, concerned were not identified by the following Monday morning and suspended from duty, I intended to refer the matter to the Complaints Investigation Bureau. I said that I was not prepared to accept an explanation of some unknown person dashing into the control room, taking a photograph and then running off, and that if this sort of story were forthcoming it would mean that all ten detectives concerned in the operation could look forward to a transfer. On Sunday afternoon I was telephoned at home by Commander Neesham to say that the detective sergeant in the control room had admitted taking photographs and passing them to someone to give to a reporter from the *Daily Express*. He said that he did this because he thought it would be good for the image of the force if a national newspaper published the pictures. He was suspended from duty pending disciplinary proceedings but resigned before these could be arranged. It was a case of *pour encourager les autres*, regrettable, but unfortunately at this time necessary.

The arrest of Davis standing on the pavement outside a bank holding a sawn-off shotgun brought the 'George Davis is innocent OK' campaign to an abrupt end. I can only hope that some of its supporters had troubled consciences and lost some of their naïvety.

Of all the many convictions for armed robbery none gave more satisfaction than that at the Old Bailey in September 1981 of a South London robber named Billy Tobin. This man, after a retrial, was sentenced to sixteen years' and three years' imprisonment, to run concurrently, for attempted robbery and possessing firearms with intent to endanger life.

The background to this case was that in November 1980 an informant told us that Tobin – at that time on bail from two charges of armed robbery – and others were planning to rob a van carrying up to £1 million one Tuesday in Alleyn Park in Dulwich, outside a large comprehensive school. The attack was to take place at about 1 P.M. and the robbers planned to ram the doors of the security van with the jib of a heavy mobile crane. The informant said they were prepared to shoot their way out of trouble and, if opportunity offered, to take children as hostages.

Complications were caused because it was suspected there was an inside agent involved and so the cash-carrying company could not be approached, and at 1 P.M. school pupils were likely to be out of classes for their lunch break. We talked to the headmaster of the school and plans were made to ensure the safety of the children. On 16 December 1980 at 1.10 P.M. the attack on the security van took place immediately outside the school gates. With the support of five other armed men Tobin was seen to ram the rear of the security vehicle with a mobile crane which the gang had hired with the driver, whom they had kidnapped.

The Robbery Squad's plan worked perfectly. All six men were arrested, and seven firearms and a large quantity of ammunition recovered. Three shots were fired by a detective sergeant when he challenged Tobin and another robber as they came towards him in the school grounds, reaching into their pockets for their revolvers, which were later found to be fully loaded. Both men fell to the ground and surrendered. They had not been hit but a bullet had passed through the collar of Tobin's jacket. After the robbers had been arrested the kidnapped crane driver was found tied up in a van used by them and, shaken but otherwise unharmed, he was released.

Photographs of the robbers, their vehicles and the weapons found on them were taken at the scene. The evidence seemed overwhelming, but when the trial began on 22 June, all six defendants pleaded not guilty. Their defence counsel exercised their individual right to object to three jurors each – well-dressed, middle-aged people were particularly singled out. Because Tobin had boasted that he knew how to fix juries – he had been acquitted on four occasions between 1976 and 1980 on robbery and firearms charges – and it was suspected that attempts might be made to interfere with this jury, the judge had directed that they be given police protection. After the jury had been sworn in it was found that no less than ten of the twelve lived in the Greenwich/Bermondsey area, the district from which Tobin and three of his fellow defendants came. On the third day of the trial a female juror told the judge that her son knew one of the defendants and he stopped the trial.

A second jury was sworn in and again eighteen objections were made to respectable-looking jurors. Later in the trial a detective recognized one of the jurors as a man with a conviction for robbery, but because he had only received a six-months' prison sentence and it was over ten years earlier, he was eligible to sit on the jury. The trial went on until August, when the jury found four men guilty, one not guilty, and could not reach agreement on Tobin. The defence by Tobin had been that he was tricked by a criminal associate in collusion with a detective to go to the scene of the attempted robbery where he had been 'given' a revolver and arrested.

During the retrial of Tobin, which took place in September, two female members of the jury complained of receiving threatening telephone calls. The defence also called a man, who had not given evidence at the first trial, to say that he had been in Alleyn Park at the time of the robbery and that the man he had seen getting down from the mobile crane was not Tobin. However, Tobin's luck had finally run out and he was found guilty, the verdict of the jury being unanimous. On the direction of the DPP, following a comment by the trial judge, inquiries were made about the evidence of the new male witness which disclosed that he had been paid to commit perjury. He was prosecuted and after pleading guilty to giving perjured evidence was jailed by the Recorder of London for three years. This sentence was upheld by the Court of Appeal, where it was stated that punishment for perjury had to be condign.

The Flying Squad continued to show that in its reorganized form it was very effective in combating robbery, and in August 1982 it was augmented by another twenty-six officers to tackle a spate of armed robberies at commercial premises such as building societies and post offices. This strategy proved to be successful. Lone individual robbers and some organized gangs specializing in this sort of robbery were arrested and the number of attacks diminished. Many anti-robbery operations were carried out jointly between C.8 Branch, the Flying Squad, and C.12 Branch, the Met's Regional Crime Squad unit, both branches being controlled by the same commander.

It was with great sadness that on 26 January 1985, less than a year after my retirement, I heard of the death by stabbing of Detective Constable John Fordham, one of the most experienced members of the C.11 surveillance unit, while he was working with the Flying Squad on an operation to find the proceeds of the £26 million gold bullion robbery from a Brinks Mat depot near Heathrow in 1983.

I had been telephoned at home on Saturday, 26 November 1983, by David Powis and told about the bullion robbery, which had taken place a few hours earlier. Commander Frank Cater, the head of the Flying Squad, had personally taken charge of the investigation and, as he always did, David Powis had visited the scene of the crime to confer with the commander. This was the second multi-million-pound robbery to be investigated by the Flying Squad in 1983, the first having been a £6,000,000 robbery of cash and travellers' cheques at a Security Express depot in the East End during the Easter weekend. Five of the armed robbers who committed this crime were subsequently arrested and convicted but only about £1½ million of the stolen money was recovered.

The gang's haul from the Heathrow depot, including three tons of gold bullion, diamonds and platinum – all awaiting shipment – was valued at £26,369,788, the biggest robbery ever in this country. The planning of such an operation would have needed good inside intelligence, and Flying Squad detectives immediately began screening the staff on duty at the time of the crime. They discovered that a security guard, Anthony Black, had a sister who was living with a notorious south London criminal named Brian Robinson, known to his associates as 'the Colonel' because of his organizing ability. Black, an ex-soldier of thirty-one with a good record, had been employed as a security guard for about three years. He was called in early in December for a reconstruction of the robbery and closely questioned. Eventually he cracked and confessed to his part in it, naming Robinson and two other criminals from south London as being amongst the robbers.

Black remained in police custody until he appeared at the Old Bailey early in 1984, when he pleaded guilty to his part in the robbery. After the Common Serjeant of London, Judge David Tudor-Price, had been told by Commander Cater of the assistance Black had already given, and that he would be a witness at the trial of three men who had been charged with the robbery, he sentenced him to six years' imprisonment. As the case against the robbers was not due to be heard until later in the year, a special application was made to the Secretary of State, in which I enlisted the aid of Mr Justice Tudor-Price, for Black to remain in police custody until after he had given evidence at this trial. We feared that if he went to prison he would be got at in some way to stop him giving evidence or to change his story. Reward money of £2 million was advertised for information leading to the recovery of the bullion but no one came forward and no gold was recovered.

The four-week trial of Robinson and the two other men ended at the Old Bailey on Sunday, 2 December 1984. Black had given his evidence well and the jury, by a 10–2 majority, convicted Robinson and a man named Michael McAvoy, and they were each jailed for twenty-five years. The third man was acquitted.

When I retired in March the search for the gold and for other members of the robbery gang was continuing and on 26 January 1985 it was reaching a climax. A Flying Squad team, with C.11 surveillance unit support, had a search warrant – one of thirty-six warrants granted by a magistrate on the previous day – and were poised to search the home of Kenneth Noye at West Kingsdown in Kent. It was dark and there was snow on the ground when at 6.15 P.M., just after a friend of Noye's, Brian Reader, had arrived at the house a decision was made to execute the search warrant.

The unarmed surveillance officers, John Fordham and Neil Murphy, wearing camouflage clothing, including balaclava helmets, and equipped with two-way personal radios, left their observation hide and entered the ten-acre grounds of Noye's house. Their job was to watch the reaction of the people inside the house, and look out for anyone escaping as other detectives gained entry and carried out the search. Inside the grounds the surveillance detectives were quickly scented by three Rottweiler dogs and they surrounded John Fordham, barking and growling. His colleague retreated, calling for assistance and attempting to draw off the dogs.

When in response to the radio messages other detectives arrived on the scene they found John Fordham lying in the snow, dying from stab wounds. He whispered to one of his colleagues, 'He has done me. He has stabbed me.' Noye, standing there holding a shotgun, pointed it at the officers and retreated into his house where they arrested him. Reader was found shortly afterwards on the main road trying to hitch a lift and he too was arrested.

Forensic evidence was given that John Fordham died from stab wounds to his back and front torso. Noye told the court that he had stabbed the detective constable ten times with a kitchen knife, using all his strength, but claimed that he did this in self-defence after being attacked by a masked man whom he believed would kill him. He also said that ten bars of gold found at his house were not stolen, but he admitted dealing in them unlawfully because they had been smuggled into the country without Value Added Tax having been paid. Reader exercised his right not to give any evidence.

The judge, Mr Justice Caulfield, ruled that the burden of disproving the defence submission by Mr John Mathew, QC, that the accused men were acting lawfully in their own self-defence and were therefore not guilty of murder, rested on the Crown. The jury found them not guilty of the murder of John Fordham. Both men remained in custody to await trial, with others, on charges arising out of the Brinks Mat gold bullion robbery.

On the night that John Fordham was killed the commander of the Flying Squad, Frank Cater, was on final leave before his retirement, but he immediately returned to duty and worked on the case until the last day of his service. I know that he was shocked and saddened that his retirement should be marked by the tragic death of this dedicated surveillance officer, but he had the satisfaction of knowing that arrests had been made and that the squad would not let up on this bullion inquiry until it had been completely resolved. Frank Cater was one of the best commanders that the Flying Squad has ever had. He was a true professional, a first-class detective of great experience and an excellent motivator of men.

There were complaints that he was somewhat reticent in communicating with the media and did not therefore fully support the official policy of the force. I defended him on that score, telling our Press Bureau people that his value as a senior detective far outweighed any inconvenience caused by his caution towards the insatiable appetite of the press for information. The regular crime reporters understood and respected him, and jokingly made a pun out of his name, referring to him as Frank non-communiCater.

The reorganization of the Flying Squad to concentrate on professional criminals engaged in armed robbery was successful. Considerable expertise was developed, and to avoid long prison sentences a number of robbers who were arrested began to turn Queen's evidence, which spread alarm amongst the criminal fraternity. This development had been anticipated by us and a detailed plan had been formulated, which is discussed in the following chapter, to ensure we got the maximum benefit from what these informers could tell us.

Probably because they are fairly consistently in the public eye, the Flying Squad has had its share of detractors and internal jealousy, but also its strong supporters. Smear, innuendo and biased comment, if repeated often enough, attain a certain credibility and become established in the mythology of those who miss no opportunity of denigrating the police.

The squad and, indeed, the other Yard specialist branches both individually and collectively, are pretty robust bodies. Most ill-informed criticism is taken in their stride but occasionally they get a little irritated and anxious. Such a situation developed in the spring of 1983 when some newspapers, speculating on plans for the Met by the recently appointed Commissioner, Sir Kenneth

Newman, carried articles saying his plans included the scrapping of central squads like the Flying Squad and the Serious Crime Squad. How these stories started I do not know, but they were a distraction that we could have done without. My staff suggested that some members of a planning team – with no experience of the importance of specialized central squads in combating serious and international crime – had thought the unthinkable and passed it on as the official plan. After checking with the Press Bureau that they had not released any such information, I immediately authorized a statement denying the assertions. At my request the Commissioner came to the next weekly informal conference of 'C' Department commanders, when he told them how much he appreciated their work, that the press comments were untrue and that there would always be a need for specialist squads in the Met.

One national newspaper, in reporting the denial of the plan, wrote, 'The Flying Squad, in particular, has been the butt of recent criticism; its officers were involved when Stephen Waldorf was mistakenly shot, and they remain the focus for vigorous allegations of corruption, despite the four-year inquiry named Operation Countryman, which ended last year.'

This was, in my view, a typical example of smear by inaccuracy and innuendo and it could not be allowed to pass unchallenged. The editor printed the following letter from me under the heading, 'A case of mistaken identity'. After repeating the offending paragraph, I added:

The facts are that no officer of the Metropolitan Police C.8 Branch (Flying Squad) was in any way involved when Stephen Waldorf was mistakenly shot. Following this incident the task of locating and arresting David Martin (for whom Mr Waldorf had been mistaken) who was wanted for the attempted murder of a policeman, was given to the Flying Squad and successfully accomplished on January 28 1983. Whilst the expression 'remains the focus for various allegations of corruption' etc., is open to interpretation, it is a fact that during the last 2½ years none of the 178 officers of the Flying Squad have been charged with corruption or any other criminal offences; none has been disciplined or suspended from duty – the procedure followed in the Metropolitan Police with allegations of corruption which are believed to have some substance. It might interest your readers to know that the Flying Squad is responsible for investigating all cases of armed robbery in the Metropolitan Police District, which this year are averaging about 25 per week. Officers of all ranks serve for periods of two to three years on this squad, which means there is a constant rotation of personnel. Those dealing with the criminals committing this sort of crime have a difficult and not infrequently dangerous job, which, although they would not claim immunity from human frailties, they carry out in a professional manner of which they are justifiably proud.

Whether or not my letter had any influence on the readers of the national daily paper concerned I do not know, but I do know that the personnel of the Flying Squad appreciated my defence of their professionalism and integrity.

They, of course, were just one of the specialist detective branches at the Yard, each with its own particular responsibilities but very much complementary to each other. Personality cults were discouraged and commanders and other senior officers of the branches were normally employed on a two-to-three-year tour of duty basis. This helped to spread experience and expertise throughout the force and avoided individuals being kept too long in particularly stressful positions and perhaps appearing to be indispensable. Keeping a finger on the pulse, to monitor both what was happening – be it robbery, fraud, terrorism, murder or other crime – and to influence people and events was a constant but fascinating challenge.

Probably because of the predictability of their targets and their methods, we were able to take some satisfaction from the success of our strategy to deal with organized armed robbers. However, the same could not be said about the problem of street robbery. How to deal effectively with this continually increasing crime, especially in tense multi-racial inner-city areas, is the problem of the 1980s which it still remains for society to resolve. In dealing with organized professional criminals, the detection methods of targeting, surveillance and arrest when sufficient evidence is obtained receives general public support. The street crime situation is a different proposition, presenting many more difficulties in formulating a policy. Much of it is opportunist crime in areas where social, political and economic tensions exist. In such districts, particularly if the policeman is continually portrayed by political activists as the symbol of oppressive authority, there is likely to be united hostility towards him by sections of the community.

In his report following the Brixton riots in the summer of 1981, Lord Scarman suggested that the police should give the preservation of public tranquillity a higher priority than the prevention of crime in order to gain the assent of the community to their policies. There was much to digest in the Scarman Report and Sir David McNee organized a weekend seminar at the Hendon Training Centre for the senior ranks of commander and above in which Lord Scarman participated.

But despite all our efforts and many local initiatives, street robbery continued to increase, especially in the Inner London boroughs. Local officers were worried and concerned that so much media comment tended to concentrate on the criticism of police that Lord Scarman had made. They felt it was unfair that they should be continually blamed for the riots while the criminality of the rioters was being explained and excused.

At the beginning of January 1982, with street crime figures rising, there was a degree of dissatisfaction in many divisions and a feeling that the Commissioner should say something publicly about the robbery situation. I called a meeting at the Yard in the second week of January on the current street crime situation. It was attended by the commanders of the nine districts most seriously affected, the DACs in charge of the four Met areas, the commander of the Community Relations Branch and DACs (Operations) of 'A' and 'C' Departments. Common agreement was reached that the police could not go it alone and that the local communities and their leaders must be involved. There was concern expressed about the threats by younger male relatives of some of the elderly street robbery victims to take revenge by attacking black youths, though so far this had been averted by strong police advice. It was also reported that the great majority of operational policemen felt there was a conspiracy of silence which was causing resentment in the community about the known disproportionate involvement in these crimes of a minority of black youths. The message from the conference was that the problem had to be publicly identified, despite the storm of criticism this would doubtless raise, so that the young criminals concerned could be isolated and have pressure brought to bear on them from within their own community. I informed the Commissioner of the view of the meeting and sent him a copy of the minutes.

The debate in the post-Scarman period about the

involvement of ethnic minorities in street crime went on both domestically and in the public arena, and our meeting had mirrored this concern. Statistics that identified by race code the assailant and the victim had been kept by the Met for some years. From time to time – mainly in answer to parliamentary questions – some of these statistics relating to specific London boroughs had been released. We were approaching March, the month when traditionally the AC (Crime) had given a press conference to release the previous year's crime statistics for the metropolis, and from various sources it became clear to me that I was likely to be questioned by the press at this first conference since the Brixton riots about the involvement of black youths in street crime. The fact that the figures of 11,239 for robbery and 7,524 for other violent theft were increases of 48 per cent and 18 per cent respectively over the 1980 totals were bound to raise questions. I was also aware that to avoid this issue would do nothing for the morale of the policemen on the streets and that to suppress the truth, which was known to us, would be wrong. I believed that to give the figures would help to dispel rumour and enlist public support – especially among the great majority of law-abiding black people who were often unfairly linked with this type of crime. In other words the motivation was realism and not racism.

I discussed my intentions with the Commissioner to get his approval. As Sir David McNee was having one of his informal meetings with the Home Secretary on 9 March, the day before the crime statistics press conference, I gave him a copy of my opening address which referred to the breakdown of these crimes by London borough and by the racial identity of the assailants, which he cleared with Mr Whitelaw.

The release of the figures – and more particularly the manner of their presentation in some newspapers – caused quite a furore. The race relations experts and various pressure groups condemned the Metropolitan Police for our action, accusing us of insensitive, provocative and inflammatory behaviour. They stopped short of saying that the figures although available should have been suppressed, but argued that they should have been 'interpreted' by me. Presumably this meant explaining them away by discussing social causes and other reasons used to excuse this type of crime. I did not intend to get into a political argument, but merely to give the accurate figures, and I stressed that robbery and other violent theft was only three per cent of the total of recorded crime and that only a small minority of black youths was involved. The actual interpretation of the figures – in some cases under sensational headlines – was carried out by newspapers, television and radio stations. To be blamed by one section of the media for the interpretation given to the statistics by another section seemed to me to be somewhat rough justice.

On the Sunday morning after the release of the crime statistics, I took part in a London Broadcasting Company phone-in programme on the subject. After the end of the one-hour programme, I was told by the producer that it had been difficult to maintain a balance because the overwhelming number of people who telephoned had agreed with what we had done. Despite the cries of outrage from some predictable quarters and perhaps some embarrassment to the Home Office – although the Home Secretary supported my action in the House of Commons – I still feel it was the right thing to have done. At grass-root level street duty officers, particularly in the troubled districts, were approached by many local residents –

both black and white – who wanted to express their understanding and stop this type of crime. Certainly the sort of siege mentality that had been growing up was dispelled and more healthy dialogue took place within the general community.

For a few months after all the publicity the incidence of street robberies declined, but by the end of the year and ever since the seemingly inexorable increase has continued. Street robbery in this country would, not so many years ago, have been considered intolerable, but a level of acceptance has developed and now it seems to have become part of the pattern of life in some districts of London – a sad reflection on twentieth-century society.

13
Reward Money and Supergrasses

There are two sources of income for the payment of rewards to the Yard's informants. The first is a sum of money allocated from the annual budget known as the Metropolitan Police Informants' Fund – the amounts paid from this are usually fairly modest. The second is reward money paid by insurance companies, the banks, the Post Office, building societies and, occasionally, private individuals for information leading to the arrest of criminals and the recovery of property stolen by them. In the latter case, it is common practice for insurance adjusters to advertise a reward of up to ten per cent of the value of the missing property.

At an appeal in 1976 against a conviction for the shotgun murder of a Luton sub-postmaster in 1969, disturbing evidence had been given. A man who was originally also charged with the murder but had the charge withdrawn when he turned Queen's evidence, had received £2,000 in reward money from the Post Office. The money had been recommended and paid on behalf of the Post Office by the officer in charge of the murder investigation, Detective Chief Superintendent Drury of the Flying Squad. Before this appeal court hearing, Jimmy Humphreys had gossiped about the payment of reward money in this case and mentioned irregularities about the administration of Informants' Fund money which he claimed some of his corrupt police friends had talked about. These general allegations had been reported at the time, but I decided when I became responsible for the Informants' Fund that a thorough review of the rules and procedures for dealing with reward monies was needed.

An immediate policy decision was made that no reward money would ever be recommended or paid by us to anyone who had turned Queen's evidence. A revised set of rules and procedures, largely the work of DAC David Powis, was agreed and circulated based on the principle that financial dealings with confidential informants in matters of crime must be scrupulously exact and capable of passing the most searching audit. One of the rules was that all correspondence and negotiations with insurance companies, assessors or other agents of losers about rewards for the recovery of stolen property would be conducted by the DAC (Crime:Operations). He would also personally make the payments to informants in the presence of the detectives controlling them in cases where commercial agents agreed to pay rewards through the police. Individual detectives were forbidden to make any personal approaches to interested parties about a reward for an informant.

In 1980 I wrote a confidential letter to all the major banks, insurance companies and loss assessors pointing out the dangers of offering rewards so large that they might in themselves generate crime. The letter also set out the basis of our new internal rules, including the prohibition on individual officers entering into negotiations, and asked for their co-operation as a matter of mutual interest. The fact that this letter had been sent was not publicized, and it brought to notice a breach of the rules by a detective chief inspector when, a few weeks later, an insurance company referred to my office his attempt to open negotiations on behalf of an informant.

The existence of clearly defined rules had an excellent

effect in establishing and maintaining a code of ethics in a difficult area. The fact that they existed, and had been strictly complied with, enabled David Powis to secure substantial damages for libel in 1985 against a national Sunday newspaper for articles they had published in 1982. The articles commented on his role in the alleged payment of £180,000 of reward money by insurance assessors after the recovery of a £3 million silver bullion cargo, and the convictions of the robbers, from an armed hold-up in Barking in 1980.

David's action was funded by the Metropolitan Police with the approval of the Home Secretary. This policy had been established in 1977 when the then head of the Obscene Publications Squad, Chief Inspector John Hoddinott, and the former head, Superintendent John Smith, were awarded substantial damages in the High Court over a libellous campaign against them in certain sex magazines alleging that they had taken the law into their own hands to intimidate and blackmail publishers. These two officers were considering taking civil action either themselves or with the help of the Police Federation, but I referred the matter to the Home Office with the recommendation that where in the opinion of counsel an attack made on the integrity of an officer carrying out his duties as required of him amounted to libel, it was in the interests of his police authority to support an action to defend his character. The Home Office agreed and during 1985, in answer to a parliamentary question, a government minister stated that since that date four such actions had been funded. No charges had fallen on the public purse because each case had been successful and the full costs had been paid by the parties against whom the libel actions had been taken. This policy is very important because surely it is right to be as quick to defend the integrity of policemen acting correctly as it is to press for the dismissal of those who betray their calling.

One of the most interesting characters amongst informants I have known personally was a woman, now dead, whom I will call Sadie. She was a prostitute's maid, and was driven to inform mainly because of her hatred of the ponces who lived off her employers, particularly if these men, as was sometimes the case, used violence. I first met her while I was at Notting Hill when, with the approval of her call girl employer, she informed on a brutal character who regularly beat up the prostitute.

As a young woman just after the First World War she had been a member of a shoplifting gang or in her parlance, a 'hoister'. 'We wore big drawers, you know, dear,' she said, 'and dropped the goods inside them.' However, a short sentence served at Holloway apparently deterred her from carrying on this occupation and she drifted into the vice world as a housekeeper and prostitute's maid. In her latter years she was what an employment agency would call a 'temp', standing-in for regular maids who were absent because of illness, holiday or any other reason. This was useful because as she moved around she was able to gather a lot of information.

Born and bred in Lambeth, where she lived with her old-age-pensioner common-law husband, Sadie knew her way around the clubs and pubs used by the south London criminal fraternity. After she finally retired and until she died in her late seventies I used to call on her at Christmas time with a small present and listen to her reminiscences – 'Give yer ears a treat, dear.' Sadie's stories – which went back to the 1920s – about the life styles of local criminals and their relationships with the law, back-street abortionists, prostitutes and vice landlords, were interesting and considerably improved my understanding of the London criminal sub-culture.

The common factor with all criminal informants is their natural desire for anonymity, and the courts have recognized that it is in the public interest for the true identity of a police informant to remain confidential. In all correspondence they are always referred to by their pseudonyms, although of course a secret record of true identities has to be kept.

There is one class of informant, however, who has become prominent in the last decade who cannot be protected by anonymity. These are characters known to the Met as RIs, or 'resident informants', but more popularly to the public as 'supergrasses'. They are professional criminals, mainly robbers, who when faced with long terms of imprisonment turn Queen's evidence and testify in their true names, with their records known and exposed, against their former criminal associates. The name 'resident informant' is used because having confessed their guilt they remain in police custody pending sentence and often after that sentence until they have given evidence in the trials of their accomplices.

There is a distinction to be made between an informer, speaking about his knowledge of crimes in which he did not take part, and a man arrested who is willing to give evidence against his accomplices in this and other crimes. The former may have any one of a number of motives, the most common of them being a financial reward or revenge. The single purpose of the man already arrested is to minimize his own punishment.

Honour amongst thieves has always been an exaggerated concept and it is certainly not in the public interest that it prevails. Although 1979 became known as the year of the supergrass – over twenty criminals changed sides –

there was nothing new about criminals attempting to save their own skins. As early as 1650 reference can be found to the plea of approvement, which was the practice of granting immunity from prosecution, or further prosecution, to accomplices willing to give evidence for the Crown.

The most modern dictum, and the most helpful to us in our efforts to deal with escalating armed robbery, was that of Lord Justice Roskill on 28 July 1977 in the Court of Criminal Appeal in the case of *Regina* v. *Lowe.* Charlie Lowe, who had informed and given evidence against fifty associates, had appealed against his own sentence of eleven and a half years' imprisonment on the basis that his assistance to the Crown had not been sufficiently recognized. In reducing the sentence to five years His Lordship said, 'It must therefore be in the public interest that the persons who have become involved in gang activities of this kind should be encouraged to give information to the police in order that others may be brought to justice and that when such information is given and acted upon, substantial credit should be given upon pleas of guilty, especially in cases where there is no other evidence against the accused than his own confession. Unless credit is given in such cases there is no encouragement for others to come forward and give information of invaluable assistance to society and the police which enables these criminals to be brought to book.'

As a judgment of the Court of Criminal Appeal, this could be cited as a precedent in other cases. Criminals and their lawyers took notice, and five years' imprisonment became the recognized tariff for our RIs.

In formulating our own internal policy and procedures I was very much influenced by the adverse publicity over our handling of the first of the modern supergrasses, Bertie Smalls, who in 1973 was given complete immunity by the then Director of Public Prosecutions, Sir Norman Skelhorn, in return for informing on twenty-seven of his associates. The document giving Smalls immunity was described by defence counsel for those charged on his evidence as an 'unholy bargain'. Lord Justice Lawton later rejected an appeal by sixteen of Smalls's accomplices against their convictions and sentences but he was critical of the indemnity undertaking, and although when the same appeal was taken to the House of Lords Lord Dilhorne supported the DPP's right to make such a decision, it was agreed that complete immunity would never be given again.

Smalls eventually told his story to a national Sunday newspaper and a picture was published that was said to have been taken at a celebration party in a police cell showing him wearing a police helmet. This glamorizing of and over-identification with a notorious criminal was something that I was determined would not happen again. Firm and detailed guidelines were laid down and a system of supervision and responsibility at senior level instituted. This included informing and consulting the DPP at an early stage of any proposal to treat an arrested criminal as a resident informant.

It had to be faced that these criminals were totally amoral people with very little regard for anyone other than themselves. They were cunning, devious and often strong personalities who, not surprisingly, were not consistent in their moods. At times, when a good rapport had been developed, they almost regarded themselves as part of the investigating team. On other occasions, when they were feeling depressed, they would insult their handlers, make threats and be generally unco-operative.

It was important to select mature, experienced and intelligent detectives to handle these men. They had to guard against becoming emotionally involved or too closely identified with their charge, to prevent a form of 'Stockholm Syndrome' developing. An important responsibility of senior supervisory officers engaged on such inquiries was to be alert to the pressures on the officers handling the informant and not to hesitate quietly to change them if this seemed necessary.

Cells in police stations are not constructed to provide long-term accommodation, so the location and adaptation of premises to provide secure temporary housing was a problem that caused some headaches. While they were actually serving their sentences, resentment against informants by other criminals created many difficulties for the prison authorities who had to ensure their protection from violence. Two prisons in fact set aside special wings to house this category of prisoner.

As part of our strategy at the Yard it was decided that once the informant had given his evidence and gone to prison the operational detectives who had controlled him would sever all connection with him. Liaison with the prison authorities, probation and after-care service concerning his new identity and rehabilitation on discharge from prison were all handled by C.5 administration branch. Detectives and, indeed, others in the criminal justice system had to be educated to accept that apart from advising him about his personal safety the Met had no special responsibility for an ex-informant.

An early breakthrough for the Robbery Squad took place in November 1977 when a man named David Edward Smith, arrested with others on suspicion of being responsible for a number of armed robberies, turned Queen's evidence. He had only been out of prison for a year after a ten-year sentence for armed robbery, so he was facing the probability of a very long sentence. He made a complete confession, was dealt with for fourteen offences, with seventy others being taken into consideration, and received five years' imprisonment.

From Smith we learned about the 'Gartree Connection', the name given to the link between a group of dangerous criminals who had met while they were serving sentences in the secure Gartree Prison in Leicestershire. The Mountbatten Inquiry in 1960 into measures required to prevent dangerous criminals from escaping from prison had recommended that as it was impossible to make all prisons completely escape-proof, two or three should be designated as high-security jails. The first contingent of high-risk prisoners from all over the country, which included Smith, was sent to Gartree. There they had struck up relationships that lasted after their release.

Smith's information led to the discovery of a cache of weapons, crash helmets and other robbery equipment and this in turn resulted in the arrest of no less than sixty-nine people. The charges against them included four for murder, 77 for robbery, 37 conspiracies to rob and 18 firearm offences committed in places as far apart as Manchester, Liverpool, Birmingham, Nottingham, Glasgow, Cardiff and London.

During the next few years others followed Smith's example and in criminal circles it became almost fashionable to be a police RI. There were critics of our policy, including some who had moral objections. My answer to them was, and still is, that there is little morality amongst hardened criminals and the 'fair play' approach is not realistic. Crimes such as terrorism, murder, armed robbery or any situation where the security of society is threatened must be vigorously tackled by all lawful means and, as I reminded questioners at crime conferences, the use of informers is lawful. Occasionally, particularly after a series of acquittals, articles were published suggesting that the system was dangerous and ineffective, but its usefulness certainly should not be measured solely by the conviction or acquittal rate. The disruption of criminal gangs, the recovery of firearms and other weapons, as well as the intelligence gleaned, are perhaps better yardsticks of the benefits of the system for police and for the public. The old adage, 'When thieves fall out honest men come into their own' is a true one.

Although detailed statistics were not religiously kept, a count in 1982 showed that during a five-year period nearly fifty men had been used as resident informants, resulting in 451 people being charged, 262 convicted, 85 acquitted, 78 awaiting trial and 32 cases not proceeded with. Technological advances in electronics, automatic camera surveillance systems and barrier materials used by commercial businesses have all helped to deter the robber. However, the vulnerability to criminal attack when cash is transferred to or from a security van across a pavement remains.

As far as I am aware the only other country in the world with an organized resident informant programme is the United States. The programme there is operated by the Federal authorities from specially constructed blocks within correction establishments in New York, Chicago and San Diego, where the informers are guarded by the US Marshall's Service. With the organized crime problems peculiar to the USA, the authorities there have found it necessary to grant complete immunity from prosecution to informers for the gravest crimes, including contract murder.

In this country contract killings are fortunately very

rare, but in two cases in recent years resident informants have given evidence against their alleged accomplices after they themselves had been sentenced to life imprisonment. One of these cases, which occurred in 1979, concerned George Piggott, who was mentioned earlier in this book as one of Rachman's strong-arm rent collectors. Piggott appeared at the Old Bailey in February 1978 and after pleading guilty to four counts of armed robbery, two counts of possessing firearms with intent to resist arrest and asking for six offences of armed robbery to be taken into consideration, was jailed for ten years.

In October 1978, while he was at Long Lartin Prison, Piggott asked for a visit from Detective Sergeant John Baker, who had arrested him for the crimes for which he was serving. Piggott told Baker he wished to confess his part in the contract murder by shooting of Alfred 'Italian Toni' Zomparelli at the Golden Goose Amusement Arcade in Soho in September 1974. He volunteered, if he could be accommodated away from the prison, to help the police clear up this murder, which he had been paid to commit, and other serious crimes in London by naming his associates. He had apparently been let down by them and was feeling bitter.

Zomparelli had been murdered within a year of his release from prison after being sentenced to four years for the manslaughter of David Knight, the twenty-three-year-old brother of Ronald Knight, the husband of the actress Barbara Windsor. David Knight had died after being stabbed in the Latin Quarter Restaurant in Wardour Street, and his brothers, Ronald and John, with a William Hickson had appeared in the dock at the Old Bailey with Zomparelli – who was additionally charged with murder – charged with fighting and making an affray which had led to the death. Zomparelli, with whom they had all been fighting, was convicted of manslaughter and Hickson was given a suspended sentence of twelve months' imprisonment on the affray charge, but the jury could not agree a verdict on the Knight brothers. A retrial was not held because prosecuting counsel told the court that as some witnesses had gone abroad and others would not voluntarily attend the court the Crown thought it proper to offer no evidence. Both men were discharged and as they left the dock Sir Carl Aarvold, then the Recorder of London, warned them to 'be careful'.

Before leaving George Piggott at Long Lartin Prison Detective Sergeant Baker asked him for some proof of his involvement in the murder of Zomparelli. Piggott described a place near the Winchester golf course in Hampshire where in 1974 he had buried the two guns used in the Golden Goose murder, a ·38 revolver and a ·22 automatic pistol. He also said that he could give details of over twenty armed robberies and a case of arson, but because he feared for his own safety if he gave this information whilst he was in prison he would only inform if he was held in police custody.

At the time of the murder a witness said she had heard four shots and afterwards saw two young men running away from the amusement arcade. The spent bullets were, of course, recovered and had been retained as forensic exhibits. Sergeant Baker visited Winchester and the two guns, by now very rusty, and some ammunition were recovered from the place described by Piggott. An examination by a ballistics expert from the Met Police Scientific Laboratory quickly established that these were the guns from which the bullets recovered at the scene of Zomparelli's murder had been fired.

A conference was held with the DPP and in view of the importance of clearing up a case of murder, and particularly murder by hired gunmen, he agreed to support an application to the Home Secretary for Piggott to be released into police custody. The necessary authority was eventually given, and on 11 April Piggott, under the alias 'John February', was detained under Rule 6 of the Prison Rules, 1964, in specially adapted cell accommodation at Twickenham police station under conditions of great secrecy. Detective Chief Superintendent Robert Wilson of C.1 Serious Crime Squad was put in charge of the inquiry.

During the next six months Piggott was interrogated by Detective Sergeant Baker and Chief Superintendent Wilson and he made a large number of statements under caution, confessing to over one hundred serious criminal offences. These included murder, attempted murder, arson, armed robberies, conspiracies to rob and stealing motor vehicles, and he named about a hundred people whom he alleged were involved with him in the commission of these crimes in a three-year period from 1974 to 1977.

We were required to subject him as far as was practicable to the same restrictions that would apply if he was in prison. Exercise was a problem and to help with this an exercise bicycle was provided in the detention suite. He was examined once a month by a police doctor and a report certifying his general fitness sent to the prison authorities. Although he had a very bad record and a propensity to use violence, Piggott had an artistic bent. He occupied much of his time in constructing elaborate pictures on such subjects as St George and the Dragon by glueing small pieces of eggshell on to a base and then painting and varnishing them.

His confessions and other statements were checked as far as was possible without alerting the people he named, but our official files soon showed that only someone deeply involved in many of the crimes would have been able to give such accurate details about them.

We learned that while serving a term of imprisonment at Albany Prison in the late 1960s and early 1970s, Piggott became friendly with another inmate who was a notorious south London criminal specializing in armed robbery. Through this man he met other professional robbers and deliberately decided on his release from prison to join in what he saw as a very lucrative area of crime, the robbing of cash-carrying security guards. His ruthlessness, willingness to use firearms and organizing ability quickly made him acceptable, and also feared, in his new circle of friends.

He claimed he was propositioned to shoot Zomparelli by a criminal associate who did it as a favour for a friend who wanted revenge because Zomparelli had killed his brother in a brawl in a West End night-club. By a coincidence Piggott knew Zomparelli, for he had sat next to him in the textiles shop at Wormwood Scrubs Prison and remembered him boasting about his light sentence of four years for murdering a man.

Piggott described how, eventually, his associate was supplied with a brand new ·38 revolver in a club at Charing Cross Road and how he himself went to Winchester to get a ·22 automatic pistol which he had hidden there after a shooting he had carried out at a North Woolwich scrap yard – this had been done to avenge a criminal friend whose wife had had an affair with the victim. The guns were hidden in a flat at Roseberry Square, Holborn, that was provided for their use by the man who wanted Zomparelli shot.

On 4 September 1974, after drinking several large

brandies, Piggott and his accomplice set out from Roseberry Square to carry out cold-blooded murder, travelling by tube train from Chancery Lane to Tottenham Court Road underground station and walking to the Golden Goose Arcade via Soho Square and Greek Street. The man with Piggott was wearing a false moustache bought from a theatrical supplier's shop near St Martin's Lane. Piggott had thrown away a false beard bought for himself because it looked ridiculous, but for disguise he wore dark glasses.

After checking that their intended victim was in the amusement arcade they went in and, according to Piggott, his companion shot Zomparelli three times in the head with the ·38 revolver. He claimed the shock of hearing the gunfire made him involuntarily pull the trigger of his own ·22 pistol and fire a shot into the floor. They ran away through the back streets of Soho and, realizing they were not being followed, removed their disguises and returned by tube to Holborn and their Roseberry Square flat. The following night they went to a West End club where, he said, they were given £250 of the £1,000 they had been promised for the murder. Piggott took the guns to his parents' house in Hampshire and later buried them in the place from which Detective Sergeant Baker recovered them some three years later.

Full details of the inquiries and copies of Piggott's statements were supplied to the Director of Public Prosecutions, and Piggott was committed on a voluntary bill to appear at the Old Bailey charged with the murder of Zomparelli, arson, wounding with intent and two robberies, and he asked that 107 other offences, including 48 robberies, be taken into consideration. The voluntary bill procedure averted the need of Piggott appearing at a magistrates' court for normal committal for trial proceedings and thus avoided alerting his accomplices. He appeared at the Old Bailey on 17 January 1980, and after pleading guilty to all the offences he was sentenced to life imprisonment for murder and concurrent terms of imprisonment for the other charges.

Immediately he had been sentenced teams of detectives arrested a number of associates. Two of them, Ronald Knight, who was said to have supplied the ·38 revolver and paid for the shooting, and Nicholas Gerrard, who was alleged to have used the revolver, were charged with the murder of Zomparelli. Their trial took place at the Old Bailey between 10 and 19 November 1980. Piggott was the principal prosecution witness, and the jury found them not guilty. In June 1982, less than two years after this acquittal, Nicky Gerrard met a violent death when he was blasted with a sawn-off shotgun in a south London gangland killing.

As the jury did not accept the evidence of Piggott the DPP decided not to take action against anyone else named by him as accomplice to criminal offences. His period of detention in police custody was immediately ended and he returned to prison to serve his life sentence. Whilst he had been held by us George Piggott had been well behaved and co-operative, although he seemed completely cynical about his involvement in murder and other violent crimes. In my view it should be many years – if ever – before such a ruthless criminal is considered suitable for parole.

In the *Sunday Times* of 1 July 1984 it was reported that Ronald Knight was living in Spain on the Costa del Sol where he had purchased two villas at a cost of £250,000 and had also bought a plot of land on which he intended to build eleven luxury apartments. In the same newspaper article the Spanish Chief Commissioner, Lorenzo Mora Conesa, was quoted as saying that Interpol had informed them that Ronald Knight and four other Englishmen also living in Spain were wanted in connection with robbery but that nothing could be done because there was no extradition treaty between Britain and Spain.[1]

Not all the Knight family were as lucky. On 10 June 1985 at the Old Bailey John Knight, another brother James, and William Hickson were three of the five men found guilty of charges arising from Britain's biggest ever cash robbery, the theft of £6 million from the headquarters of the Security Express at Easter 1983. The judge commented that this armed robbery – where one guard had petrol poured over him and was threatened with being turned into a human torch if the vault keys were not handed over – had involved a year of planning by a team of professional criminals who decided to go to war on society. He jailed John Knight for 22 years, James Knight for eight years and William Hickson for six years.

When it was decided as a matter of policy to have a resident informants programme we faced the fact that it might reveal some skeletons in the constabulary cupboard. Instructions were given that any information or complaints from the informants about lack of police integrity were to be reported immediately in order that an investigation could be carried out by the Complaints Investigation Bureau.

It was a report from the commander of the Flying Squad in August 1978 that an RI detained at Finchley

[1] A treaty was signed in 1985, but under Spanish law there is no retrospection. However, should a British subject resident in Spain at the time the treaty was signed subsequently leave the country and then return, he, or she, would then be subject to the provisions of the new treaty.

had made serious allegations against City of London police detectives that launched the inquiry styled 'Operation Countryman'. As the original allegations were confined to City of London officers the Deputy Commissioner informed Peter Marshall, the City of London Police Commissioner, and he appointed Mr Leonard Burt, an assistant chief constable of Dorset, to conduct the inquiry. When it seemed that Metropolitan detectives were also involved, Mr Burt was asked to extend his inquiry to cover both police forces. The complaints were of bribery, corruption and conspiracy with particular reference to two recent major crimes in the City of London, a £175,000 robbery at the *Daily Express* building and a wages snatch at the *Daily Mirror* offices when a security guard was shot dead by the robbers.

Inevitably the Met in its role of big brother in the police world soon became the focal point for publicity in this inquiry, whose very name seemed to stimulate journalistic interest. Even calling it 'Operation Countryman' had created a precedent, for up to that time, and since, code names have not been used for internal inquiries. The shadow of it hung over the force like a giant albatross until the end of 1982 – over five years. The inquiry cost the taxpayer about £3 million and finally resulted in the conviction of a detective chief inspector and a detective inspector of the City of London force for two offences of conspiracy to contravene the provisions of the Prevention of Corruption Acts. Eight Met detectives, the highest in rank a detective inspector, were prosecuted for separate offences such as conspiracy to pervert the course of justice, but all were acquitted. Of these eight three were dismissed as the result of disciplinary proceedings, one resigned and four resumed duty.

During those five years some newspaper and TV

journalists, anticipating sensational developments that never materialized, became obsessive in condemning the Met without any real evidence. The media helped to convert an inquiry that should, if only for reasons of efficiency, have had specific terms of reference, into a self-appointed, all-embracing anti-corruption squad willing to receive gossip from any criminal. Leaks and rumours under headlines such as '12 "super informers" aid search for corrupt policemen' and 'Senior Yard man took bribes from robbers' appeared with great regularity. The latter story was said to feature in a sworn affidavit from a Mrs Vivienne Wilde, described as a former lover of one of the robbers. Allegations about bribing the 'top detective' – neither his rank nor name were given, no doubt for fear of libel action – were printed on the front page of a newspaper, and the article stated that the affidavit would be passed to the Assistant Chief Constable of Dorset. What was not said in the newspaper article was that Mrs Wilde was the wife of a man then serving a long sentence for bank robbery and that a prison warder had been charged – and was later convicted – of conspiring and being bribed to aid her husband's prison escape.

The 'top detective', although not named, identified himself and protested about this smear om his good name. If he could have been discredited, Mrs Wilde's husband and her former lover would both have walked free – he was involved in prosecuting both of them and had there been a prima-facie case of corruption he would have been suspended from duty.

However, this lurid story and others like it could not be substantiated, but this did not deter our critics. The BBC joined the bandwagon and produced a programme called 'Countryman'. Sir David McNee issued a statement pointing out that the programme showed anonymous criminals making allegations of corrupt behaviour against unidentified police officers. He was concerned about fair play and the presentation to the public of anonymous, untested allegations from criminal sources in relation to an inquiry before it was settled what criminal proceedings might, or might not, be brought.

It seemed to the force at that time that our friends were thin on the ground, although Mr Eldon Griffiths, MP, did write a strong letter to the *Daily Telegraph* taking the BBC to task. He accused certain producers of again and again stabbing the police in the back, quite likely without realizing the impression their programmes created. Broadcasting time had been given to unsubstantiated allegations that many policemen were racists, extortionists, perjurors and planners of crime, which they, bound as they were by the rules of evidence, had no means of refuting. Allegations like this, Mr Griffiths pointed out, led the public to believe that the police as a whole were deliberately covering up crooks in their own ranks and removed from individual policemen that assumption of innocence until there is proof of guilt that applies to all other citizens.

In my position as AC (Crime) I was committed to getting rid of any detective who behaved criminally or unethically, and I continued to demonstrate this. But I also had a duty to support the great majority who were honest and hard working. Detectives are men of the world, not shrinking violets, and as long as they have the confidence that their own senior officers are being fair, they are not deterred from doing their job. I was personally put to the test over this in the autumn of 1979. I had just returned from an overseas Interpol meeting when representations were made to me about the unfairness of a peremptory transfer from CID duties of a detective superintendent and a detective chief inspector, both attached to the Complaints Investigation Bureau. It was alleged, and this was published in the press, that a senior member of the Countryman team had complained that one of the investigations they had carried out for the Bureau had been inadequate. I examined the investigation file and, while it was not perfect, there did not seem to be any gross neglect or evidence of dishonesty that would normally be necessary to justify a summary transfer without any disciplinary proceedings being taken.

With the consent of the Deputy Commissioner, Pat Kavanagh, I asked DAC John Radley, who had not long joined the Met from the West Midlands Police, to carry out a thorough review of the case. His findings were that, bearing in mind the pressure of other work allocated to these two detectives, there was no reason to doubt that the inquiry they had been engaged on had been carried out efficiently and honestly. In the light of this finding the Deputy Commissioner agreed that they could be transferred back to CID duties. I should mention that during the period their case was being reviewed both men had given complete satisfaction in carrying out their duties in uniform, behaving with dignity and an absence of animosity. Some time later the detective superintendent retired normally on pension and the detective chief inspector, who was a younger man, is now a detective chief superintendent. Although the reappointment to CID duties of these officers may seem only a minor domestic matter, it had, because it was seen by them and many of their colleagues as the correcting of an injustice, a certain symbolic significance and was good for morale.

Knowing from experience the problems of a major corruption inquiry where the complainants and witnesses are men with criminal records, I was saddened to hear rumours and to read press reports that the Countryman inquiry team leaders were complaining about the Director of Public Prosecutions. A report appeared in the *Sunday Times* in November 1979 saying that Mr Burt was angry about obstacles being placed in his way by the Met and by the DPP.

In his book *McNee's Law*, Sir David McNee relates how, having established with him that the *Sunday Times* article was untrue, Mr Burt, after some delay, complied with his request to issue a press statement denying categorically that the inquiry had been obstructed. However, some idea of the underlying tensions can be sensed from the fact that some two years later, after he had retired, Burt's chief constable, Arthur Hambleton, qualified this by saying that if the denial statement had not been issued the inquiry would have folded up, though I am sure the Commissioner would not have let this happen. David McNee also mentions a meeting at the Home Office in February 1980 when Hambleton said that the DPP was not helping Countryman and, indeed, was actually obstructing it, and he comments that the Chief Constable seemed bent on conducting a private war against the Director and the Attorney-General.

Some journalists were having a Roman holiday reporting dissension between those who should have been united, and clearly there were inspired leaks to prompt them. Inevitably this did nothing to help the inquiry and merely fuelled further extravagant speculation. Then there was the embarrassment of a public rebuff to Mr Burt when the DPP found it necessary for lack of evidence to withdraw at St Albans Magistrates' Court so-called 'holding charges' for handling stolen property against Detective Chief Inspector Cuthbert of the City of London Police which had been preferred earlier without any consultation with the Director. Some two years later Cuthbert was charged and convicted of corruption offences which were part of the original allegations the inquiry was set up to investigate.

The final straw, which in my view destroyed the credibility of this inquiry and left the police world gasping with astonishment – not to mention anger – came in February 1980 when, on the eve of his retirement, Arthur Hambleton gave a TV interview about the inquiry's progress. It was unprecedented that an uncompleted criminal inquiry should be publicly discussed in considerable detail, and that speculation should be indulged in about its possible outcome – including a forecast that up to twenty policemen would be charged with corruption offences. I felt sorry for the working detectives on the investigation team who must have been as incensed by this as the rest of us.

There were by then more than eighty investigating officers on the Countryman team, which seemed to me to be excessive. It is essential in complex corruption investigations to have a reasonably compact team of selected officers working closely with the senior policeman in charge who must control and co-ordinate their activities, though it goes without saying that the statutory positions of the deputy chief officer of the force initiating the inquiry and the DPP must be strictly observed. Both have specific responsibilities under the Police Act and the advice and assistance of the Director's staff is invaluable in maintaining a dispassionate and professional approach. After all, it is the Director's statutory responsibility – subject to the Attorney-General's consent – to brief Treasury counsel to prosecute in all corruption cases. For a police officer to challenge or in any way undermine the authority of the Director of Public Prosecutions is almost a form of anarchy.

I breathed a sigh of relief when in May 1980 I was asked to make DAC Ron Steventon, whose experience in this field was unrivalled, available to assist Sir Peter Matthews, the Chief Constable of Surrey who had taken over the direction of the Countryman inquiry. The bickering and backbiting through the media faded, the team was reduced to a reasonable size and, working closely with the representatives of the DPP, it got on with its task. The inquiry was finally concluded in 1982 with, as I have already mentioned, the jailing of Detective Chief Inspector Cuthbert and a detective inspector of the City of London Police.

It was not surprising that with all the allegations and media speculation that had been going on for the last five years – sometimes in 'faction' programmes amounting to condemnation without trial – the fact there were only two convictions, both City of London detectives, was seen by some as evidence of a cover-up. The Met was in a no-win situation and some MPs were reluctant to let the matter drop.

The Liberal Party, in the person of Mr Stephen Ross, MP for the Isle of Wight where his constituents include the inmates of the Albany and Parkhurst prisons, started the ball rolling, and he was later supported by his leader, Mr David Steel. I was having my breakfast at 7 A.M. on Friday, 23 July, when on the Independent Radio News broadcast the newsreader announced:

> A new scandal is threatening the Metropolitan Police. Stephen Ross, the Liberal MP for the Isle of Wight, is claiming that twenty police officers up to the rank of Assistant Commissioner should be investigated on corruption charges. He has called for

a royal commission to investigate police corruption in London after following up information given to him by prisoners on the Isle of Wight, and Mr Ross says he is hoping to meet the Home Secretary to discuss the allegations next week.

Nobody wants to criticize [second voice now speaking – presumably Ross] the police unreasonably at a time when they are under pressure, particularly after the recent bombings. But I don't think anybody, any citizen of this country, can be happy at some of the accusations that have been made and they have come from so many different sources that I think that this is a time now to clean the whole thing up. If we are going to reorganize the Metropolitan Police, well, for God's sake let's do it properly this time.

When I reached the Yard I discussed this with the Commissioner and with David O'Shea, the Met's solicitor, after which the following message was sent to the editor of the IRN Company:

Referring to news item(s) involving Stephen Ross, MP, of 23.7.82, your attention is drawn to the apology printed in *The Times* newspaper of 17 February 1982 following a similar defamatory allegation made in *The Times* Diary. Would you please ensure that a retraction is made at once whilst the legal position of the assistant commissioners is considered.

A reply was received later in the day that a retraction and an apology would be transmitted on the following Monday's news bulletins at 7, 8 and 9 A.M. – the same bulletins which had carried the original news item. I was advised that the original broadcast was defamatory but in view of the retraction and prompt apology I did not consider legal action for damages necessary.

As far as the Met was concerned the Countryman inquiry was over, there was no longer any *sub judice* restraint and in my view a vigorous response to the repetition of general innuendo about corruption in the force was justified. A political campaign was building up to try and persuade the Home Secretary to set up an independent inquiry into alleged corruption in the Metropolitan Police in the aftermath of the Countryman investigation and I believed that such an inquiry would mainly be used to score political points, that it would be harmful to the Met and would do nothing to help the public of London. I was determined to do what I could to prevent it taking place.

Mr Steel gave a press conference after he and Mr Ross had met the Home Secretary, Mr Whitelaw, on 30 July. Much comment was made in the press about the list of names gathered by Mr Ross of police officers alleged to be corrupt, though Mr Steel made a point of saying that there was a very high standard of integrity within the police force and the allegations concerned just a small section of one force.

Newspaper articles quoted Mr Ross as saying that he would be more than prepared to raise the matter on the floor of the House if things did not move a bit. Parliamentary privilege, it was pointed out, would protect any MP who chose to list in the House the names of police officers alleged to have been corrupt. I am pleased that no MP abused his privilege by taking such action.

As part of the counter-attack to the extensive reporting and discussion of these unsubstantiated allegations made to the MP by anonymous criminals against police officers whose names were not disclosed, I gave an exclusive interview to Tom Sandrock, crime reporter of the *Daily Telegraph*. He reported on what had been done over a five-year period to secure effective operational control and direction of the CID, and pointed out that attitudes in the Met towards the active rejection of corruption, and pride in its professionalism, had never been better. Once again the Met's own in-house newspaper, *The Job*, helped by printing Mr Sandrock's unedited report with my explanatory remarks. I could not help likening the list of names of corrupt officers to the list that Senator McCarthy claimed he had had in the United States and which all liberals detested as unfair witch-hunting.

At the end of September the Deputy Commissioner, Pat Kavanagh, and I went to a meeting with the Home Secretary and his senior civil servants at the Home Office. We discussed the current situation in the force and I gave a brief historical overview of corruption in the Met and the reasons why I believed the measures we had taken were successful. I told the Home Secretary that while a poor salary was no excuse for being corrupt, the origin of many of the bad practices stemmed from the days of very poor pay. The acceptance of the Edmund Davies Committee pay recommendations had for the first time placed policemen on a proper salary scale appropriate to their responsibilities and they were responding. I described how individual officers – following the example of those who gave evidence in the porn trials – were coming forward and reporting dishonesty by colleagues, and I gave details of some specific cases. I also told the Home Secretary that I had made a point of talking to all these detectives some time after they had given evidence, to let them know how much their moral courage was appreciated and also to learn the reaction of individuals and their colleagues to this experience. Without exception they had found it a traumatic experience that they hoped would not have to be repeated, but they all spoke highly of the almost unanimous support of their colleagues. There is no doubt that peer group pressures are of vital importance in establishing a healthy climate and all the signs were encouraging.

Late in October, in a reply which was released to the press, the Home Secretary wrote at length to Mr Steel. In rejecting the Liberal Party leader's call for an independent inquiry, he stressed all the consultations he had carried out. He said that he was entirely satisfied that senior officers of the Metropolitan Police and City forces were rightly giving the highest priority to the prevention and detection of corruption, and had succeeded in creating a climate which led to its exposure and rejection. In concluding the letter, he hoped that everyone concerned would keep this matter in perspective and remember that, for every police officer who was shown to have abused the trust placed in him, there were thousands who carried out their duties with the honesty and dedication that society rightly expects of them and who continued to deserve our fullest support.

The letter was vintage William Whitelaw, warm but firm, decisive and supportive, and it was good for our morale at a difficult time. I felt some satisfaction that the few vultures waiting to pounce on the carcass of the Met had been driven off.

There was one more attempt to get a new inquiry in a debate in the House of Commons on 18 November. After turning down a request from Mr Campbell-Savours, MP, the Home Secretary said in answer to another question from Mr Winnick, MP:

> I must decide what is the best way to prevent corruption in the Metropolitan Police and, at the same time, as the Honourable Gentleman said, do what is best for the police and for their morale. I have concluded it would be wrong to have an enquiry. It is right to back the new Commissioner, the Deputy Commissioner and the Assistant Commissioner for Crime. A great deal has been done in recent years to root out corruption in the Metropolitan Police. They have my full confidence in doing so. I want them to get on with the job.

Politically, I believed this marked the final watershed effect of the porn and other corruption trials, and from then onwards it became clear that politicians accepted there was nothing to be gained from attacking the integrity of the Met by flogging the corpse of Countryman.

14
Terrorism and Kidnapping

Of all the responsibilities borne by the Yard's central office detective branches, none is more important or more onerous than that of C.13, better known as the Anti-Terrorist Branch. This is the youngest of the branches, founded in 1971, to investigate bombing outrages by a group of anarchists who called themselves the 'Angry Brigade'. At the time it was thought to be only a temporary measure and the name 'Bomb Squad' was an obvious title – the incident that caused alarm and gave the Angry Brigade the most publicity was a bomb attack on 12 January 1971 on the Barnet home of the then Mr Robert Carr, Minister of Employment.

Unfortunately the hope that this squad could be disbanded after the arrest of the group of anarchists did not materialize. Political terrorism brought murder by shooting and bombings to the streets of London, and in April 1976 the Bomb Squad was renamed the Anti-Terrorist Branch. This name better reflected its function because many of its investigations involved criminal offences by various national and international terrorist factions.

The then United Nations Secretary General, Kurt Waldheim, said in an address to the Security Council in July 1976: 'The world community is now required to deal with unprecedented problems arising from acts of international terrorism . . . which raise many issues of a humanitarian, moral, legal and political character for which, at the present time, no commonly agreed rules or solutions exist.' Although some political progress has been made, this statement remains largely true, and it is against this background that a domestic police force, the Metropolitan Police, has had to work.

Without publicity terrorist acts would lose much of their effect, for it is the media that give them their power to command attention and, some claim, this tends to legitimize terror groups by familiarization. This is a difficult and contentious area, very much brought to the fore by public discussion, particularly in the United States, by the massive TV coverage given to the Islamic extremist hi-jackers of the TWA aircraft with its crew and passengers held as hostages in Beirut in June 1985. Academic discussions on such matters are important but, of course, they make very little immediate impact on police operational problems.

It was my experience that the responsive and co-operative attitude of the press in making known dangers and alerting and stimulating the public to give their utmost help to the police in combating terrorism was excellent. The only area of irritation was the occasional sensational report about alleged disagreements between the Met and the Royal Ulster Constabulary, or even internal differences within the Yard itself, that had little or no basis in fact. Following the newspaper reports after the assassination of Airey Neave that the RUC had passed a 'death list' to the Met which we had failed to act on, the Home Secretary of the day, Merlyn Rees, said in Parliament in April 1979: 'I could also add that unsubstantiated and mischievous rumours of this kind are not just a disservice to those who seek to protect their fellow citizens, but they also divert them from their essential tasks.' The amount of time that was spent by me, and by senior operational officers in the Met and the

RUC, in dealing with this sort of accusation was sometimes frustrating.

From its inception an essential part of the Anti-Terrorist Branch has been its complement of Special Branch detectives. For a period before his promotion, Detective Chief Superintendent Peter Phelan, a career Special Branch officer, was second in command to Commander Peter Duffy. The Metropolitan Police Special Branch was founded in 1883, when it was known as the Special Irish Branch, to deal with terrorist activities by the Fenians and, whilst it has certain national responsibilities for Irish terrorist activities, it is, contrary to much mythology, one of the CID branches at the Yard. This branch has built up an extensive intelligence network, including, since 1976, a small European Liaison Section. The formation of this section was made necessary because the International Criminal Police Organization (Interpol) is precluded by charter from handling intelligence that concerns politically motivated crime.

An essential part of the responsibility of the Assistant Commissioner (Crime)[1] is to co-ordinate the activities of his various branches, and the judicious selection of branch commanders and deputies who respond to the leadership of their DACs can be a great help in this. Anti-Terrorist Branch detectives are essentially like any other detective, in that they are investigators of crimes committed or about to be committed but they rely for their intelligence on their Special Branch colleagues. Special Branch detectives differ from their colleagues in as much as once they are selected, usually after two or three years' service in uniform, they normally remain in this branch of about 400 officers for the rest of their careers. Some interchange

[1] His suffix has now become SO (Special Operations).

takes place on promotion, particularly among the higher ranks, but the importance of continuity in this sensitive area of police work makes it necessary for a high degree of specialization. The ordinary detective, on the other hand, usually serves up to three years in a central branch before being transferred to CID duties in a territorial division or another central office branch. Of course, they are frequently selected to return for further tours of duty – usually in a higher rank – when their background is valuable in establishing their effectiveness. This generalist approach has proved itself over the years by improving efficiency through the development and spread of expertise and experience, and at times of emergency it automatically provides a reserve of trained officers on which to draw.

One problem which has to be taken into account in planning anti-terrorism is the spasmodic nature of this type of crime. The branch has a basic establishment of officers, and a contingency plan provides for rapid reinforcements when the scale of incidents makes this necessary, but in order to make the best use of these scarce resources, this branch was also given the responsibility of investigating the comparatively rare crime in this country of kidnapping. This foresight paid off when, in the first half of 1983, three kidnappings – none of them political – took place and were successfully investigated.

At times when there has been a welcome lull in terrorist activity, teams of detectives from the branch have been used to help their hard-pressed colleagues in the territorial division. For example, the major part of the investigation into the arson, looting and burglary that took place during the Brixton riots of 1981 was undertaken by Commander Michael Richards and his Anti-Terrorist detectives.

The success achieved by the Anti-Terrorist Branch –

and it has been considerable – is a tribute to their professionalism and to the general team spirit. Parts of the team supporting them, in addition to the Special Branch, have been the Special Patrol Group, C.7 Technical Resources, C.11 Surveillance Squad, the Fingerprint and Photographic Branches, the Metropolitan Police Scientific Laboratory and that brave band of ex-servicemen who continually risk their lives to deal with bombs and other explosive devices, the Explosives Officers. In some administrative tidying up the Explosives Officers became part of the Anti-Terrorist Branch rather than C.7, and in 1984 the Fingerprint and Photographic Branches rejoined their alma mater, the CID, after five years in the unfamiliar fold of 'B' Department, which was mainly concerned with traffic and communications matters.

During my period of office as AC (Crime) I was served by four different commanders of C.13 Branch. They were all career detectives with proven track records and each of them made a special contribution to the exacting work of their branch. One of them was promoted and is serving as a DAC in charge of a territorial area; two others, although not reaching their age limit, completed over thirty years' service – the requirement for maximum pension entitlement – and accepted offers of commercial employment. The last one, Commander Bill Hucklesby, who was in charge for two and three-quarter years, after attending a one-year Imperial Defence College Course, is now occupying a senior administrative post as commander of C.2/5 Branches.

Forensic evidence has played a vital role in the detection of terrorists and the investigating detective owes much of his success to the skill and expertise of the forensic scientist and the fingerprint expert. During the operations of the Provisional IRA bombers in the middle

1970s a series of fingerprints kept coming up at scenes of crime, houses used by terrorists, on documents and correspondence and on cars coming into our possession. These fingerprints were set up on a special type of graph and although the identities of the terrorists were not known at that point, it was obvious that comparatively few people were responsible for a whole series of outrages. When some suspects finally came into police custody they were identified and subsequently convicted – mainly on fingerprint evidence – of a large number of crimes arising from terrorist incidents.

There is little doubt that terrorists have learned much about our methods of detection from the technical evidence given at trials. It is rather like being a conjuror when having astounded the audience with the trick, one is then required to show exactly where the cards were hidden. Irish terrorists now wear surgical gloves when they are constructing explosive devices so that fingerprint evidence will not be found on them. Their anti-surveillance tactics have also become very sophisticated after hearing evidence of how other terrorists have been followed and observed. Much of this detail has been deliberately elicited in intensive cross-examination by the defence counsel at various trials.

Perhaps the most sinister and bizarre act of terrorism in London was the murder in September 1978 of Georgi Markov, a 49-year-old Bulgarian defector who came to the United Kingdom in 1970. Mr Markov worked for the BBC as a broadcaster in the Overseas Service and some of his broadcasts to Bulgaria had apparently included material critical of Bulgarian political figures.

On 7 September, having parked his car near Waterloo Bridge, Mr Markov was waiting at a bus stop on his way to his office at Bush House, Aldwych, when he was jabbed in the thigh with an umbrella by an unknown man. The man apologized and disappeared into a taxi, but later in the day Markov felt ill and mentioned the incident to his wife. Shortly after he lapsed into a coma and died four days later. The pathologist who carried out the post-mortem examination, prompted by Mrs Markov's report, found in his thigh a tiny metal sphere 68-thousandths of an inch in diameter – slightly smaller than a pin head. The sphere was made of an alloy containing a mixture of ninety per cent platinum and ten per cent iridium, with two holes, each 16-thousandths of an inch, drilled through it.

Publicity about the death of Mr Markov jogged the memory of another Bulgarian defector, a Mr Vladimir Kostov who was living in Paris. He recalled that he had been ill for several days after being prodded in the back with an umbrella on 26 August as he was leaving a Metro train. Liaison was established with the Paris police and Anti-Terrorist detectives went to France to talk to Mr Kostov. He agreed to be medically examined and to have a small surgical operation, when a metal sphere, identical to the one found in Markov's thigh, was removed from the lower part of his back. The French authorities and Mr Kostov agreed that our officers should bring the sphere back to London for forensic examination.

I wanted to trace witnesses and generally alert the public, here and abroad, to this type of assassination. On the evening of 29 September I gave a press conference at the Yard with Commander Jim Nevill, the head of the Anti-Terrorist Squad, who, because of the political implications, had taken over the Markov murder inquiry from divisional detectives.

Although there was vast publicity we received very little information, and the murder remains unsolved.

Scientists say that although there were no traces left on either of the spheres, the circumstances and the symptoms of the victims strongly suggest that Georgi Markov was murdered by poisoning with ricin. A minute quantity of this poison introduced into the bloodstream would be fatal and virtually untraceable as it would be completely absorbed. If Mr Markov had not mentioned being jabbed in the thigh with an umbrella, or had this information not been passed on to the pathologist, it is highly likely that his murder and the attempt on Mr Kostov would have gone undetected. No other murders by this method have since been reported anywhere in the world.

The most sensational act of terrorism during my serice as AC (Crime), played out in front of TV cameras giving world coverage, was the Iranian Embassy siege which began at 11.25 A.M. on Wednesday, 30 April 1980, and ended six days later with the embassy being stormed by a unit of the Special Air Services regiment, after the Arab terrorists – who called themselves the 'Group of the Martyr' – had shot a hostage. The assault on the embassy was launched after the Home Secretary – responding to a request from the Commissioner after the murder of one hostage and threats of further killings by the hour – gave his authority for the military action. With the exception of one other hostage, shot dead only moments before the SAS went in, all the remaining nineteen hostages, including PC Trevor Lock, were rescued and five of the six terrorists were killed. This was a brilliant operation by the Special Air Services Regiment which won world-wide acclaim.

Much has been written about this six-day ordeal, including a book by a BBC reporter, Simon Harris, who was one of the hostages. He and everyone else agreed that the hero of the siege was Constable Lock, who was on protection duty at the embassy when the terrorists struck and took him as one of the hostages. How he assumed leadership, negotiated with his captors and successfully concealed from them that he was armed with a revolver is now legend. For his outstanding devotion to duty and great bravery he was subsequently honoured by Her Majesty the Queen with the award of the George Medal.

Sir David McNee, the Commissioner, in his book *McNee's Law* describes his direction of the operation. He chaired twice-daily conferences with his deputy and four assistant commissioners, plus the two DACs, John Dellow and Edgar Maybanks, who, one by day and the other by night, were at the forward control in charge of the operation. The assistant commissioners were on a rota to give 24-hour support to the operational commanders but the Commissioner himself remained on call and also spent a lot of time at the forward control.

On the morning of the final day, which was a bank holiday, I attended the Commissioner's morning meeting at Prince's Gate. Then after spending some time with Commander Peter Duffy of C.13 Branch and Commander John Wilson of Special Branch, who with their specialist staff were collating evidence and providing an intelligence service to the operational commander, I went home. There was every indication that the siege would reach a climax that day and it was impossible to relax. I spent most of the day listening to the radio and waiting for the telephone to ring. In common with millions of others, just before 7.30 P.M. I saw on the television screen the dramatic filming of the SAS assault on the Iranian Embassy, and I went immediately to the Yard.

It had been agreed that as soon as PC Lock was rescued he would be taken to my office and Mrs Lock brought from their home to meet him there. As I reached my office on the fifth floor, a C.13 detective told me that Trevor Lock was safe and well and was in the cloakroom next to the office having a shower. As I went through the communicating door he was standing naked there towelling himself down. He gave me the ritual police greeting, 'All correct, sir,' adding, 'Sorry I'm not properly dressed!' He looked in pretty good shape, although he had lost several pounds in weight during those six terrible days, and I shook his hand telling him it didn't matter to me how he was dressed as long as he was alive and well.

After dressing he sat in my office and we talked about the siege until his wife, Doreen, arrived. Then I left the room so that they could have a few moments alone together. Shortly afterwards, Sir David McNee came from Prince's Gate and congratulated PC Lock on his bravery and presence of mind during the time he had been held as a hostage.

DAC Peter Neivens, the Director of Information, reported that the media were clamouring to interview the Locks. However, after six days as a hostage, and as he had not yet been debriefed, he was not ready for a press conference. This was explained to the reporters who, although they were disappointed, understood and agreed to wait until the following day. As some of them had collected outside the Locks' home, I asked a member of C.13 to book a room for them in a central London hotel under an assumed name. Later I was told that a reservation had been made, but it was not until the next day that I learned the assumed name used was Mr and Mrs Duffy, the name of their commander. Perhaps this was done to ensure that he got the bill!

The end of the siege and the safe release of the hostages was regarded as the end of the operation by the general public and, indeed, by some policemen, but this was far from the case. At that point the search began in earnest for weapons and forensic and other clues that could be used in evidence to prosecute the one surviving terrorist and at the inquests of the two dead hostages and five dead terrorists. I left the Yard just after midnight and on the way home called at Prince's Gate. Peter Duffy, who had been on duty since early morning the previous day, was still at the Iranian Embassy supervising the securing of the building until the search could begin the following day. There were also other premises to be searched that the surviving terrorist, Fowzi Badavi Nejad, told us he and his associates had used.

The crumbling embassy building, with small fires still spasmodically breaking out and with the ever-present likelihood of detonating explosives or hand grenades, made the search dangerous and difficult. It took a C.13 recovery team helped by a laboratory liaison officer and an explosives officer three days to complete the task. In addition to recovering the bodies of the dead terrorists and the one hostage shot just before the rescue operation, they found eight weapons, five hand grenades and about four hundred potential exhibits. A reel of film on the body of one of the dead terrorists provided evidence of the positions of the hostages and terrorists in the embassy before the SAS assault.

All the SAS men who took part in the assault had to be interviewed and statements taken for the coroner's inquest. We also took possession of all the firearms that had been used so that ballistic tests could be carried out on them at the Metropolitan Police Forensic Laboratory. The necessity for all this was well understood by the military authorities and we received their full co-operation.

Fowzi Badavi Nejad was charged on the evening of

Wednesday, 7 May, and appeared the next day at Horseferry Road Metropolitan Magistrates' Court. During the next four and a half months he appeared at weekly intervals at the high-security Lambeth Magistrates' Court while C.13 officers prepared the case papers for the Director of Public Prosecutions. Committal proceedings took place on 25 September and Nejad's trial at the Central Criminal Court began on 13 January 1981 and ended on the 22nd on the following indictment:

FIRST COUNT
On the 5th day of May 1980 murdered Abbas LAVASINI.
SECOND COUNT
On the 5th day of May 1980 murdered Akbar SAMADZADEH.
THIRD COUNT
On and before the 5th day of May 1980 conspired with other persons, in particular with persons known as Salem, Abbas, Shai, Makki, Jassem and Sami, to commit murder in the execution and pursuance of their unlawful occupation of the Iranian Embassy, Prince's Gate in London and in the pursuance of their demands published during the course of the said occupation.
Contrary to Section 1(1) of the Criminal Law Act, 1977
FOURTH COUNT
Between the 29th day of April 1980 and the 6th day of May 1980 unlawfully and injuriously imprisoned Trevor James Lock and detained him against his will.
FIFTH COUNT
Between the 29th day of April 1980 and the 6th day of May 1980 had in his possession certain firearms and ammunition, namely, 2 Polish WZ63 sub-machine guns, 3 9mm Parabellum Browning self-loading pistols, a ·38 Special Astra revolver and ammunition suitable for use in the said firearms, with intent by means thereof to endanger life.
Contrary to Section 16 of the Firearms Act 1968

Nejad pleaded guilty to Counts 3, 4 and 5 and not guilty to Counts 1 and 2. On the sixth day of the trial, following consultations between the prosecution and defence, he applied to change his plea to guilty of manslaughter on the first two counts. This was accepted by the court and he was sentenced to life imprisonment on each of the five counts.

The inquest into all seven deaths was opened on 9 May 1980. In accordance with Section 20(1)(b) of the Coroners Amendment Act, 1926, as substituted by Schedule 10 of the Criminal Law Act, 1977, HM Coroner had been requested by the Director of Public Prosecutions to postpone the inquest until the criminal proceedings had been completed.

The inquest into the deaths of the two hostages was satisfied by the findings of the Central Criminal Court. The inquest into the deaths of the five terrorists was resumed on Monday 3 February 1981 and a verdict of 'justifiable homicide' was reached in each case.

There were extensive debriefing conferences so that we could get the maximum benefit from the siege experience and update our contingency plans. Although the safe release of hostages is the overriding concern in any incident, it is also vitally important to gather intelligence and evidence for the eventual prosecution of the terrorists and their associates. C.13 and the supporting branches who work closely with them have developed considerable expertise in this.

It must be unique for the Commissioner and the Assistant Commissioner (Crime) both to be present at the scene of a terrorist attack. This was the situation on Thursday 3 June 1982, just after 11 P.M. when as His Excellency Shlomo Argov, the Israeli Ambassador, was leaving the Dorchester Hotel in Park Lane where he had been attending a diplomatic dinner, an attempt was made to assassinate him. Sir David McNee and I had also been guests at this dinner and were still inside the hotel when the Arab assassin, Ghassov Said, a twenty-two-year-old member of the Al-Asifa terrorist group, shot the ambassador in the head as he was about to get into his car in Park Lane.

I was in the foyer of the hotel when the news was broken to me by the personal assistant to an executive of the company hosting the dinner. Her actual words, a typical example of British understatement, were, 'Excuse me, Mr Kelland, but I think you ought to know that the Israeli Ambassador has been shot outside.' As can be imagined, my exit from the hotel into Park Lane was rapid. A few yards north of the hotel entrance I saw the ambassador lying in the gutter between his parked car and the pavement with a white-haired man bending over him. As I reached them I recognized Lord Richardson, a former Chairman of the General Medical Council and for many years Consulting Physician to the Metropolitan Police. Although I could see the ambassador was unconscious and had a nasty head wound, I asked the obvious question, 'How is he, Lord Richardson?' which was answered by another piece of understatement, 'He is not very well, Mr Kelland, but the good news is that the blood is clotting. We will leave him where he is until the ambulance comes.'

Police officers were already busy cordoning off the area and standing by Mr Argov's car was Detective Constable Colin Simpson, his Special Branch protection officer. He quickly told me what had happened, concluding with, 'And I shot the assassin who is lying around the corner being guarded by a uniformed constable.' I went around into South Street and found the assassin, who had a head wound but was conscious and being given first aid by one of the three constables with him. Introducing myself – I was wearing a dinner jacket with medals – I told them to hold on to the man and that the first ambulance to arrive was to be sent to Park Lane for Mr Argov. Returning to the hotel I met the Commissioner and a few minutes later an ambulance arrived and took Mr Argov to hospital.

Our contingency plan was working well, the area was cordoned off pending the arrival of Anti-Terrorist Branch officers and details of a yellow Fiat 127 that had been seen driving off at high speed by a hotel security officer had been circulated over the radio network to all officers. Anti-Terrorist personnel arrived and began collecting evidence at the scene of the crime. I sent Detective Constable Simpson to the Yard and followed him there shortly afterwards.

At the Yard in the fifth-floor C.13 operations room I met DAC David Powis and Commander Bill Hucklesby, both of whom had come from their homes in response to telephone messages. I also received the good news that the yellow Fiat had been stopped on Brixton Hill and its two male Arab occupants arrested. Later at Brixton police station I met constables Blake and Rickard, members of the night-duty crew of an 'L' District R/T car, who, unarmed, had seized an automatic pistol carried in a briefcase by one of the men and arrested both of them. Their presence of mind meant that within two hours of the attempted assassination the criminals responsible had been arrested and two guns seized. Very shortly afterwards Anti-Terrorist Branch detectives searched a room at the YMCA hostel at Wimbledon where one of the Arabs had been living and found another WZ 63 machine pistol – identical to the assassination weapon – and four hand grenades complete with ignition sets.

When I reached my home to snatch some sleep before returning to Scotland Yard, dawn was breaking. I recall feeling immensely proud of the team work and professionalism of the Metropolitan Police that I had witnessed in the past few hours. Later I was to learn that Detective Constable Simpson had been very lucky. After the assassin Said had fired one shot at him – which smashed the side window of a car in South Street – his automatic machine pistol had jammed, leaving twenty-three bullets in the magazine.

The arrest of the assassin near the scene of the crime with the weapons he had used still in his possession would be regarded by a reasonable person as conclusive evidence. The Anti-Terrorist Branch, by finding other weapons, fingerprints and documents – including a hit list – linking all three men, presented a very strong case. There were also charges of possession of the firearms and grenades, as well as further charges against Said of attempting to murder Detective Constable Simpson and possessing an automatic pistol with intent to resist arrest.

The three Arabs appeared at the Old Bailey in February 1983. They were, of course, all legally represented and entered pleas of not guilty. The trial lasted five weeks and on Saturday, 5 March, after they had been found guilty of attempting to murder the Israeli Ambassador, Mr Justice Mars-Jones sentenced each to thirty years' imprisonment. There were additional concurrent sentences for possession of the firearms and the grenades. However, the jury found Said – who had fired his automatic pistol at Colin Simpson – not guilty of either attempted murder or of possessing a pistol with intent to resist arrest. I can only say that this verdict seems to me as extraordinary as was the proposition, put to DC Simpson by defence counsel during the trial, that he had shot Said who was passing by at the time in mistake for the real assassin. Colin Simpson accepted all this with equanimity and afterwards resumed his low-profile role with his branch.

Thanks to the skill of the surgeons and his own tenacity, Mr Argov did not die. He recovered sufficiently to be able to return home, but is permanently paralysed from the neck down. I was reminded of his tragedy when early in 1984, shortly before I retired, I met the man who replaced him as Israeli Ambassador, His Excellency Yehuda Avner, and asked after Mr Argov. It took Mr Avner a few seconds to compose himself and then he described to me the courage of his friend. He told me how active his mind was and of the devotion of his wife who read to him every day. Mr Avner told me that it was because of his great regard for Mr Argov, and because he expressly wished it, that he himself had agreed to become the Israeli Ambassador at the Court of St James.

Most terrorist incidents in London emanating from the Middle East have involved assassination, or attempted assassination, by shooting at close range. This form of attack means that the gunmen have to show themselves and such has been the response of the Metropolitan Police and of brave and alert members of the public that a high percentage of them have been arrested. Foreign diplomats resident in or visiting London who are thought to be at risk are protected by armed Special Branch detectives. This precaution does make would-be assassins think twice, and although Mr Argov's attacker was not deterred, the fact that he was shot by the protection officer will have been noted by terrorist organizations. I believe this is the only time a Special Branch detective has had to use a firearm to protect his principal.

By contrast the PIRA and INLA groups have almost always in this country used explosive devices to perpetrate their assaults – the shooting of Ross McWhirter the journalist on his doorstep was a notable exception. This vicious and cowardly method enables the terrorists to be well away from the scene when havoc is created by the explosion of their bombs.

These attacks have caused the deaths of about eighty people in mainland Britain since 1969. Unacceptable though this number of murders is, the fact is that they are out of a population of 55 million. It is a sobering thought that during the same period in Northern Ireland 2,000 people have been killed out of a population of 1½ million. The scale of atrocities and the problems faced in preventing and detecting them by the Royal Ulster Constabulary are immense.

During the last decade the co-operation between the Metropolitan Police, the RUC and the An Garda Siochana to combat the violence of the common enemy has become increasingly effective. Government initiatives have helped, but much is also due to personal contacts and mutual confidence established between individual members of the respective police forces. This co-operation was never better illustrated than by the success of a complex anti-terrorist operation at the end of 1978 code-named 'Otis'.

At that time Brian Pascall Keenan was in Brixton Prison awaiting trial for offences of conspiracy to cause explosions. Keenan, who was believed to have been the PIRA's director of operations, had been arrested in Northern Ireland in March 1979 and brought to the mainland by C.13 Branch officers to be charged. His value to the PIRA was such that they embarked on an audacious plan to rescue him from Brixton Prison by using a helicopter.

In September Richard Glenholmes, a known member of the PIRA, and a colleague who was identified as

Robert Campbell came to London via Liverpool and were traced to the house of a Mrs Margaret Parrott, a cousin of Campbell, at Southgate in London. At this time we did not know the purpose of their visit, but their status indicated that it was likely to be some important terrorist activity. Glenholmes had succeeded Keenan as director of PIRA operations and Campbell, who was released from prison in 1977 after serving six years of an eleven-year sentence for a £60,000 armed robbery in Belfast, was a senior member of the PIRA Belfast Brigade. We decided not to arrest them until we knew more about their plans but to mount a comprehensive surveillance operation which involved several police forces.

Early in October both men went separately to Dublin. Campbell returned to his cousin's house on 14 October and that evening they both met Glenholmes at Southgate underground station. Glenholmes was not immediately recognized because he had changed his appearance by altering the style and colour of his hair, beard and moustache. During the next few days both men visited various estate agents in central London looking for a two-bedroomed flat to rent for three months, for which they were prepared to pay up to £70 a week. They also met Keenan's wife Christine and Jacqueline Ann O'Malley who was known as an Irish Republican political activist and lived in West London.

Both Glenholmes and Campbell were suspicious that they might be followed, and the officers on the surveillance operation did a superb job in keeping them under observation without alarming them. On 24 October the two men went by train to Liverpool, arriving back at Euston station at 2.30 A.M. where they were met by

O'Malley. At this stage they moved from Margaret Parrott's house in Southgate to stay with Jacqueline O'Malley at Wilsham Street in west London.

On 26 October Glenholmes went to the Southgate address and came out after about half an hour with his hair and beard dyed. The following day Campbell returned to Dublin via Liverpool, where he boarded the ferry as a seaman after obtaining an identity card from a member of the ferry staff at Liverpool. Three days later Glenholmes went to Dublin by the same route and also used a seaman's identity card.

I held frequent informal conferences with the three 'C' Department DACs, David Powis, Ronald Steventon and Colin Hewitt, and Commanders of C.13 and Special Branch (Ops), Peter Duffy and John Wilson, where we assessed intelligence, reviewed progress and agonized about the risks of leaving these dangerous men free.

Early in November our Royal Ulster Constabulary colleagues let us know that Campbell was returning to the mainland. He came back and some time later was seen to visit a model aircraft shop where, after asking about walkie-talkie equipment that the assistant told him it was illegal to use, he bought for £45 a 2-channel radio system. These sets are easily adapted for use in radio-controlled bombs and for this reason were not available in Northern Ireland. At this stage, although we had accumulated a wealth of intelligence, we still had no definite information about what these high-ranking PIRA members intended. The regular association with Christine Keenan did indicate the possibility of planning the escape of her husband from Brixton Prison, and close liaison was established with the police adviser to the Prison Service, who was Commander Bill Hucklesby. Campbell was still making inquiries about renting a flat and our information was that their plan had reached an advanced stage.

Then we had an internal complication. Margaret Parrott was employed as a secretary at a bank and was separated from her husband. A detective who had had an inquiry involving the bank some months before Campbell and Glenholmes came on the scene had met Parrott and had started an affair with her. He visited her fairly frequently – always during his off-duty periods – but never when her cousin Campbell was staying with her. We decided that this situation had to be allowed to continue, for any sudden end to his visits or his interest might arouse Parrott's suspicions, while the risks involved in taking him into our confidence and asking him to continue the affair were unacceptable.

After she was arrested, Margaret Parrott admitted that she had told her cousin about her detective boyfriend and that he had discussed with Glenholmes the possibility of her planting a bomb at a CID Christmas office party to which she and other members of the bank staff had been invited. Fortunately Glenholmes vetoed the idea in case it complicated and jeopardized the Brixton Prison escape operation.

On 4 December Campbell arranged to rent a top-floor flat at 38 Holland Park and gave a bank reference provided by his cousin to the letting agency. It looked as if matters were coming to a head and this view was reinforced when on Saturday 8 December Glenholmes arrived at Jackie O'Malley's address. Late that night he left the house with Campbell and a third man who was identified as Robert Storey, a known PIRA gunman. A senior member of the reputable flat-letting agency had been contacted and through him Commander Duffy obtained keys to the street door and to Flat 11 on the top floor.

I chaired a conference of senior detectives on the following Monday when we agreed that a unit of senior PIRA members had assembled to release Keenan from Brixton Prison and possibly also plan some diversionary bombing attacks. The risk of loss of life or serious injury was now too great to allow these terrorist suspects to remain at liberty. An operational plan was prepared for co-ordinated police raids to take place on addresses which had been identified during the inquiry in London, Liverpool, Manchester, the West Midlands and Hampshire, at 4 A.M. on Wednesday 12 December. The operation went smoothly and twenty-eight people were arrested under the Prevention of Terrorism Act. Of these, eleven of the principal suspects were subsequently charged with a variety of criminal offences.

When armed police from the D.11 firearms unit entered Flat 11 at 38 Holland Park, the four men who had been asleep there surrendered, were handcuffed and arrested by C.13 detectives. In bedside cabinets there were two loaded 9mm Browning pistols and 196 rounds of ammunition. When, in addition to Campbell, Glenholmes and Storey, the fourth man arrested was identified as Gerard Anthony Tuite, advertised on wanted posters all over the country for his involvement in the December 1978 series of bombings in London, we realized what a blow had been dealt to the PIRA.

On the domestic front, Mrs Parrott's detective friend was interviewed and we were satisfied that he knew nothing of her PIRA associations. It was a very subdued and chastened man who emerged from the office of DAC Ron Steventon after he had learned the potential danger of his amorous adventure. In fact, this particular relationship was responsible for the operation being code-named 'Otis', which is a slight variation on the CID expression 'OTS', an acronym for 'over the side', a slang description for an extra-marital relationship. There was some in-house amusement when a crime reporter attributed the use of the name Otis to the fact that it was the trade name of a passenger-lift manufacturer, and of course the terrorists had been 'lifted'!

Documentary and other evidence seized at Holland Park and the other addresses fully confirmed our suspicions that the plan to release Keenan from Brixton Prison was well advanced. We learned that on the day before the arrests Jackie O'Malley, using a false name, had made a booking to hire a helicopter for £250 to fly herself and two men from Battersea Heliport to Folkestone and return on 13 December. We believed this trip was intended as a trial run to see if the carrying of firearms on the hired helicopter was likely to be detected. Markings on an A–Z map of London found in Margaret Parrott's flat showed that on the actual rescue flight they had intended to land the hi-jacked helicopter in Finsbury Park after the escape, and we believed that Storey had been brought over to shoot the pilot after he had served their purpose. In Campbell's room we found an accurate map of Brixton prison showing a proposed route for the helicopter, with notes on the layout and height of buildings. The handwriting proved to be that of Brian Keenan and, although she would not admit it, we believed the map and the notes had been smuggled out of Brixton Prison by Christine Keenan after one of her visits to her husband.

The seaman's pass used to board the Liverpool–Dublin ferry was found and the rightful owner, after pleading guilty to withholding information under the Prevention of Terrorism Act, received a sentence of three months' imprisonment.

At the Old Bailey in March 1981 Brian and Christine Keenan, Campbell, Glenholmes, Storey, Parrott and O'Malley were tried for various offences including conspiracy to aid the release of Brian Keenan from Brixton Prison, possessing firearms with intent to endanger life and conspiracy to cause explosions. Campbell and Glenholmes received fifteen years' imprisonment, Brian Keenan had three years added to the eighteen years he was already serving for offences of conspiracy to cause explosions in the United Kingdom, Parrott was sentenced to twelve months' imprisonment suspended for three years and fined £1,000 and Jacqueline O'Malley was also fined £1,000 and sentenced to eighteen months' imprisonment suspended for three years. Robert Storey was found not guilty and he returned to Northern Ireland where within a year he was arrested in possession of an Armalite rifle after a shooting incident and was subsequently sentenced to fifteen years' imprisonment.

Gerard Anthony Tuite did not appear to stand trial because during the early hours of 16 December 1980, one year after his arrest at Holland Park, he escaped from Brixton Prison with two notorious London criminals, Alfred Moody and Stanley Thompson. The three men were in adjoining cells in 'D' wing of the prison and each made a hole in his cell wall – the hole in the last cell wall, which was Tuite's, gave access to a flat roof. It was discovered afterwards that Moody initiated the escape, using various small tools smuggled to him by his brother during visits to tunnel through the walls. Moody was lodged in the inside cell and it was fortuitous for Tuite that he was in the cell with an external wall and so had to be brought into Moody's plan. Each of the men put a dummy figure made up of clothing stuffed with newspapers in his bed on the night of the escape. This deceived the night duty warders inspecting the cells and it was not until 5 A.M., when a prison warder on outside patrol found a plank of wood against the security fence, that the alarm was raised. As the result of inquiries a minicab driver was found who at about 4 A.M. had driven three men from near Brixton Prison to East Dulwich.

The escape by Tuite was a bitter disappointment but eventually when he was arrested in March 1982 at Drogheda in the Irish Republic he was the test case for the Irish Criminal Law (Jurisdiction) Act, 1976. This Act was designed to overcome the problem of the Irish Republican courts refusing to extradite alleged criminals who claimed they were wanted for politically motivated offences. Much preparatory work had been done and agreement reached with the legal authorities in Dublin because a person arrested in the Republic must be charged and taken before a court within forty-eight hours.

Tuite appeared before a no-jury three-judge court, known as the Special Criminal Court, which sits in Dublin and deals with all terrorist offences. He was charged with two offences at a flat in Trafalgar Road, Greenwich, between June 1978 and March 1979 of possessing explosives and conspiracy to cause explosions, both contrary to Section 4 of the Irish Criminal Law (Jurisdiction) Act, 1976.

As this was the first time this legislation had been used in respect of offences committed in England, there were problems to be faced. The charge included the words 'being an Irish citizen outside the State' and so it was necessary to prove Tuite's nationality. His birth certificate was produced and proved but this was insufficient. However, the evidence from a retired police sergeant that in 1975 at Mountnugent, Co. Cavan, where Tuite lived, he had been on duty when in a passport application he had witnessed Tuite signing a declaration that he was Irish, was accepted as being conclusive. The defence claimed double jeopardy because he was still wanted in the United Kingdom for these offences, and the court resolved this by asking Tuite where he wished to be tried, Dublin or London – not surprisingly he elected for Dublin.

Apart from the forensic evidence it was vital to produce the prosecution witnesses in Dublin. A team of C.13 detectives carried out the delicate task of interviewing over 150 potential witnesses and getting their agreement to travel to Eire to give evidence. Only one person refused. Witnesses cannot be compelled to travel out of this country and it would certainly be beneficial if legislation provided, as it does with witnesses north or south of the Irish border, for the High Court judges to hear evidence where the witness is domiciled. The Dublin court required the attendance of fifty-eight witnesses and C.13 detectives arranged for their travel, in some cases going with them to reassure them about their safety.

There were over 500 exhibits, about 250 of them taken from the various bomb scenes, the remainder from the safe houses and bomb factories in and around London. Each exhibit, including firearms and explosive traces, when produced to the court had to be strictly proved in accordance with Irish Law. A C.13 detective was sworn in as the exhibits officer and made accountable for the continuity and security of the exhibits. To assist the court a schedule was prepared covering a three-year period, showing the movement of each exhibit, by whom it was handled and where it was stored. This document, which took eight weeks to prepare, was invaluable in proving the exhibits and making them admissible as evidence.

Then a further complication developed. At the time of Tuite's arrest another member of his 1978/9 gang, John McComb, was arrested in Belfast, brought to London and charged with identical offences. This meant that the same exhibits would be required in both courts, but we could get no firm undertaking either from the Special Criminal Court in Dublin or the Central Criminal Court in London that exhibits after production to their court would be released before the conclusion of the respective trials. However, in due course the Central Criminal Court did give consent for the exhibits, first produced there in the trial of McComb, to be taken to Dublin.

As can be imagined, the C.13 manpower commitment in connection with these two trials, especially that of Tuite, was very considerable. This is, of course, a problem with all major criminal trials where key operational detectives are often tied up for several weeks preparing for the case and attending the court.

The Dublin Special Criminal Court eventually found Tuite guilty on the count of possessing explosives and sentenced him to ten years' imprisonment. They adjourned the conspiracy to cause explosions charge without pronouncing upon it. At the end of the trial both the court and the defence counsel commended the C.13 exhibits officer for the professional way in which he had helped the hearing.

Tuite appealed against his conviction but in May 1983 the Court of Criminal Appeal in Dublin upheld the decision and the authority of the three-judge Special Criminal Court and dismissed his appeal. An application to appeal to the Irish Supreme Court on grounds that the case raised a point of law of exceptional public importance was also refused.

This prosecution under the Irish Criminal Law (Jurisdiction) Act is important because it has established that provided evidence of an offence against the Explosive Substances Act, 1883, or of murder can be produced, a terrorist born in the Irish Republic can no longer regard his homeland as a safe haven.

Whilst all terrorist attacks involving loss of life and injury are obscene, none, in the eyes of policemen, are more so than those where their colleagues are victims and, although by comparison with the RUC the Met casualty list is minuscule, the deaths still cause a deep anger. The longest outstanding case of the murder of a Met policeman by a terrorist is that of twenty-year-old Stephen Tibble in Fulham in 1975. This newly married young officer was shot dead when he joined in a chase by other policemen to stop a man running in the street. There had been seven PIRA bombings in London during the previous month and evidence was later found linking the assassin with these crimes.

As the result of inquiries by the Anti-Terrorist Branch, a William Joseph Quinn, alias Rogers, born in 1948 and an American citizen was circulated as wanted for Stephen Tibble's murder. In 1981 he was traced to San Francisco and early in the morning of 30 September, at the request of New Scotland Yard, agents of the Federal Bureau of Investigation arrested him for the offences of murdering Constable Stephen Tibble on 26 February 1975 and for conspiring to cause explosions in London during 1974 and 1975.

There then followed long extradition hearings where our case was vigorously and skilfully presented by an

American Federal attorney acting on behalf of the Director of Public Prosecutions and briefed by Anti-Terrorist Branch detectives. The Californian magistrate hearing the case eventually made an order for Quinn's extradition to the United Kingdom. However, Quinn appealed against this decision and those representing him argued that the alleged offences were 'political' crimes. As a result his appeal was allowed. The Federal authorities have further appealed against this ruling to the Supreme Court, Quinn is in custody and to date (1986) the case has still not been resolved.

During 1985 a revised treaty between Britain and the United States was signed, a supplement to one signed in 1972, in an attempt to close legal loopholes which have enabled terrorists to avoid extradition by pleading that their crimes were political. Its principal provision identifies specific crimes such as murder, kidnapping and hijacking as being non-political. Before this treaty can become operative it has to be ratified by the United States Senate, where a group of Democrats – including the powerful Irish lobby – are raising all sorts of questions and holding up the treaty's progress. This is hardly in accord with the many strident speeches made by political leaders on both sides of the Atlantic on the need to stand firm and united against all forms of terrorism, and law enforcement agencies could perhaps be forgiven for suggesting that in international matters the unspoken caveat, 'Unless it is politically expedient not to do so', too often applies.

The memory of Stephen Tibble, who was posthumously awarded the Queen's Police Medal for gallantry, is kept alive in the Met by a boxing trophy presented by his parents, which is competed for annually at the Metropolitan Police Athletic Association's Novice Lafone Cup competition and awarded to the boxer judged to have given the best performance. Mr and Mrs Tibble have several times attended the competition and presented the trophy to the winner at the Hammersmith Palais, less than a mile from where their son tragically lost his life in the course of duty. They are rightly very proud of their son, and of his service with the Met, and share the wish of all his former colleagues that the man accused of his murder should stand trial at the Old Bailey.

It was with considerable satisfaction that at my retirement party at the Yard on the evening of the last day of my service on 16 March 1984 I heard of the arrest of Paul Kavanagh by the RUC in Belfast. Kavanagh was wanted by us for being a principal in the October 1981 wave of bombings. In one month a PIRA terrorist group set off a nail bomb outside Chelsea Barracks, intended for the Irish Guards but killing a man and a woman who were passing at the time; planted two booby-trapped time bombs in Oxford Street shops, one of which killed Kenneth Howarth, a Met explosives officer, when he was attempting to dismantle it; seriously injured Sir Steuart Pringle, Commandant-General of the Royal Marines in an attempted assassination by planting an explosive device in his car while it was parked outside his Dulwich home, and bombed the Wimbledon home of the Attorney-General, Sir Michael Havers, when, fortunately, he and his wife were not sleeping there.

Kenneth Howarth's act of bravery was recognized by the posthumous award of the George Medal. He was a keen cricketer and in keeping with the sporting traditions of the Met in his memory there is an annual six-a-side cricket competition between civil staff branches for a trophy donated by his wife, Mrs Ann Howarth.

Kavanagh was known to be living in Eire but, as the

RUC had thought likely, he made the fatal mistake of returning to Belfast to see his wife and four-year-old daughter and they arrested him. During January 1984 some brilliant work by our Special Branch surveillance unit had identified Kavanagh and another man, Natalino Vella, when they followed them to Annesley Forest in Nottinghamshire and Salcey Forest in Northamptonshire. At both places subsequent searches revealed arms and explosive caches inside plastic dustbins buried in the ground. There was disappointment that after being followed to the arms caches Kavanagh and Vella had slipped through the net and escaped to Ireland, largely because it was necessary to give them a long rein until the last moment. However, not only did the discovery of the PIRA's arms store prevent another bombing campaign but when they were eventually arrested the forensic evidence from the surveillance proved most valuable.

Another similar cache of arms had been discovered earlier in October 1983 near the village of Whitechurch in Oxfordshire by a forestry worker while he was clearing some undergrowth. In this store, as well as guns, explosives and batteries, two sets of car keys were found. These proved to belong to the white Commer van used for the car bomb at Chelsea Barracks and to a green Volkswagen seen by witnesses nearby at the time of the attack on the barracks. Meticulous planning had taken place months before the bombings: the gang had obtained birth certificates and other documentation to establish false identities and registered the ownership of a vehicle under a false name and address. Having gone to such elaborate lengths and then having blown up the van and abandoned the Volkswagen, the retention of their keys is inexplicable. However, their mistake provided useful evidence in linking them with the bombings.

Another of the October gang, Thomas Quigley, had already been arrested and charged, having been brought to London from Belfast in December 1982. Kavanagh joined him in the dock, and later Natalino Vella, the PIRA messenger, was also arrested. The three men were finally convicted at the Old Bailey in March 1985 after a trial lasting nearly three weeks. Quigley and Kavanagh, both aged twenty-nine, were given five life terms for the three murders, placing an explosive device at Debenham's in Oxford Street, and for a bombing attack on the home of the Attorney-General on the night of 13 November 1981. The judge, Mr Justice McCowan, also gave them twenty years each for possessing the Oxfordshire cache and Kavanagh received a further twenty years in respect of the Salcey and Annesley Forest caches. A recommendation that a minimum of thirty-five years be served by each of them was made. Vella, who had pleaded guilty to two charges of possessing arms and explosives at the forest caches, was jailed for a total of fifteen years. Once again, patient methodical detective work over a long period backed up by expert forensic evidence had resulted in a terrorist gang being brought to justice.

Kidnapping for ransom is fortunately a very rare crime in the United Kingdom. In the decade before my retirement in 1984 there had only been six in London – five during my period of office as AC (Crime), and three of them between January and April 1983. Every case was successfully concluded: the victims were freed unharmed, no ransom money was paid and the criminals concerned were arrested and jailed.

In 1978 David Powis, my deputy, chaired a small working party which revised the Met's contingency plan for dealing with kidnapping. The Anti-Terrorist Branch

(C.13) were nominated – provided they were not fully committed on anti-terrorist operations – to be responsible for the investigation of all kidnap-for-ransom crimes as well as the investigation of all political kidnappings. In fact the April 1983 case was taken on by C.1 Serious Crime Squad because C.13 were already fully stretched with the January and March cases.

The major contributory factors to our success in clearing up these serious crimes were having a good plan, the complete co-operation of the relatives of the victims and the agreement of the media to maintain a news embargo until the victims were safe. The media were given full and frank briefings at regular intervals – sometimes twice daily – and informed immediately there was no longer any danger to the life of the victims.

The latter proviso is essential because it forms the basis of a relationship of mutual trust. It was the condition made by news media editors and accepted by Sir Robert Mark when he chaired a conference in 1975 to find a formula for a news blackout after the tragic murder in Staffordshire of the kidnap victim Lesley Whittle by Donald Neilson, the Black Panther.

There can be circumstances where there is a big temptation for operational officers to delay informing the press that the victim has been freed. I recall the case in March 1983 of the kidnapping of eighteen-year-old Robert Goldstein at Ilford in Essex. The kidnappers, believing that his family was wealthy, made a ransom demand of £200,000 and on the evening of the second day after his abduction his father, responding to their directions and in co-operation with C.13 Branch, set out to deliver the money. He was directed by messages left under the coin boxes of three different telephone boxes to Chigwell, Wanstead, Redbridge and then to the junction of the M11 motorway with the A113 where, obeying instructions, he left the parcel containing the money and went home.

Just before midnight his son telephoned him to say he was free and at a telephone call box at Wanstead. Mr Goldstein immediately drove there and brought his son, who was unharmed, back to their home at Chigwell. The ransom money was being kept under covert surveillance by detectives, but no attempt had yet been made to collect it. I was telephoned at home at about 1 A.M. and told what had happened and that the intention was to maintain the watch on the ransom money until dawn. If by this time no attempt had been made to collect it, without the cover of darkness the presence of police would become obvious.

I instructed that our Press Bureau should be informed immediately that Robert Goldstein was free so that the news could be passed to the media without delay. It was pointed out to me that early publicity might alert the kidnappers who would not then come for the ransom money. I did not think this was an acceptable argument for not releasing the news, for the basis of the agreement with journalists only provided for a blackout if life was in actual danger. Fortunately, though, the news was too late for publication in the morning papers and therefore the only possibility of publicity before dawn came from the all-night London radio news broadcasts. The representatives of the agencies concerned were told we were anxious not to have any publicity before dawn and that we would appreciate their co-operation in keeping a blackout until then. No mention of the kidnap case was made therefore until the 7 A.M. news broadcasts, by which time the criminals had still not attemped to collect the money and it was recovered.

I chaired a press conference at the Yard at eleven

o'clock attended by Mr and Mrs Goldstein and Robert. In the course of it Mr Goldstein said, 'I'm very grateful to the press for holding off any stories about this which enabled our son to return safely to us. I would advise anyone to go to the police. I would never consider giving any money without involving the police. Initially I was very alarmed but subsequently very reassured by the attitude and advice of the police.'

During his period of detention Robert Goldstein was bound and blindfolded, so he was unable to help by giving any description of his captors or of the place where he was held. Based on an estimate of the time between the kidnapping and arrival at the address where he was kept the investigating officers had the thankless task of looking for a place anywhere within a ten- to fifteen-mile radius of his work at Gants Hill. However, Robert was able to provide a very useful clue – he remembered hearing a helicopter flying over at fairly regular intervals. The C.13 detectives quickly realized that the only regular helicopter flights in this area were those of our police helicopter – India 99 – from its base at Lippetts Hill near Epping Forest, and with the co-operation of the pilot the search area was narrowed. Eventually they focused on the motel where the kidnappers had rented accommodation and held Robert Goldstein. Further inquiries eventually led to the arrest of two men who were convicted and jailed for the crime.

Voluntary news blackouts to protect life have been a remarkable development and there is no doubt that it has contributed immensely to a greater understanding between the Yard and journalists. However, it is essential, if this situation is to be maintained, for the police always to be absolutely frank and never to delay releasing news once the life of a victim is no longer at risk.

An official spanner was almost thrown into the works when the Director of Public Prosecutions drew up guidelines to prevent breaches of the Contempt of Court Act, 1981, after the furore caused by reporting of the arrest of the multiple murderer known as the 'Yorkshire Ripper' and the press conference that followed it. The Home Office issued a circular to all chief police officers repeating the advice of the Director, which included a ban on press conferences once an arrest had been made. A Home Office circular is in theory an advisory document because constitutionally chief police officers cannot be given operational orders by the executive. However, in practice these circulars are regarded as directives and the advice given in them – which is usually published after consultation with the Association of Chief Police Officers – is invariably acted upon.

In April 1983, after the Home Office circular had been issued but before a copy had reached my desk, I held a press conference at the close of the third kidnapping operation that year which involved a Mrs Shirley Goodwin.

Mrs Goodwin, whose husband John had only just begun to serve a seven-year sentence for jury nobbling – his conviction was later quashed on appeal – was taken from her Hackney flat at 10.30 P.M. on 21 April at gun point by four masked men. They also robbed her of £1,500 from a wall safe which they forced her to open. Her eighteen-year-old son, Spencer, who was at home when his mother was kidnapped, telephoned a family friend, Mr Peter Gough, who told him to go to the police. He did not do so and it was not until 5 P.M. on the following day, when Mr Gough came to the Yard, that we learned of the kidnapping. Detective Chief Superintendent John George of C.1 Serious Crime Squad was put in charge of the investigation and he was told by Spencer Goodwin that the kidnappers had telephoned demanding a £50,000 ransom for his mother's release and telling him not to contact the police.

For the next six days negotiations by telephone went on between the criminal gang – who were unaware that the police had been called in – and members of the Goodwin family, and tape-recorded messages from Mrs Goodwin pleading with her sons to do what the kidnappers wanted were delivered to the flat. This development, coupled with information from John Goodwin when he was interviewed in Wandsworth Prison that he had had a long-standing quarrel with a Walworth criminal named Charlie Pitts, had helped the investigation to make good progress. The Goodwins had agreed a reduced ransom of £10,000 with the kidnappers and at 8 P.M. on 27 April as the money was about to be handed over in a car park near the Elephant and Castle an arrest operation was put into action. Between then and 10 P.M. five men, including Charlie Pitts, and four women were arrested and a number of addresses in the Walworth area were searched. Mrs Goodwin was not found, but from one of those arrested we learned that she was being held at a holiday chalet on the Isle of Sheppey in Kent.

At about 11.15 P.M. while Kent County Constabulary officers were on their way to the Isle of Sheppey, Mrs Goodwin, still dressed in the nightdress and dressing-gown she had been wearing when she was kidnapped, walked into Mitcham police station. She told us her captors had brought her to London in the boot of a car and released her in the car park of a public house quite near to the police station. She was taken immediately to the Yard where she was examined by a doctor and seen by her solicitor before being interviewed and then driven to her home. She was suffering from shock and stress but was otherwise unharmed.

The media had once again co-operated in maintaining a news embargo and I felt that it was fair and important to continue to give the facts about our operation. I believed that, as in earlier cases, this could be done without offending against the 1981 Contempt of Court Act. I understand that the TV broadcast of the press conference was monitored at the Home Office, but I never received any criticism and when I pointed out to them the special position of the media in kidnap cases, and the need to maintain their co-operation, it was agreed that a relaxation could be made in the advice ruling out press conferences after an arrest. Of course there is normally no exemption for the police, or the media, from the observance of the Contempt of Court Act and the legal position has not changed since the issue of the Home Office circular.

The sequel to the Shirley Goodwin case was that in June 1984 Charles Pitts was jailed for eighteen years for kidnapping and his son-in-law, Sean McDonald, also from Walworth, who pleaded guilty to false imprisonment, blackmail and robbery of Mrs Goodwin, received a sentence of eight years' imprisonment. Inquiries continued to trace the other members of the gang and in May 1985 at the Old Bailey William Davies was jailed for fourteen years for his part in the kidnapping. An unusual piece of evidence was given at his trial when a phonetics expert identified the voice of Davies on one of the tape-recorded ransom messages.

Police operations to deal with kidnapping are very manpower intensive because speed is vital. Something in the region of 120 detectives, with vehicles, radios and other equipment, are usually deployed, and the C.11

Surveillance Squad proved its value in every one of the three successful 1983 operations. Confidence in, and co-operation with, the police by the relatives of victims is, I am sure, a deterrent to those who might be tempted to try their hand at kidnapping for it has meant that there has been a nil success rate for the crime in this country. Long may this confidence between members of the public and the police continue.

15
International and Organized Crime

In recent years there has been a significant increase in the United Kingdom of international organized crime. With our common language it is not surprising that major criminal elements in the United States have from time to time attempted to get a foothold in London and they are aided now by the speed of communication and transportation. Although one high-value jewellery robbery, which will be mentioned later, was carried out by two American criminals with Mafia connections, in the main they have concentrated on the so-called victim-less crimes such as gambling, pornography, drugs and fraud, all criminal enterprises they have found lucrative in their own country.

Organized crime has been described as the product of self-perpetuating criminal conspiracies to wring exorbitant profits from our society by any means – fair or foul, legal or illegal – and undoubtedly vast profits have been made from well-organized international ventures. It is by definition on a vastly different plane to the majority of crimes known to the police, and the problem is, how do you recognize it? In a report on criminal activity in the State of New South Wales published in 1972 a High Court judge of that State, the Honourable Justice Moffitt, commented: 'There seems to be a very real danger that organized crime from overseas will infiltrate this country in a substantial fashion. If it does there will be little appearance of its arrival or activities of armed gangsters with black shirts and white ties. More likely it will arrive within the Trojan horse of legitimate business, fashioned for concealment and apparent respectability by the witting or unwitting aid of expert accountants, lawyers and businessmen.' The judge's observation sums up the insidious nature of organized crime and it could be equally applicable to London or any other major international English-speaking city.

While the majority of crimes are poorly planned, frequently violent and generally not enormously financially rewarding, organized crime, committed by rational and intelligent individuals, is well planned and always aimed at an immense financial gain. In this country the law at the moment prevents the deterrent of stripping them of their assets.

To combat serious crime, and particularly international organized crime, an efficient intelligence system is essential. When I took over 'C' Department in 1977, I asked for the organization of C.11 Criminal Intelligence Branch to be reviewed, for I had misgivings about the minuscule international section after my experiences in the West End in the 1960s when casino gaming was legalized, and by spin-offs from the Humphreys inquiry.

In the middle 1960s, when casino gaming had been legalized but before the Gaming Board of Great Britain was set up, Juda Binstock had been a part owner of the Victoria Sporting Club and, through Angelo Bruno, a well-known American Mafia figure, had flown parties of punters across the Atlantic to gamble at his casino. In 1968/9 Binstock relinquished his interest in the company, apparently fearing that the new Gaming Board would not grant a certificate of consent for it to apply for a casino licence while he was a principal shareholder. At about the same time a C.11 detective inspector, who had been responsible for intelligence concerning gambling and casinos, resigned before reaching pensionable service and was immediately employed by Binstock. Because of Binstock's association with American criminals the move by the detective was regarded with some suspicion. Later on, when Binstock was charged with stockbroker Lewis Altman and others in a £2 million currency fraud but fled the country and failed to stand his trial, these suspicions were not allayed.

While they were showing an interest in the Victoria Sporting Club through Binstock, American organized crime figures also had a financial stake in the Colony Club casino in Berkeley Square. George Raft, the film star, was a director of the Colony and Freddie Ayoub, another American and a former casino manager in the States, was the company secretary, while other American citizens from New York, Philadelphia, Florida and Cleveland were shareholders. After prosecutions in 1969 for illegal gaming at the Colony Club, the company owning it went into voluntary liquidation. As the result of the prosecution and the subsequent inquiries, links with the Mafia were established and George Raft was 'gated', that is, he was placed on the list of persons designated by the Home Secretary as not allowed to enter the United Kingdom.

There was also another significant prosecution in May 1969 when the Villa Casino Club in the Bayswater Road, which was leased to some Americans for £1,000 a week, was raided and seven people – all of them Americans – were arrested and charged with conspiracy to obtain property by deception. They had been arranging gambling junkets, flying punters to London and then cheating them at the three gaming tables by using loaded dice. I have reason to believe this club was 'shopped' by rival Americans with gambling interests who hoped to curry favour with our international criminal intelligence section.

These two prosecutions, followed by the introduction of the Gaming Board of Great Britain as the statutory regulatory authority, made these clubs the last examples of any overt investment by American organized crime interests in London casinos.

A spin-off from the Humphreys inquiry that disturbed me concerned two C.11 officers, a detective chief inspector and a detective sergeant, who after being investigated had been disciplined and required to resign. The case against the former arose from the inept prosecution of an American pornographer arrested for passing forged dollar bills which a prostitute acquaintance had attempted to change in a casino; and the sergeant had been compromised by a Soho pornographer.

After much thought and discussions with my immediate deputies I agreed in 1978 to a proposal from David Powis to form a new special intelligence section (SIS) that would be responsible for international crime matters. Great care was taken in selecting people to serve in the new intelligence section. An injection of fresh blood into the junior detective ranks was achieved by transferring some members of the fairly recently established West End Central vice intelligence section. Two men who came from this unit, constables Frank Pulley and John Summers, had been known to me personally for over twenty years. Their vast knowledge of the Soho and Mayfair gambling and vice scene, coupled with their ability and reputation for integrity, made them very effective intelligence officers.

Although I was more than satisfied with Commander Harvey's direction of C.11 Branch it was decided that the new SIS should be part of C.1 Branch and thus under the control of DAC 'C' (Operations), whereas C.11 was responsible to DAC 'C' (Support). The separation of this aspect of intelligence from the mainstream was an unusual decision and not universally popular, or understood. It was made because of my experiences and a gut feeling, shared by David Powis, that some elements of international organized crime might have penetrated our existing intelligence system. I envisaged this separation as a temporary measure – albeit perhaps a fairly lengthy one – with full integration with C.11 when all our fears had been allayed. It was a full six years later, in 1984, that this integration finally took place.

Some further justification for the action came after the suicide of the property tycoon Sir Eric Miller in 1979, when some C.11 confidential documents were found among his papers that related to his friend Juda Binstock, who was wanted for exchange control offences and had fled to France. A detective superintendent who had been a member of C.11 eventually appeared at the Old Bailey charged with corruption and, under the Official Secrets Act, for passing the papers about Binstock to Sir Eric. He was acquitted on the corruption charge but convicted on the Official Secrets Act offence and fined £500.

Sir Eric Miller, it will be recalled, was the flamboyant chairman of the Peachey Property corporation who received his knighthood in Harold Wilson's controversial 1976 resignation honours list. On 22 September 1977, after he had been removed as the chairman of his property company and was under investigation by the Met Fraud Squad and the Board of Trade, he committed suicide in the garden of his house at Little Boltons in Chelsea by shooting himself. A Board of Trade report published in 1979 chronicled his many extravagances and the lavish spending of his company's money which, had he lived, would have meant prosecution for theft and fraud.

One of the earliest tasks of the new SIS was to take an

in-depth look at London casinos. It was ironical that just at the start of this examination, which was to show that all was not well with the gaming industry, a Royal Commission on gambling chaired by Lord Rothschild after a three-year inquiry produced its final report. A paragraph in this report stated, 'The Gaming Board has been particularly successful in dealing with casinos in which, before the 1968 Act, the criminal threat was perceived to be the greatest. The situation has now changed markedly and in future we envisage that the Board's role will have to change and develop somewhat away from the crime-busting one with which it now tends to be identified.' They could not have been more wrong.

Acting on information collated by the new intelligence section, C.1 Serious Crime Squad between December 1978 and February 1981 executed search warrants and raided fourteen London casinos – about twenty-five per cent of the total. The investigations that followed disclosed widespread dishonesty and malpractice on the part of some casino company directors and their managers that deprived their shareholders of millions of pounds. The prosecutions were in most cases contested but convictions were obtained and usually resulted in heavy fines. However, the most feared penalty was the loss of the casino licence. Eight casinos closed down because they were unable to renew their licences and in two cases the premises were also disqualified from being used as casinos for three years. The remainder, after changing hands, were relicensed under new managements. Share values of operating companies were affected and the Commissioner, Sir David McNee, told me that comments had been made to him that our actions had harmed pension fund investments.

There was no direct evidence of any American-based

crime involvement, but some of the practices we uncovered such as 'skimming' – that is, diverting monies out of the companies without their passing through any accounting procedures – were typical of Mafia methods. Casinos have long been recognized by criminals as being useful for 'laundering' hot money so that it can then be claimed as legitimate gambling winnings. There are two ways of doing this, by purchasing gaming chips and later exchanging them for cash or a casino cheque, or a straight change of cash at a discount rate. The second method requires the connivance of the casino management and in one of the raids on a West End casino bundles of bank notes each to the value of £925 were found in a safe. Although there were no admissions, our information led us to conclude that these bundles of notes had been made up ready to exchange for amounts of £1,000. Criminals would regard this as a fair rate of interest for the service provided.

These operations against casinos were quite expensive in terms of resources, particularly in tying up experienced detectives for long periods. I had no doubt, however, that the time and effort were very worthwhile, both in their effect on attitudes to honesty in the industry and as a warning to the international criminal fraternity that London was not to be regarded as a soft touch. One inquiry took detectives to the USA where, with the help of the FBI, a former casino deputy managing director who had absconded some five years earlier after 'skimming' at least £400,000, was located and interviewed. The Director of Public Prosecutions agreed to his extradition from California and he eventually stood trial at the Central Criminal Court, was found guilty and jailed for two and a half years.

As a result of the rapport we developed with various

American law enforcement agencies, a number of the SIS staff and David Powis attended criminal intelligence analysis systems and management courses run by Colonel Dintino of the State of New Jersey Police Department which helped to improve our efficiency. Colonel Dintino, who later visited us at the Yard, was responsible for pioneering work on the subject of criminal intelligence, is the author of many professional articles and is much respected in legal circles as an expert in this area.

I was very amused after the return in 1983 of a member of the SIS from the United States, where he had carried out some inquiries on behalf of the Gaming Board, when he reported that some dubious character there had discovered that the salaries of the part-time chairman and members of the Board were £7,000 and £5,000 respectively. 'What's the problem in getting a deal with guys paid chicken feed like that?' he had remarked. He, of course, had never heard of the British system of 'the great and the good'. At this time the chairman of the Board was the Lord Allen of Abbeydale, a former permanent under secretary at the Home Office, and a member was Sir James Starritt, former Deputy Commissioner of the Metropolitan Police. I could not help reflecting that an interview between the cynical American and these two formidable gentlemen – although probably very short – would have been more than interesting.

The fact that expert observers and students of criminology everywhere regard gambling as the life blood of organized crime – the ultimate in low risk/high profit business – made the rash of casino prosecutions in London of worldwide interest. One result of it was that in November 1982 David Powis gave evidence in Melbourne at the request of the State of Victoria before a Board of Inquiry into casinos chaired by the Honourable F. X.

Connor, QC. The Board, charged with recommending for or against casinos, was concerned that money from organized crime would arrive with the introduction of legalized gaming. The chairman also commented on the situation in neighbouring New South Wales, as it was documented in a report by Justice Moffitt on criminal activity in that State. The decision went against having licensed casinos in Melbourne.

One domestic problem that arose out of the casino prosecutions was the discovery of what appeared to be another attempt to penetrate the C.11 intelligence branch. Examination of the books of a casino showed that the company had discussed with a detective inspector, who was at that time – before the formation of the SIS – responsible for international crime and casino intelligence, the question of offering him a job. Further inquiry revealed that he had been abroad on holiday with the casino accountant whom he had met in the course of his duties. Although there was no evidence of any criminal offence this relationship did not, to say the least, inspire confidence and the inspector, after being given some advice, was transferred to a less sensitive post. Shortly afterwards he voluntarily resigned and I was told he had gone to Sun City in Bophuthatswana, to work in the casino industry there. However, the fact that despite the anticipated high internal security risk there had been no leaks or whispers of any kind about the casino operations from the wrong quarter more than compensated for this incident.

I was reminded that the Met had no monopoly on the 'enemy within' syndrome by experiences I had when I was in charge of the Clubs Office in the West End during the early 1960s. Within a short period a sergeant and a constable had been lent on separate occasions to the then

Manchester City and Southend Borough police forces to keep undercover observations on large clubs where betting, gambling and licensing offences were suspected. On each occasion, after the observations had been successfully kept and search warrants obtained by local senior officers, our Clubs Office staff had told us that shortly before the raiding party was due at the clubs the management announced that police were expected at any minute and requested all non-members immediately to fill in application for membership forms! Clearly there were eleventh-hour leaks and attemps to nobble the operations.

The case initiated by the SIS that most clearly and unequivocally showed the involvement of American organized crime concerned the Soho pornography trade. It was also an example of first-class team work between the intelligence section, the Serious Crime Squad, the Obscene Publications Squad, HM Customs and Excise and the FBI.

In 1981 a London family named Holloway, despite many prosecutions and seizures of magazines, films, video cassettes and sex aids, had continued to expand their business and flout the law through various companies owning shops and other premises. Through their legal advisers they contested every case and caused as much delay as possible in their cases coming before the courts – there were instances of three years elapsing between the execution of a search warrant and the eventual trials. They were in fact making a mockery of the Obscene Publications Act.

At about this time the intelligence section discovered that two Americans, Reubin Sturman, alleged to be the world's biggest pornographer, and an associate called Ronald Braverman had met the Holloways in London. Sturman, together with about fifty others, was at this time on bail from the US Federal Court in Miami after their arrest by the FBI in their project code-named 'Operation Miporn'. It was alleged that Sturman was one of the main figures in a syndicate that included all five New York Mafia families and controlled the major part of a nationwide distribution of obscene materials. The SIS made a complete analysis of all the intelligence data on these pornographers and the complete dossier was passed to Commander Len Gillert of the Serious Crime Squad.

Sturman and Braverman returned to America after their meeting with the Holloways, and in November 1981 another business associate of Sturman's, a man named Scott Dormen, landed at Heathrow Airport. He was carrying papers which showed that he and Sturman had a business relationship with the Holloway brothers, and immigration officers refused him permission to enter the UK. In January 1982 with a new passport Dormen again arrived at Heathrow, and as this time his passport was 'clean' he was allowed to enter the country as a visitor. He immediately linked up with the Holloways and became active in their pornography business. We established that Sturman was a partner with a member of the Holloway family in the then well-known West End 'Doc Johnson' sex shops under the umbrella of a company named Stonerealm Ltd. Dormen was Sturman's business manager and his role, apart from looking after the interests of his boss, was to arrange for obscene master tapes to be imported from the United States or from Sturman's Amsterdam-based companies. The Holloway organization made reproductions from the master tapes and distributed the obscene material through their market outlets all over Britain.

After discussions with the Director of Public Prosecutions, proceedings were authorized for conspiracies to contravene the Obscene Publications Act contrary to Section 1 of the Criminal Law Act, 1977. These 'overlord' conspiracy charges provided for more serious penalties than those normally imposed for breaches of the Obscene Publications Act of which at that time there were over three hundred outstanding against the Holloway empire. On 29 April 1982 a major operation was launched. Dormen and six members of the Holloway family were arrested and tons of obscene material seized.

Dormen was remanded in custody because it was believed that he would flee the country if he were granted bail, but after a month a High Court judge granted a bail application on the condition that he found four sureties in sums totalling £150,000, that he made a cash deposit of £50,000, surrendered his passport and reported daily to the police. Even so, we calculated that these conditions were unlikely to stop him jumping bail, and it came as no surprise when on 19 August, just a few days before the trial was due to start at the Old Bailey, I was told that Dormen had not reported that day and it was believed he had left the country. He was eventually located at his mother's home in the United States, but could not be extradited because the offence with which he was charged is not included in our treaty with the USA. However, the conviction and jailing of the Holloway family at the Old Bailey later in the month successfully demolished the Holloway/Sturman pornography syndicate and, with the prospect of being arrested and charged should they ever enter the country, Sturman and Dormen are effectively barred from Britain.

Other cases with international dimensions, which after being developed by the intelligence section resulted in arrests and successful prosecutions, included the criminal association of British and American fraudsmen handling stolen bonds, and a conspiracy to steal from a commercial bank. The training of a number of specially selected detectives and members of the civil staff in intelligence analysis systems by Anacapa Sciences Incorporated of California, coupled with the use of a modern computer, contributed immensely to the efficiency of the intelligence unit. Good intelligence helped to make better use of valuable detective resources and made it possible to move in a pro-active way rather than the normal – and usually inevitable – reactive approach after a complaint of crime had been received. The development of the special unit to gather and analyse intelligence about international crime made an important contribution to the Yard's crime-fighting capability. I am confident that it will continue to help identify and understand the ramifications of organized crime and I believe will highlight the need for new legislation – especially regarding the forfeiture of the assets of criminals – to deal with the problem.

While a planned approach to the problem of serious crime is essential, information from alert and co-operative members of the public is something that will always be valuable. Such alertness was shown by an accountant, Colin Protheroe, while he was out shopping with his girlfriend in Knightsbridge one morning in September 1980. He became suspicious when he saw a false beard become detached from the chin of a man outside the shop of Graffs the jewellers, and he watched as the man and a companion carried out an armed robbery there. In a few minutes they had seized a dozen rings, a pendant and a necklace containing the famous Marlborough Diamond, a haul worth £1·4 million. Mr Protheroe followed the men after the robbery and saw them drive away in a green Fiat Mirafiori which had been parked in nearby Sloane Street. He wrote the registration number of the car on the back of his hand, returned to the jeweller's shop and passed it on to a policeman.

It transpired that he had recorded one letter of the car registration wrongly, but this did not prevent a lady identifying the car when she heard its details being broadcast by London's Capital Radio station. She was an employee of a car hire firm and she quickly checked on the Fiat and notified the Yard that it had been on hire to an American staying at the Mount Royal Hotel near Marble Arch. Flying Squad officers who rushed to the hotel found that the car hirer, a Joseph Scalise and his companion, Arthur Rachel, both from Chicago, appeared to have left their room in a hurry. Their descriptions, which were quite distinctive since Scalise had a withered hand and Rachel a prominent scar on his face, matched those given of the jewel robbers. A telephone call to British Airways at Heathrow brought the news that the two men were somewhere over the Atlantic on their way home to Chicago.

The FBI representative at the American Embassy, Bob Moore, was contacted and within a short time he was able to tell us that both men were known to the Bureau and that Scalise had Mafia connections. A reception party was organized by the FBI and when they landed in their home city at O'Hare Airport the two robbers were promptly arrested. They did not have the jewels on them, but in Scalise's luggage the FBI agents found a pair of white gloves he had worn during the robbery when he had threatened the staff with what he claimed was a hand grenade. A taxi driver was later traced who described how two men whom he had driven from Victoria – where the Fiat had been found abandoned – to Heathrow just after the time of the robbery had asked him to post a parcel to an address in New York. Unfortunately our luck ran out here, for the post office clerk, who had just started work that day, had not recorded the full details of the parcel's destination and the jewels have never been recovered.

The Flying Squad quickly prepared the case papers and the Director of Public Prosecutions successfully applied for extradition, although the two criminals, who were unable to satisfy the conditions of bail set by the Federal judge and so remained in prison, used all possible avenues to appeal against it. On 6 August 1984, nearly four years after the robbery, Joseph Scalise, aged forty-six, and Arthur Rachel, aged forty-five, were found guilty at the Old Bailey and sentenced to fifteen years' imprisonment each. The judge gave a £500 reward to Mr Protheroe, £250 to the taxi driver, who had been offered bribes and received threats in an attempt to prevent him from giving evidence, and £100 to the post office clerk as tokens of appreciation of their public-spirited behaviour. When making these awards from public funds he said, 'American gangsters planning raids in this country should know they are likely to come up against such public-spiritedness, people who will put themselves to enormous inconvenience to bring the perpetrators to justice.'

The London cabby has long been a valuable ally of Met detectives and therefore it was no surprise when one day a member of this alert fraternity got in touch about an American whom he thought was behaving very suspiciously. The man was staying at a hotel in Park Lane and had hired a cab for two successive days to drive around London and to Oxford. Our informant's suspicions had been aroused by the surreptitious manner in which the American was going about trying to locate an

Arab businessman and to establish whether this man's son was a university student.

After some preliminary inquiries to establish the identity of the American and to eliminate him from possible terrorist activities, he was invited to have a chat with the Serious Crime Squad. He turned out to be a debt collector from a Las Vegas casino who was looking for the Arab to collect a gambling debt incurred there. A warning to him about keeping within the laws of the UK, and a telephone call to Las Vegas to check on his credentials, had the desired effect – he left for home within hours of being interviewed.

I have already mentioned several times the lack of legislation in this country to ensure the forfeiture of the proceeds of crime, and the difficulties of devising adequate laws become more acute when organized crime syndicates set out systematically to launder their ill-gotten gains. A straightforward casino cash exchange has already been touched upon, but a more sophisticated method of passing money through the accounts of an apparently legitimate business controlled by the criminals has been identified in the United States. These funds are declared for tax purposes as part of business turnover and the method has the effect of increasing the value of the company's shares by artificially inflating its profitability. The type of business chosen is usually one with little or no stock but a high cash flow, such as hotels, restaurants, bars or service industries. The Customs and Excise case of *Regina* v. *Bromley* in 1981 is an example of the laundering of money from this country. It was discovered that large sums of money, the 'skimmed' takings from machines installed in West End amusement arcades, were being taken by couriers to Switzerland. The Customs authorities were informed and eventually the people concerned agreed to pay £1 million as an alternative to a prosecution for the evasion of Value Added Tax.

An essential part of any forfeiture legislation would be regulations to enable the proceeds of crime to be identified and traced. Since exchange control regulations were lifted in 1979/80 there has been no legal requirement to report the transfer of funds in or out of the United Kingdom. By contrast, the US Government has introduced regulations requiring certain financial transactions to be reported to the Treasury Department. For example, the United States Currency and Foreign Transactions Reporting Act requires financial institutions to report within forty-five days all transfers of credit outside the United States as well as payments from outside the country of more than $10,000. Similarly, the US Bank Secrecy Act specifies that persons importing or exporting currency or monetary instruments such as securities issued where the value is in excess of $5,000 must complete Customs declarations. All this data is stored in a computer and analysed in conjunction with the Treasury Department's records and if suspicious patterns emerge inquiries are taken up by Treasury or Customs investigators.

Special legislation to attack organized crime has also been introduced in America, the Racketeer Influenced and Corrupt Organizations (RICO) Statute. Racketeering activity is defined as any act or threat involving murder, kidnapping, gambling, arson, robbery, extortion or dealing in drugs which is punishable under State law with more than one year's imprisonment. Under the RICO legislation both criminal forfeiture and civil penalties, including the winding up of the enterprise and private right of action for treble damages to persons injured by reason of a violation of the Statute, are provided for. The penalties include fines of up to £25,000 per count, prison sentences of up to twenty years and forfeiture of any interest acquired or maintained in violation of the Statute. This legislation is an indication of how seriously a free and democratic country takes the threat of organized crime. Although I believe there was some initial difficulty in enforcing it, including defendants who concealed and transferred their assets before conviction, it has been successfully used and in many cases forfeitures have been ordered.

Although the organized crime situation in the United Kingdom is fortunately not on the scale found in the United States, it does exist and, if it is not unhindered, is likely to expand. At the same time there is nothing in our existing criminal legislation which is expressly designed to help deal effectively with it. However, long-overdue legislation in the form of the Drug Trafficking Offences Bill, designed to enable the proceeds of drug trafficking and the assets of drug traffickers to be confiscated, is before Parliament and will be enacted in 1986. The Home Secretary has also announced his intention of introducing legislation to implement the recommendations the Roskill Committee considered necessary to deal with serious fraud. I am sure these measures will be welcomed by the specialist squads at New Scotland Yard.

16
Beyond 1984

For students of George Orwell the year 1984 probably had all sorts of connotations, 'newspeak', 'doublethink', and 'thought police' no doubt among them. While we might be forgiven for thinking that some politicians had occasionally flirted with the first two, thank goodness no rational person had any reason to fear the development of the last. The Met in the period since 1949, when Orwell's book was first published, had moved increasingly into the public eye. Often under fire, it was occasionally found wanting but – on the evidence of several opinion polls – it was supported by the majority of the population and generally in a more healthy state than at any time in its history.

For me the year meant that after nearly thirty-eight years of being closely involved with the policing of London, and having become the longest-serving officer in the force, the time had come to call it a day and retire. At sixty I had reached the statutory age limit and had no option but to pass on my share of the burden of responsibility – although I was not conscious of it weighing too heavily. I looked forward to enjoying more time with my family: the prospect of becoming a professional grandfather and enjoying power without much responsibility had a certain amount of appeal! However, there were regrets at leaving the force which, warts and all, I had grown to love and respect. I knew that besides missing my colleagues I would also miss the stimulus of the regular doses of adrenalin to which I had become accustomed.

In this book I have deliberately written about some of the warts which had grown and developed in the Met's CID. It is regarded as bad form for members of a family to wash their dirty linen in public, but I believe that to stifle publicity where the integrity of a public body or political life is concerned is both wrong and dangerous. Publicity enables the informed discussion to take place which is essential to the understanding and prevention of such developments. History is of vital importance, and the past, no matter how painful, should be chronicled for the benefit of the future.

Neglect by authority to identify and tackle problems that should have been recognized, ignorance of detail – particularly of the scale of profit from certain types of crime – as well as failures in communication and historical organizational factors, all contributed to the insidious growth of corruption. The malaise, although it was serious, only affected a minority – albeit a substantial one – and the great majority, when the problem was brought to their attention, gave their unqualified support to remedial action. Sir Robert Mark made this point in his memories, *In the Office of Constable*, when he referred to a post-retirement BBC interview: 'On reflection, I am sorry that I did not make the point that the great majority of the CID must not only have been honest, but anxious to reform. Were that not so, reform would clearly have been impossible. It could not have been achieved without the wide measure of support it was given by the CID generally.' It was my good fortune to take over 'C' Department when the climate for change – in which I had played a part – was well developed.

To be effective, individuals leading law enforcement agencies need staying power, year in and year out, and much patience. Progress is inevitably slow, but the important thing is to keep moving forward. The development of the Met illustrates this: commissioners come and go, some leaving their mark and others forgotten, but the durability of the force is there for all to see. By its very size and the number of stations and specialist branches, local traditions and loyalties have developed, but all if they are properly harnessed contribute to the vitality of the whole. There is a saying, 'Look at your past to see the future – if you don't you may have lost your future.' This is very important when making any major innovations in what is basically a conservative organization with a history dating to 1829.

It would be unhealthy for the hierarchy of the Met to be a closed shop, but equally dangerous to exclude from its senior ranks those whose careers have been entirely in London. It is always necessary to strike a balance, with enough officers filling senior positions who are used to the pressures of London and have proven track records, who are known to the force and enjoy its confidence. In recent years professionalism in the police service has grown, but sometimes this can lead to a confusion with careerism. The two things are poles apart and the tendency needs watching. High-fliers, never remaining in operational commands long enough to be really tested, sometimes turn out to be articulate but ineffective leaders who do not enjoy the confidence of their men.

Policing in a democracy can only be carried out satisfactorily with the consent and co-operation of the public. This means close involvement with people at local level and, whether policemen like it or not, working with elected local authority politicians. The Met, unlike all other police forces, does not have a police committee to which it is accountable and on which local elected representatives sit. Since 1829 the Home Secretary has personally been the Police Authority for the Metropolis, but there is increasing dissatisfaction with this system and pressure for the establishment of an authority like those elsewhere in the country. In 1965 when the Greater London Boroughs were formed the Commissioner of the day, Sir Joseph Simpson, aligned the police territorial divisional boundaries with those of the new local authorities, and since then the Met has made increasing efforts to identify on a London borough basis. It is interesting to note that Sir Joseph was farsighted enough to appoint at that time a community relations officer for each borough.

Sir David McNee during his term of office as Commissioner worked hard at supplementing the established relationships between divisional police commanders[1] and their boroughs by organizing regular meetings between himself and his Policy Committee with representatives of the London Boroughs Association. From my own participation in those meetings, I know that there was frankness on both sides, very little emphasis on party politics and there was a strong feeling that a very useful forum of communication was developing. With the addition of the Home Secretary and his nominees, it seemed to me to point the way towards a possible formula for a Metropolitan Police Committee. I am sure that ultimately political pressure from local authorities will bring about the establishment of such a body.

The Home Secretary is a busy man and it is understandable that his national responsibilities limit the time he has available to spend on the personal duty of Police Authority for the Metropolitan Police. Senior civil servants at the Home Office act on his behalf and assume aspects of his personal role which, it could be argued, is not strictly

[1] Later renamed district commanders.

constitutional and sometimes can lead to strained relations with the senior police officers. I remember Sir David McNee's anger when in July 1981, after the arrest of the intruder Michael Fagin in the Queen's bedroom at Buckingham Palace, the Permanent Under Secretary at the Home Office visited him and pressed for his resignation.

In my constabulary travels, and particularly close to home in the City of London which has its own police force, I have often been impressed by the close relationships between members of the local police authority and their senior police officers. Some Home Secretaries and ministers of state have made great efforts to get to know senior officers in the Met as well as the Commissioner, and from personal experience I place Mr Merlyn Rees, Lord Whitelaw and Lord Harris of Greenwich in this category, but with their demanding ministerial responsibilities they could never spare the amount of time devoted by members of local authorities. Over the years I have often attended the County Hall when the Lord Lieutenant of London, on behalf of the Queen, has presented awards to Met officers for gallantry and distinguished service, but I have never known any Home Secretary or other Home Office minister to be present. Nor do I believe that there is any other police authority in the country where the chairman is either too busy, or not interested enough, to give a personal welcome, or to say goodbye, to a chief officer of equivalent rank to assistant commissioner on appointment or upon retirement. I am sure it would be beneficial if Home Office politicians, who often talk about the importance of staff and community relations, found the time to identify a little more closely with their own police force.

However, the memories that will remain with me for

the rest of my life will be not so much of politicians but of my former colleagues, men and women from constables to commissioners with whom I was privileged to serve. Their friendship – much of which will continue – their loyalty and support in good times and bad and their dedication to giving an around-the-clock service every day was nothing short of an inspiration. Outstanding events that ranged from happy occasions like the Coronation, royal weddings, the Queen's Jubilee celebrations and various State ceremonials to the solemnity of State funerals, will also stay with me. Public meetings and demonstrations are an integral part of London's history. Most of them were good-natured and peaceful but some bad-tempered and threatening, and the experience has left me with some understanding of crowd psychology and a lasting interest in current affairs.

Not unnaturally, many of my most vivid recollections are of events that occurred during my period of office as Assistant Commissioner (Crime). The mass media, catering for the public interest, constantly seeks information on the most sensational incidents, and is always demanding details of crimes and arrests so that it is said that the detective is at the glamorous end of policing. However, although he never receives the amount of publicity he deserves, it must never be forgotten that it is the beat constable who is the key figure in our policing system. He is a symbol of the tradition of service to the public, he contributes immensely to the detection of crime and he and the detective are complementary to one another as members of a team with a common purpose.

Most experiences enrich life, although it is true that a few could be said to debase it, but all are valuable in gaining a better understanding of human nature. A policeman has to learn to be dispassionate and unemotional, or his efficiency would be impaired. However, he would be less than human if, on occasions, his experiences did not engender strong emotions. I can relate the whole span of human feelings to events in which I was involved in the later years of my career.

There was joy and elation, shared with others, in the Yard's CID operations room, as we heard over the radio link a report of the recovery of a little girl, unharmed, and of the arrest of her kidnappers.

There was despair when I interviewed the male prostitute Michael Rauch in a sleazy flat at Cleveland Square, Paddington, and realized that the allegations he had already made to a newspaper reporter would lead to a scandal that would wreck the career of a senior colleague who was the Queen's personal protection officer.

There was anger and a sense of outrage when I saw scenes of terrorist activity that had resulted in the death and injury of innocent people. Saturday, 18 December 1983, was such an occasion. With Sir Kenneth Newman I went with the Prime Minister and Mr Thatcher to Harrods in Knightsbridge, where a PIRA car bomb had killed five people, including two policemen. Ninety-one people had been injured including a number of policemen, one of whom died later from his injuries. The appalling scene was made more poignant by the sight, amongst all the damage and debris, of police dog Queenie lying dead in the gutter – her handler, Constable John Gordon, had been seriously injured and eventually lost both his legs.

I sometimes felt fear when our intelligence sources revealed assassination plots – which for security reasons can never be publicly discussed – and wondered whether despite all our precautionary measures the terrorist might succeed.

Since my retirement Parliament has passed the new

Police and Criminal Evidence Act, violent crime has continued to rise and more legislation is proposed to deal with the problems of drugs, disorder and riot. A new national prosecution system, which it has already been admitted was seriously underestimated in cost when it was presented in Parliament, is about to be introduced. I am sure the taxpayer will find it a very expensive addition to the present ever-increasing legal aid budget.

The role of the police in our criminal justice system has been closely examined by Royal Commissions and various committees, but other parts of the system such as the administration of the courts, juries and lawyers have not been subjected to quite the same intense scrutiny. Perhaps one day, although we shall probably have to wait until there are fewer lawyers in both Houses of Parliament, a serious look will be taken at the advantages of the inquisitorial system – seeking after truth – as practised on the Continent, as opposed to our own adversary system. After all, France and Germany are both democratic and civilized countries.

There is still cause for concern about the jury system despite the introduction of the 10–2 majority verdicts in 1967, largely the result of lobbying by Sir Robert Mark which was opposed by both the Bar Council and the Law Society, and the recent long-overdue Juries (Disqualification) Act, 1984, introduced originally by the SDP peers Lords Harris and Wigoder after details were given by the Met of the presence of convicted criminals on juries. The ability of defence counsel to influence the composition of the jury by exercising the right to object to up to three jurors without giving any reason, and the difficulty experienced by some jurors in understanding long and complex fraud trials, are current issues. The right of silence by defendants at their trials, the inordinate length of some criminal trials – a phenomenon that has developed since the introduction of the present legal aid system – and the facilities for witnesses at courts are all matters worthy of inquiry.

Clearly, for the foreseeable future, the responsibility of the Met for the prevention and detection of crime is going to be a heavy one. Unfortunately, it will not be lightened by the increasing politicization of law and order matters. The force will need to draw on all its experience, courage and innovative ability to continue the tradition of keeping the Queen's Peace and of maintaining the rule of law without fear or favour, regardless of class, creed or race to ensure that London remains one of the safest and most civilized capital cities in the world. In this task they will need the continuing help and support of the general public whom they have served for over 150 years.

Appendix I
Assistant Commissioners (Crime)

Charles Edward Howard VINCENT (Knighted 1896)	6.3.1878–14.6.1884
James MONROE	8.7.1884–31.8.1888
Robert ANDERSON (Knighted 1901)	1.9.1888–30.5.1901
Edward R. HENRY (Knighted 1918)	31.5.1901–4.3.1903
Melville Leslie MacNAGHTEN (Knighted 1907)	19.3.1903–12.6.1913
Basil Home THOMSON (Knighted 1919) (Director of Intelligence during World War I)	23.6.1913–30.11.1921
Hon. Trevor R. BIGHAM (Knighted 1929)	29.1.1914–28.1.1931
Borlase Elward Wyndham CHILDS (Knighted 1919)	5.12.1921–5.12.1928
Norman KENDAL (Knighted 1937)	6.12.1928–28.2.1945
Ronald Martin HOWE (Knighted 1955)	1.3.1945–12.8.1953

Richard Leofric JACKSON (Knighted 1963)	13.8.1953–31.10.1963
Ranulph Maunsell BACON (Knighted 1966)	1.11.1963–8.4.1966
Peter E. BRODIE, O.B.E.	9.4.1966–16.4.1972
Colin Philip Joseph WOODS (Knighted 1977)	17.4.1972–16.5.1975
John Spark WILSON, C.B.E.	17.5.1975–31.7.1977
Gilbert James KELLAND, C.B.E., Q.P.M.	1.8.1977–16.3.1984

Appendix II
'C' Department (February 1984)

C.1 Serious Crimes Branch
Organized Crime
Cheque/Credit Card Fraud
Forged Currency
Dangerous Drugs
Extradition
Art & Antiques
Complex Enquiries/Reserve Squad

C.2 Case Papers & Correspondence

C.3 Fingerprints & Photographic

C.4 National Identification Bureau
National Criminal Record Office
National Fingerprint Collection

C.5 Policy & Administration
Crime, Policy & Legislation
Interpol Office
Language Services

C.6 Met. & City Police Fraud Branch
Commercial Fraud
Public Sector
Corruption Index

C.7 Technical Support Branch
Laboratory Liaison
Equipment Unit
Scenes of Crime Officers

C.8 Flying Squad
Central Robbery Squads

C.10 Stolen Vehicle Investigation Branch

C.11 Criminal Intelligence Branch
Criminal Intelligence
Central Drugs Intelligence Unit

C.12 No.9 Regional Crime Squad

C.13 Anti-Terrorist Branch
Terrorist Crimes
Kidnapping
Explosives Officers

Special Branch
Counter Subversion
VIP Protection
Naturalization Enquiries

Forensic Science Laboratory

Index

Abbreviation of police ranks used in Index are as follows:
PC = Police Constable; DPC = Detective Police Constable; Sgt = Sergeant; D Sgt = Detective Sergeant; SPS = Station Police Sergeant; D Insp = Detective Inspector; C Insp = Chief Inspector; DC Insp = Detective Chief Inspector; D Supt = Detective Superintendent; Supt = Superintendent; C Supt = Chief Superintendent; DC Supt = Detective Chief Superintendent; DAC = Deputy Assistant Commissioner; AC = Assistant Commissioner; DC = Deputy Commissioner